THE UNIVERSITY
OF MISSISSIPPI
• SCHOOL OF LAW

THE UNIVERSITY OF MISSISSIPPI SCHOOL OF LAW

A SESQUICENTENNIAL HISTORY

MICHAEL DE L. LANDON

PUBLISHED FOR THE UNIVERSITY OF MISSISSIPPI SCHOOL OF LAW
BY UNIVERSITY PRESS OF MISSISSIPPI/JACKSON

www.upress.state.ms.us

The University Press of Mississippi is a member of the Association of American University Presses.

Photographs courtesy of the University of Mississippi School of Law.

First edition 2006

Library of Congress Cataloging-in-Publication Data

Landon, Michael de L.
   The University of Mississippi School of Law : a sesquicentennial history / Michael de L. Landon. — 1st ed.
   p. cm.
   Includes bibliographical references and index.
   ISBN-13: 978-1-57806-918-7 (cloth : alk. paper)
   ISBN-10: 1-57806-918-1 (cloth : alk. paper) 1. University of Mississippi. School of Law—History. 2. Law schools—Mississippi—History. 3. Law—Study and teaching—Mississippi—History. I. Title.
   KF292.M57L36 2006
   340.071'176283—dc22

                                                                                                    2006017535

British Library Cataloging-in-Publication Data available

Book design: David Alcorn, Alcorn Publication Design

CONTENTS

PREFACE

The author owes a lot of thanks to a large number of people for a great deal of help in researching and writing this sesquicentennial history. My thanks go first to Law Center Dean Samuel M. Davis for having invited me to undertake what has turned out to be a very interesting research and writing project. Second, I wish to thank Law Alumni Officer Timothy Walsh for much assistance and encouragement in getting this history written and also all of the membership of the Lamar Order (the foundation of which has been one of the most fortunate events in the recent history of the law school) for paying me very generously for doing so.

The sesquicentennial historian of the university, that master of Mississippi history Dr. David G. Sansing, has assisted me very generously with regard to both the content and the editing of this work. Law Professors Larry Bush, John Robin Bradley, George Cochran, Michael Hoffheimer, and Joanne Gabrynowicz have all helped by providing me with a lot of very valuable inside information, and, indeed, every member of the law faculty has been most kind and helpful when called upon for assistance.

The Law Center staff has also been extremely kind and very helpful. Assistant to the Dean John Sobotka has acted as my host in the law building for the last thirty months and has always taken care of all my needs with regard to both office space and storage room and also provided a lot of very useful background information. Administrative Coordinator Connie Lamb and Registrar Connie Parham have found much very useful research material for me. And Joyce Whittington, Peggy Nail, Julie Baker, and Niler Franklin have all been very helpful to me at various times in various ways.

The staff of the Mississippi Room in the Main University Library has provided me with most of my research material for this history. Librarians Jennifer Ford and Leigh McWhite have both done a magnificent job of searching out and providing me with relevant material of every kind. Librarian Jennifer Aronson and staff member Fisher Fleming have also been very helpful and supportive. Off campus, two ladies very much interested in Oxford and Lafayette County local history, Patricia Young and Anne Davis Percy, have helped me a great deal, especially with regard to the life and career of Professor William Stearns.

I also very much want to thank Law Library Director Kristy Gilliland and all of her staff both for making me feel very much at home in their library and for providing me with a tremendous amount of very valuable advice and assistance with regard to my research and writing tasks. Julianna Davis, Scott DeLeve, Jessica Dupont, Stacey Lane, Macey Edmondson, Lynn E. Murray, Christopher J. Noe, and James E. Pitts have all been particularly kind and helpful.

Finally, and very important, warmest thanks to my wife, Carole Prather Landon, for providing me with a loving, comfortable, and happy home life while I was working on this very important project.

THE UNIVERSITY
OF MISSISSIPPI
SCHOOL OF LAW

CHAPTER I

The Early Days (1854–1874)

On Monday, October 2, in 1854, seven students assembled in a classroom in the University of Mississippi's Lyceum building, ready to participate in the first class on common law ever to be taught on its campus. They were Flavius Josephus Lovejoy and Lafayette Washington Reasons from Calhoun County, Benjamin Jay Clanton from Panola County, James Alemeth Green, from Tippah County, John Townes Moseley, from Kemper County, James Stephens Terral, from Jasper County, and Albert Hiram Thomas, from right there in Oxford, Lafayette County.[1] Their professor was William Forbes Stearns, a distinguished member of the Mississippi bar, from up north in Holly Springs. Their university was then just beginning its seventh year of operation. Chartered by an act of the state legislature in 1844, it had first opened its doors to students in 1848, and, until then, had only offered a curriculum in the general liberal arts leading, after four years of study, to a possible B.A. degree. A major motive for the legislature's founding and funding of it—at Oxford, where the comparatively high elevation and cooler conditions might be expected to provide healthier living conditions than were available at other suggested sites and which was comparably safely far away from any very sizeable urban area which might offer more temptations than many of the students could possibly resist—was the fact that—like many other "Southern" states around that same time—they wanted to encourage Mississippi's young men to stay close to home for their higher education rather than having them attend institutions of higher learning in "Northern" states, where they might be exposed to too many wrong ideas about the South's "peculiar institution" of Negro slavery. The fact that ten of the thirteen original members of the university's self-perpetuating board of trustees were members of the legal profession also had undoubtedly played a part in bringing into being, very early in its history, the new law department, the very existence of which made much more justifiable calling the institution of higher learning at Oxford not merely a college but a "university."[2]

Not that the study of law had been entirely neglected during the university's first seven years of operation. From 1848 to 1854, its presidents' titles had included that of "Professor of the Law of Nations," and the prescribed junior year curriculum had included a course on "National Law," the textbook for which was Vattel's *Law of Nations*.[3] Furthermore, the university's first two presidents were thoroughly qualified law instructors. George Frederick Holmes (1848–49) was a member of the South Carolina Bar, and Augustus Baldwin Longstreet (1849–56), after graduating from Yale University in 1813, had spent fourteen months studying at the historic Tapping Reeve Law School in Litchfield, Connecticut, before being admitted to practice at the bar in Georgia in 1815.[4] It also happened to be the case that the university's first professor of mathematics and astronomy, Albert Taylor Bledsoe, before coming to Oxford in 1848, had spent several years practicing law in Springfield, Illinois, where one of his closest friends and associates was his fellow Kentucky native, Mr. Abraham Lincoln. So it was not totally inappropriate that the University of Mississippi's first ever honorary degree was an LL.D. conferred on Bledsoe in the spring of 1854, shortly before he departed to take up the chair of mathematics at the University of Virginia.[5]

From 1850 to 1852, Bledsoe had been assisted in his teaching work by a young adjunct professor of mathematics named Lucius Quintus Cincinnatus Lamar.[6] An 1845 graduate of Emory University in his native Georgia, Lamar had, soon afterward, been admitted to the Georgia bar and in 1849 had followed his father-in-law, President Longstreet, to Oxford, Mississippi. In Oxford, besides teaching mathematics in the university, he also practiced some law. (Being the university president's son-in-law probably helped a bit in attracting clients.) And he also became very friendly with Alexander H. Pegues, a prominent Oxford city founder, Lafayette County landowner, and original member of the university's board of trustees. Before long, Pegues had begun taking "the poor school teacher" (as members of the Pegues family had taken to calling him) along with him to various "political meetings" around the northern area of the state. And he must have made a very good impression on those whom he met at them, for, in 1857, he was elected to the United States Congress in Washington, D.C.[7]

Pegues was one of the ten lawyers on the university's original thirteen-member board of trustees.[8] Another was Andrew M. Clayton (its president, 1844–53), a native Virginian who had served for a while as a United States judge in the Arkansas Territory before becoming a highly successful planter and lawyer in Mississippi's Marshall County.[9] And yet another was James M. Howry, also a Virginian by birth, who had come to Mississippi via Tennessee, become a leading member of the bar and a circuit judge, and who would serve on the board until 1870.[10] Howry's son, Charles B. Howry, after service as an officer in the Confederate army, would graduate from the law department in 1867 and climax a very successful professional career by being appointed to serve on the Court of Claims in Washington, D.C., in 1897.[11] In his old age, some twenty-five years later, he would write a memoir on the origins and early history of his law school. In his 37-page account of "The Rise and Progress of the University of Mississippi School of Government Science and Law," he would recall that "the bar of Mississippi had much to do in establishing and supporting the School of Law in the University" and that, indeed, "but for the zeal and interest of the profession there would have been no [law school] for another generation."[12]

A major reason for the leadership of the Mississippi bar wanting a law school, Howry explained, was that during the first few decades of the state's existence there was a great deal of confusion as to just what laws and legal systems were in force and applicable in the state. Back in colonial days, some maps of Georgia showed Georgia's western boundary running along the east bank of the Mississippi river. Did Georgia law still have force? Through the eighteenth century and into the early nineteenth century, both French and Spanish law had also been in effect in different areas at different times, and some grants of real estate were still in effect that had been made under either Choctaw or Chickasaw Indian law.[13]

In Mississippi, and in most of the rest of the United States into the 1850s, the most common method of training for admission to the bar was the apprenticeship system. The would-be lawyer would read law and observe the legal profession being practiced in the office of some established member of the bar, who would, assuming all went well, eventually recommend him to the bench for admission to the bar. Would-be lawyers in Mississippi and other southern states in the 1840s who desired a more formal legal education usually attended the prestigious University of Virginia Law School founded in 1826. By 1850, only Virginia and two other public institutions of higher learning in the United States had law schools: the University of Maryland (since 1816) and the University of Pennsylvania (founded in 1850). The University of Mississippi was destined, therefore, to be only the fourth to have one.[14]

Meeting in Oxford on January 12, 1854, the university's lawyer-dominated board of trustees drafted a report to be submitted to the upcoming session of the state legislature which included the statement: "The University greatly needs a professorship of Law." Its graduates, they noted, "often aspire to act in the counsels of their country; and history and observation both teach them to look at the Bar as the place of preparation and of trial, to vindicate their fitness for the Halls of legislation." Wherever the common law of England has prevailed: "The Bar has been the great road to the dignities, the titles, the places and the power of the politician." Right then, in Mississippi, "our ambitious youth go to the East for instruction in this department, for it is to be found there alone." The schools they were presently attending might or might not be "antagonistic . . . to Southern views of the right philosophy of government." But, if Mississippi had its own school, they could be sure it would "never disseminate views of society and government, which would prove prejudiced to Southern interests." In that school, furthermore, "the Philosophy of Government should [also] be taught . . . and history, which is philosophy teaching by example." Besides instruction in law, government, and history, they would want to add "instruction . . . in international law." They were also of the opinion that "a single professor would be adequate to discharge the combined duties that are here indicated."15 The position, however, obviously could be filled by "no ordinary man." Fortunately there was still in existence the small, real estate—invested "seminary fund," which had been created by the legislature several decades earlier, when publicly funded higher education was first being contemplated. If all the lands belonging to the fund were sold, the money brought in ought to be enough to earn an investment income of "about fifteen hundred dollars." And, "with such tuition fees as a Law professor, well known to be qualified for his duties, might command, and a payment annually of two thousand dollars as a fixed salary," they thought it "probable" that the right kind of man could be recruited.16

Less than eight weeks later, on February 27, 1854, down in Jackson, the state legislature approved "AN ACT to create in the University of Mississippi a Professorship of Governmental Science and Law." Its first paragraph ordered "the Trustees of said Institution to elect a Professor to fill the same, who shall lecture [the classes in those fields] under such rules and restrictions as the Board of Trustees may prescribe." Its second further authorized the Trustees "to fix the salary of said Professor and to regulate its payment" and added that "the sum of two thousand dollars per annum" was to be "hereby appropriated out of any funds in the treasury not otherwise appropriated, to be applied towards the payment of the salary of said Professor."[17] The university *Catalogue* for 1853–54, published a few weeks later, included the title "Professor of Governmental Science and Law" in its listing of faculty but left the space for his name blank. A few pages later, it was noted that "the Board of Trustees will, at their meeting in July, proceed to fill the chair. This will add greatly to the advantages of the University."[18]

And, indeed, at a board meeting in Oxford on Tuesday, July 11, an election by ballot was held. After the ballots had been counted, "it appeared that the Hon. Edward C. Wilkinson was elected to fill said chair." A Yazoo City resident and a sometime circuit judge for the state's Second District, Wilkinson was one of the board's own members and had been serving on it since its creation ten years earlier. Remembered as having been "a consummate scholar, an erudite lawyer, and an upright and pious gentleman," he seems to have been highly qualified to fill the position. However, perhaps because he was suffering from ill-health—he would die less than eighteen months later—the very next day he turned the offer down. So the board met again, just a few days later, on Saturday July 15. This time they elected the Honorable Carswell R. Clifton, who, evidently, also eventually declined their offer of the position.[19] It was some six weeks later, on August 29, less than three weeks before the start of the next year's classes, that they met yet again and "William F. Stearns of Marshall County" was unanimously elected "Professor of Governmental Science and Law."[20]

Like many of Mississippi's outstanding leaders in the mid-nineteenth century, Stearns was originally from out of state. He was in fact from farther away than most of them, having been born, on November 11, 1817, in Bennington, Vermont. Orphaned before the age of ten, raised by a number of his New England relatives, and educated only in the local common schools, he had come down to Mississippi in 1836, at the age of nineteen, and settled first in Pontotoc and later in Holly Springs. There he "read law" in Alexander Clayton's office, and, being a voracious reader, quickly transformed himself into a learned lawyer, "one of the best equity lawyers in Mississippi" in fact. Much consulted by other north Mississippi lawyers, he was eventually taken on as a partner by Clayton.[21] Their professional relationship, plus the fact that Stearns had by then become the grand orator of the local Masonic Order, would explain why he had already played a major role in the pre-history of the university by being invited to be the principal speaker in the Masonic grand ceremony, on July 14, 1846, wherein, with great fanfare, the cornerstone of the Lyceum was laid. In his speech on that occasion, he said: "Let this Institution succeed, and no man can estimate the influence that will be exerted for good, through its agency, upon the generations who are to succeed us. It will be demonstrated that our youth may be educated at home as well as abroad; and the example, thus afforded, will be contagious throughout this and adjacent states."[22]

Stearns did not accept the offer of the professorship immediately or eagerly. He was, in fact, "reluctant to retire from his practice." Years later, Clayton would confide to Howry that two members of the board of trustees "were constrained to visit him in his office to exert their powers of persuasion to induce him to accept the place." To that first class meeting, on October 2, 1854, he confessed: "I have had no experience in the work of instruction, except . . . in directing the legal studies of a few individual students in my office." And, having been elected just a few days before the university's 1854–55 session was due to start, his time since had been "occupied by domestic duties growing out of the removal of my family to this place." Consequently, he said that he had not yet "had time to procure all the books of reference that I require, or to peruse all the books of reference that I require, or to peruse the few I have been able to obtain." Having finally accepted the position, however, he "threw himself into the work with great enthusiasm."[23]

Meanwhile, two other major events in the history of the university were happening that same year. One of them was a grant by the board of some land on the eastern edge of the campus to the Mississippi Central Railroad to build a depot and run a railroad line through Oxford. Completed in 1860, the line, running up from Canton through Oxford and Holly Springs to Grand Junction, Tennessee, linked Oxford up with the Illinois Central Railway and other major railway systems. That, of course, made the university and its law department much more accessible from around the state, the region, and, indeed, the entire nation.[24] The other occurrence was the arrival on campus of Dr. Frederick A. P. Barnard to fill the chair of mathematics and astronomy vacated by the departing Dr. Bledsoe.[25]

Just two years later, Barnard succeeded Dr. Longstreet as the University's third president. He would serve with that title from 1856 to 1858, and as Chancellor from 1858 to 1861. Like both of his predecessors (and like Bledsoe), Barnard was someone "learned in the law." A native of Massachusetts, he had graduated from Yale University in 1828 and had spent the next few years working as a teacher at the secondary level in Hartford, Connecticut. While there he had also read law in the office of a leading member of the local bar, intending to make the law his profession. By 1837, however, he was a professor on the faculty of the University of Alabama, teaching science and mathematics. And he taught there for seventeen years before transferring to the University of Mississippi.[26]

In March 1858, President Barnard addressed a letter to the board of trustees outlining his dream of a great institution in which all of the sciences, mathematics, classical and oriental studies, civil and political history and law would be researched and taught. Professor Stearns was his firm friend and ally and shared his dream. Two months later, when Barnard traveled back to his Yale alma mater to serve as the alumni speaker at their commencement ceremonies, he took Stearns with him and introduced him to the Yale faculty as "the best-read man he had met in the South." They responded by conferring on the slightly embarrassed Stearns, who had never received any formal higher education, an honorary LL.D. degree.[27]

Back home, meanwhile, the University of Mississippi's law program was slowly expanding and growing. Three of its original seven students, Clanton, Lovejoy, and Reasons, received their LL.B. degrees in the 1856 commencement ceremonies, as did three other students, Henry J. Harper from Yalobusha County (already a University of Mississippi B.A.) and Charles Purvis Neilson and Hugh Eugene Weathersby, both of whom were from Amite County. They had evidently transferred into the law class sometime during the 1854–55 academic year. Harper and Weathersby were destined to die in battle, fighting for the Confederacy, just a few years later. The other four of the original seven law students, Green, Moseley, Terral, and Thomas, never did graduate from the program. Terral did, nevertheless, become a district attorney and later a colonel in the Confederate Army before being killed in action on October 4, 1864. Green, who had earned a B.A. at the University before enrolling in the law program, survived military service in the Civil War to become a circuit court judge operating out of Corinth. From 1876 to 1894, he served as a member of the university's board of trustees.[28] Nine more LL.B. degrees were conferred in 1857, nine in 1858, nine in 1859 (including Robert Edward Barksdale of Helena, Arkansas, and William Robert Barksdale, of Grenada). Twenty-two were conferred in 1860 (including one on James Word Falkner, of Tippah County, destined to reach, a few years later, the rank of lieutenant colonel in the Confederate Army), and ten in 1861. So the total number of antebellum law program graduates was sixty-five out of a total enrollment of 170. Of that total number, forty-two had also earned a B.A. from the university.[29]

On July 13, 1858, the university's alumni association, by then three years old, had voted to admit graduates of the law department "into the Association on the same footing as graduates of the academic department." Just a few years later, a total of ten law graduates, along with many more of the university's alumni, would lose their lives fighting in the armed forces of the Confederacy.[30]

Almost all of the students were from Mississippi, though a small number were not. The 1860–61 *Catalogue*'s list of law students includes one senior from Yell County, Arkansas, two juniors from Memphis, and one from Princess Anne, Maryland.[31] The recruiting of students for his program, from anywhere and everywhere, was of course one of Stearns's major concerns. On August 7, 1857, he wrote a letter, apparently at the request of the young man's parents, to William Cooper Nelson of Holly Springs, who was thinking very seriously of going up north to enroll in Yale University. "My Dear Boy," he inquired, was not his sole reason for planning to do so, because "you suppose its diploma would be regarded by all those who know you had obtained it, as conferring upon you a more elevated rank, among educated men, than you would be entitled to claim as a graduate of any Southern College? . . . the University of Mississippi, for example." The University of Mississippi might be a very new and still comparatively unknown institution, Stearns wrote, but, "for every valuable purpose, our education is as thorough as that of Yale." Its faculty was "as able, and learned, and competent to teach, as the men who fill corresponding positions in any of the Colleges of America." True, its libraries still needed to be greatly expanded, "but with respect to most of the departments of collegiate instruction, our means for imparting knowledge and illustrating science are fully equal to those of any other College in the United States." Graduates of both Yale and Harvard had, very recently, personally assured him of that.[32]

There were certain other very important points Master Nelson should consider as well: He was a native Mississippian and one born with a somewhat delicate constitution. "If you become ill, how long must you languish for the presence of your mother, before, even with all haste she can employ, she will be able to reach the sick bed of her suffering son? And, above all, how can you endure; day after day, for years, the studied insults which your fellow students, your instructors, and the fanatical people of Connecticut will be continually heaping upon you, and upon the land of your birth, and its people and institutions?" And later, when he was ready to "go forth as a man and engage in the great struggle of life, it will not be a matter of trivial moment whether you have numerous, attached and influential friends among the educated men of every County in the State, or whether you are to undertake your weary task alone, or with such companionship only as you may pick up by the wayside, among strangers."[33]

In spite of those very moving arguments, however, William C. Nelson apparently never was enrolled in any program at the University of Mississippi. Undoubtedly, many of the dozens who did enroll in the law program in the later 1850s were motivated, in part at least, by a provision that was included in an "Act in Relation to Attorneys and Counselors at Law" passed by the state legislature early in 1857. It said that "a diploma granted by the State University conferring the degree of bachelor at law upon students of the law class shall be equivalent to a license granted by a court as aforesaid." And that meant a license "to practice as an attorney and counselor at law in all the courts of this State."[34]

Successive university *Catalogues* informed the would-be "attorney and counselor" as to what he must do to attain his diploma. Applicants for admission to the law program had to be at least nineteen years of age (presumably, in part at least, so that they would be legal adults when they graduated), and "if not graduates of some college" were "required to exhibit satisfactory testimonials of good moral character."[35] The "course of study" was made up of "two terms of ten months each." The "term," or academic year, back then, ran from the second Thursday in September to the second Monday in July, with only brief breaks for Christmas and other major holidays. Law students in their first term belonged to the "junior class." Those in their second term made up the "senior class." The two classes (the 1854–55 *Catalogue* announced under the heading: "LAW SCHOOL. Department of Governmental Science and Law") pursued "together, under the instruction of the Law Professor the studies of International and Constitutional Law." An annual tuition fee of fifty dollars was paid directly to the law professor.[36]

Each student had to "furnish his own textbooks," however. The textbooks required for the two years course of studies were: Blackstone's *Commentaries*, Kent's *Commentaries*, Story on *Bailments*, *Agency*, *Partnership*, and *Conflict of Laws*, Smith on *Contracts*, Byles on *Bills*, Stephen on *Pleading*, Angell and Ames on *Corporations*, Greenleaf on *Evidence*, Adam's *Equity*, Gresley's *Equity Evidence*, and Wharton's *American Criminal Law*.

In a circular dated July 1855 that was aimed at prospective law students, Stearns explained that he had "adopted as text books the works of the most approved elementary writers; preferring—other things being equal—such as are least encumbered with minuteness of detail, in order to avoid that overloading of the memory, and consequent confusion of ideas, which is involved in the perusal, by the student, of those voluminous works which were compiled for the use of the practitioner." Over the next seven years, the reading list remained substantially the same, with only minor changes. Gresley was gone by 1857, and, by 1858, Wharton had been replaced by Bishop on *Criminal Law*, and the Revised Mississippi Code of 1857 had been added.[37]

As was the custom at Harvard and other law schools in America at that time, the textbooks were studied individually, in sequence, rather than several simultaneously, so that a student could, in fact, embark on his course of study at almost any stage in the academic term.[38] In class, the 1855 *Catalogue* explained, the students were "examined daily upon their reading of the textbook under perusal, and such explanations are then afforded, as are requisite in order to show wherein the general principles, laid down by the author, have been modified by local statutes or adjudications." In addition, "occasional lectures [were] given to the Seniors, illustrating the local law and practice peculiar to Mississippi." Also, moot courts were held weekly, in which the seniors were "exercised in the practical application of the legal principles they [had] been taught," and they were "made familiar with the duties of Clerks and Sheriffs, and the systems of pleading and practice applicable to cases of every description in the various courts of the state."[39]

In addition to the textbooks that the students were required to purchase for themselves and read, the 1854–55 *Catalogue* announced that, "for purposes of consultation and reference, the private library of the Law Professor [was] accessible to the students, as well as the University Library." Just two years later, however, in a meeting held on July 15, 1856, in conjunction with that year's commencement exercises, the university's board of trustees pledged to raise, in the coming year, $32,000 to meet several urgent equipment needs. Out of that $32,000, $2,000 was to be used "for the purchase of Law Books for the Law Department" In a follow-up meeting held two days later, the trustees voted to leave the choice of those books up to the law professor.[40] In response Stearns recommended that the university purchase his own "private library," which he offered "to sell . . . to the Board for the Law Library of the University." And, at their meeting a year later, on July 14, 1857, the board received a very favorable report from a committee, chaired by board member C. Pinckney Smith, LL.D., that they had "appointed . . . for the purpose of ascertaining the character, condition and value of the . . . Library of Prof. Wm. F. Stearns for the Law Library of the University." "As a lot," the committee members reported, "they have been well and judiciously selected and constitute a valuable collection" Furthermore, they added, "the specific sum which Professor Stearns offers to take, as the price of the Library, is so low as to present a strong inducement to the purchase." In their opinion, "it would certainly be difficult, . . . and probably impossible, elsewhere to procure for the same amount of money, the same books, in similar good condition." After hearing the committee's report, the board voted to pay to Stearns, for the 626 volumes he was offering, the sum of $1,627.33. They further stipulated, however, that that amount must come out of the $2,000 they had voted to spend for a Law Library the year before and that any outstanding orders for books, from any outside source, that would raise the total expenditure beyond that budgeted amount must be canceled immediately.[41] But, probably because of the expanding size of the law classes in the last two years of the decade, just one year later, on July 9, 1858, they voted to use university funds to purchase not only the current Reports of the United States Supreme Court but also the New York and Tennessee Reports "not now in the Law Library." And, on June 25, 1860, the board approved spending $150 "to keep up the sets of Law Reports now in the Law Library, and in the purchase of such other books as in [the law professor's] discretion may be necessary."[42]

The growing number of law students, meanwhile, when not attending lectures, participating in moot courts, or studying in the law library, would often be looking for recreational opportunities, both on campus and in downtown Oxford in and around the Square. Until 1857, the "Department of Law" section in the successive university *Catalogues*, briefly cautioned law students that, while they were not subject to any other university regulations, they were bound by those that "relate to moral conduct." The 1857–58 *Catalogue*, however, had a lot more to say on the subject. "The Faculty of Arts," it announced, have been relieved from the exercise of their former jurisdiction over the law students in matters of discipline; . . . hereafter, that jurisdiction will pertain to the Law Professor and the President of the University." And any law student who, after being "privately and kindly admonished," failed to mend his ways, would be "excluded from the University," though "without public censure." Furthermore, "for offences of great enormity, such as the municipal law would visit with infamous punishment, the offending student [would] be expelled."[43]

Both the jurisdictional and procedural changes and the more explicit language had been brought about by the case of James Gustavus Minter of Yalobusha County, a member of the 1856–57 law class. On February 16, 1857, he was expelled by the faculty for having drawn a pistol on an undergraduate student named Wilson in the course of a quarrel they had had in the Oxford city hall. Wilson, who had responded by drawing his own pistol, was merely suspended for three months. The very next day, February 17, however, the faculty was again called into session by President Barnard, who read to them a memorandum from the law student body addressed to the board of trustees, on Minter's behalf. In it they argued that the undergraduate code of conduct was inapplicable to the circumstances of professional students and, in other universities across the nation, was not applied with regard to them. Since Professor Stearns was, at the time, away in New Orleans on business, L. Q. C. Lamar, "acting [the minutes noted] as Law Prof.," addressed his colleagues in support of the memorandum's arguments. His colleagues, for the most part, were not persuaded by them but did agree to suspend Minter's expulsion, pending action by the board with regard to it.[44]

The board, in fact, did not meet again until July 10, just a few days before the 1857 commencement ceremonies were due to begin. At that time, the majority of them refused to remove the law students from under jurisdiction of the general faculty with regard to disciplinary matters. They did, however, recommend a rehearing of Minter's case and a review by the faculty of their policies with regard to "the use of deadly weapons." A few days later, the faculty met and voted that Minter's suspension (which had apparently been extended, pending a decision by the board) should end immediately. Furthermore, though his diploma would not actually be formally granted until two months later, on September 15, he would "be permitted to present himself with his class, and be presented with a blank Diploma," which he would be required to "return after the close of the exercise"[45]

In the weeks immediately following, board members must have given the matter of law school discipline some further and deeper consideration for at the beginning of the new school year that fall Professor Stearns was able to tell the assembled law student body that the board, much impressed by the "clear and forcible reasoning" of their memorandum, were now prepared to agree that, henceforth, "the disciplinary code applicable to Law Students [would] be administered by the Law Professor, associated with the President of the University." Furthermore, a new code had been approved specifically for them that was "not encumbered by any list of offences . . . specifically denounced." Rather, it assumed their "capacity to govern [themselves and allowed them] the fullest liberty to do whatever [they thought] fit," so long as they conducted themselves "like gentlemen." "Ordinarily, . . . except for offences of such grave enormity as will never be committed by any save the most profligate and abandoned," the penalty of expulsion would no longer be inflicted. "Venial faults" would be "visited with private admonition, graver discrepancies with exclusion—which is a lot more censure than suspension." The students clearly could "thus perceive that, in regard to [their] government, the code . . . provided by the Trustees [was] one of exceeding liberality."[46]

Although a majority of them were also lawyers, the trustees' respect for their "Law Professor" is indicated by the fact that even they, on occasion, would ask for his legal advice. For example, at a meeting on July 2, 1859, they passed a resolution: "That the Law Professor be requested to investigate the legal question involved in the loss of the chemical steam apparatus recently purchased, & to adopt such steps as he may deem necessary to recover compensation or damages from the party chargeable with the loss."[47]

Less than a year later the board would need to again call upon his professional skills with regard to a much more serious matter. On the night of May 12, 1859, while Chancellor Barnard and his wife were out of town attending a meeting in Vicksburg, two students had sneaked into their on-campus residence, and one of them, Samuel Humphreys had beat and raped their slave girl, Jane. At a called meeting of the faculty nine days later, after hearing Jane's testimony, Stearns—because, under Mississippi law, a slave could not testify against a white person in any court proceeding—joined with the majority of his colleagues in voting that Humphreys was "not guilty."[48] Since he was accustomed to explaining to his students that, while the institution of slavery certainly was contrary to the principles expressed in the Declaration of Independence, it was not in any way contrary to the Constitution of the United States or the Bible,[49] his vote was a reasonable one. A few minutes later, he voted, again with the majority of the faculty, that Humphreys was, nevertheless, undoubtedly "morally" guilty. Soon afterward, Barnard asked Humphreys's parents to withdraw him from the university, which they did. When he applied for readmission in the next session,

Barnard turned him down. That led to serious trouble in which the board soon became involved.[50]

The University of Mississippi's 1859–60 academic year would later be described by a historian of the university as one in which "both among students and faculty perhaps more bitterness and animosity were never engendered in one year before or since."[51] One major manifestation of the prevailing embittered atmosphere was the accusation made by a son-in-law of the university's former president A. B. Longstreet and brother-in-law of L. Q. C. Lamar, Oxford physician Henry B. Branham, that Chancellor Barnard—as evidenced by his handling of the Humphrey's case—was "unsound on slavery." Convinced that Barnard had played a part in forcing his father-in-law out of office four years earlier, Branham apparently now hoped that his accusation—a very serious one to make in the emotion-charged atmosphere of 1860—would quickly cause Barnard to suffer the same fate. But Barnard responded by appealing to his board of trustees in Oxford on March 1 and 2, 1860, to investigate the charges against him. At their opening session the board members proposed that Professor Stearns—"he being the only Phonographic [shorthand] reporter in or near Oxford"—be asked to take down a verbatim report of their proceedings. At first, Stearns, who was there ready to speak in defense of his good friend Barnard, "asked to be excused, upon the ground, that being a witness in the case, he felt a delicacy in acting as reporter." Finally it was agreed that he should be the first witness to testify and would thereafter record and eventually present a report on what was testified to by every subsequent witness. Two days later, the board members voted unanimously in Barnard's favor, and they also voted that the complete transcript of their proceedings should be circulated throughout the state.[52]

The editor of Oxford's only newspaper at that time, the *Mercury*, was J. D. Stevenson, a radical states' rights advocate. He strongly supported Branham's campaign against Barnard and urged that the university be moved out of Oxford and down to Jackson, where the State's establishment could monitor it more effectively. Friends of Barnard and the university responded to his attacks by promoting the start-up of a rival newspaper in Oxford called the *Intelligencer*.[53] Its editor was Howard Falconer, who had received a B.A. (with honors) from the university in 1859 and was the son of Colonel Thomas Falconer of Holly Springs, a publisher of several newspapers in north Mississippi. He began publication of the *Intelligencer* in June 1860, and it soon was being denounced by

Stevenson in the *Mercury* as "the organ of the University clique." Its editorials strongly praised and defended Chancellor Barnard, the university as a whole, and particularly the law department, which Stevenson was accustomed to referring to disparagingly as a "manufactory" of lawyers.[54]

Stearns, in response to Stevenson's attacks, mailed a circular letter out to the more than six hundred lawyers around the state, defending the law department. In it he argued that the advantages offered to law students in professional schools were much superior to what apprenticeships in lawyers' offices gave them. Whereas a successful and busy practitioner could only, at best, provide an apprentice in his office with a somewhat limited and very disorganized sampling of legal literature, a law school student received a thorough, systematic and in-depth introduction to it. At the same time, through the moot court system, he received a thorough grounding in both the organization and the procedures of the local state and federal court systems. The seventeenth century English founding father of the modern common law, Sir Edward Coke, he reminded them, had remarked that for the law student "there are two things to be avoided—distorted reading and precipitate practice." And finally, Stearns insisted, using essentially the same arguments that he had used in his letter three years earlier to young William Nelson of Holly Springs, for "Mississippi students the Law School of the University of Mississippi presented advantages superior, on the whole, to those of any other law school in the United States."[55]

Indeed, in spite of some external hostility, with enrollment now treble what it had been in the first few years and a substantial law library now in place, the future looked bright for the Department of Law in the spring of 1860. Stearns now was the senior professor on the faculty; only Chancellor Barnard outranked him. Just five years earlier, when there were then still fewer than two dozen law students enrolled, the board, not surprising, had ruled that, in the 1855–56 academic year, Law Professor Stearns must also teach an undergraduate class in "Political Economy" (economics). By July 1858, however, the trustees were considering relieving the law department of responsibility for the teaching of international law. Indeed, just a year later, they voted that responsibility for teaching it would "be imposed on the Professor of Ethics," George W. Carter, D.D. Then, in 1860, the state legislature passed an act creating a second professorship of law and government at the university. And the board, meeting in Oxford on June 27 of that year, elected James F. Trotter to fill the new position. Born in Brunswick County, Virginia, in 1802 and educated privately in East

Tennessee, Trotter had begun practicing law in Monroe County, Mississippi, in 1824. Over the next 36 years, he had several times represented Monroe County in the State Senate, been appointed in 1838 to finish out the term of resigned Senator John Black in the United States Senate, and had served as a circuit court judge, as a member of the High Court of Errors and Appeals, and as vice chancellor of the northern district. When that office was abolished in 1857, he had taken up the practice of law in Holly Springs. So Trotter was certainly well known to many of the board members and also to Professor Stearns. "Affable, upright, courageous, firm—his was a most attractive character," his contemporaries later recalled. Meanwhile, at their June 27, 1860, meeting the board also ruled that both law professors were henceforth to be regarded in every way as regular "members of the Faculty." Furthermore, to replace the departing George Carter (a disgruntled Branham supporter) as professor of ethics they chose Congressman L. Q. C. Lamar, who thus now became the one responsible for teaching International Law. And, at a second meeting two days later, on June 29, the board voted to transfer responsibility for teaching Constitutional Law to the holder of the ethics chair also. So there were three professors with law teaching duties in the 1860–61 academic year.[56]

The board at the same time acknowledged, however, that they understood that Professor Lamar would be away in Washington, D.C., from December 1 to March 10, 1861 "to serve out his time in the next session of the Congress of the United States."[57] Former board member Jacob Thompson, meanwhile, had been living in Washington since 1857, serving as the secretary of the interior in President Buchanan's cabinet. In a letter written in the spring of 1860 to board member James Howry, Thompson had expressed his regret at hearing that their fellow Lafayette County landowner and Oxford businessman William F. Avent was on the verge of bankruptcy. It is perhaps not too surprising, therefore, that the board—having voted in their June meeting that year "to contract for suitable rooms for a year or term of years," somewhere in Oxford, "for a lecture room, Law Library room and a room for the Law Professors Study"—very soon afterward secured a set of rooms to meet those needs in the Avent and Lyles bank building on the northwest corner of the Oxford Square.[58]

Just fourteen months later, however, in an emergency meeting held on August 2, 1861, the board would have to instruct its executive committee "to surrender the rooms rented from William F. Avent Esq. . . & to pay him a reasonable amount for the time they have been occupied." Only the law library might stay in his building, "at a reasonable sum," if that seemed "expedient."[59] For, by then, everything had fallen apart. In his introductory lecture to that first law class nearly seven years earlier, on October 2, 1854, Stearns, after commenting on the then on-going "Crimean War" between three of the great powers of Europe, had remarked to the seven students present: "And when we survey our own political horizon, we find that dark and threatening clouds portend a coming storm. Blind, ferocious and remorseless fanaticism, for a long time regardless of the spirit of the Constitution, now pours contempt upon its very letter, and openly avows its full intention *never* to relax its effort until the dearest rights of the South, solemnly guaranteed to us by that instrument, shall be given to the winds; our property torn from our grasp; 'fire-brands, arrows and death scattered' through our habitations, and our beautiful land made desolate."[60]

Five years later, on October 24, 1859, with the prospect of secession looming ever closer, some of the university students sought, and were given, permission by the faculty to organize a "military company" that would later come to be known as the "University Greys." And in the town of Oxford another company was organized that would eventually be named the "Lamar Rifles" in honor of their strongly pro-secessionist former United States congressman. By the spring of 1861, in fact, the atmosphere on campus had become so bellicose and violent that Professor Stearns's faculty colleagues requested that he draw up a stricter and more precise version of the ban on firearms on campus. He did, and they approved it immediately. But then Fort Sumter happened on April 12, and soon most of the students were marching off to war. The board, at their June 1861, meeting conferred B.A. and LL.B. degrees on the senior students recommended by the faculty. They declined, however, a faculty suggestion that they should confer an honorary LL.D. on the Confederacy's provisional president, Jefferson Davis, deeming it "inexpedient" to do so just then.[61]

In the same emergency meeting held at the beginning of August 1861, in which they voted to move most of the law department out of the downtown rooms rented from William Avent, the members of the board of trustees learned from Chancellor Barnard that only four students were pre-enrolled for the academic year due to start just a few weeks later. They also were proffered the chancellor's resignation, along with those of several professors, including Stearns, Trotter, and Lamar, all of which they immediately accepted. Stearns was told that he might retain control over the law library as long as he remained in Oxford, and apparently he intended to do so indefinitely. But very soon a strong "sectional feeling" that had developed among Mississippi's population (and those of its neighboring states as well), Charles Howry many years later recalled, caused anyone "of northern birth" to become hated and despised. And so Stearns was driven into exile to Peru, New York, the hometown of his second wife, Mary Jane Feriss Stearns, whom he had met on a steamboat cruise and married in 1858. His colleague, James Trotter, returned to his law practice in Holly Springs and soon was serving again on the circuit bench. Professor Lamar, having been commissioned a lieutenant colonel in the Confederate Army in that autumn of 1861, left Oxford and traveled to Richmond, Virginia.[62]

In 1863, Stearns and his wife returned briefly to Oxford, by then occupied by Union troops, but found no reason to remain. Instead, they moved to Chicago, Illinois, where he was very soon building up a profitable law practice. Shortly after the Civil War ended, he again briefly returned to Oxford and, while there, retained Charles Howry (who had been serving as a lieutenant in the Confederate Army) to manage his local affairs. During the war years his Oxford properties had apparently been carefully tended and protected by his sometime slave servant, Harrison Stearns, who was by then, of course, a "freedman of Lafayette County." On December 1, 1865, Stearns signed a deed conveying to Harrison Stearns—because he was "indebted" to him for his "labor heretofore performed"—one lot of land in Oxford. Sadly, in May 1865, Stearns had been the victim of a savage robbery and beating. The wounds he suffered from that assault triggered periodic bouts of severe depression, and, on September 8, 1867, while on a business trip to Albert Lea, Minnesota, he took his own life. On January 2, 1868, his widow, Mary J. Stearns, "of Cook County, Illinois," deeded two more lots over to Harrison Stearns. Harrison Stearns himself, on March 20, 1869, for one hundred dollars, deeded one of those two lots over to Oxford's Methodist Episcopal Church, for which he was one of the three trustees. Today that lot is the designated historical site known as the "Burns 'Belfry' Church" site.[63]

In March 1866, Judge Trotter died from natural causes at his home up in Holly Springs. Lamar, however, did come back to Oxford in the late spring of 1865, straight from Appomattox Court House, under a federal parole. During the intervening four years, he had experienced both the savagery of front-line combat as a Confederate officer and the luxury of European high society, in both London and Paris, as the Confederacy's commissioner to the Czar of Russia. The Oxford he came back to was still in a semi-ruinous condition, with the downtown area around the Square virtually burned out. Though his father-in-law, Judge A. B. Longstreet, was now back in town, living in retirement. Neither of his two brothers, who had earlier joined him in Oxford, nor either of his two law partners from a decade earlier, had survived the war, and the university was still closed. So Lamar soon moved with his family thirty miles south to Coffeeville, the county seat of Yalobusha County and a railroad town, and there began a law practice in partnership with General Edward Cary Walthall, who twenty years later, would succeed him in the United States Senate.[64]

Meanwhile, the university had reopened in the autumn of 1865 with a student body totaling just fewer than one hundred, many of whom were Confederate Army veterans. Its new chancellor was John Newton Waddel, who had served from 1848 to 1857 as the professor of Greek and Latin. By the time of their June 1866 meeting, its reactivated board of trustees was sufficiently confident that more students would be enrolling in the coming academic year to invite Lamar to take up again the professorship of ethics. He did so and returned to Oxford that fall. At the same time, the board voted to offer the chair of law to Horatio F. Simrall, a prominent Wilkinson county lawyer and politician who from 1857 to 1861 had been in his native state of Kentucky teaching law at the University of Louisville. They had forgotten, perhaps, that Simrall, twenty years earlier, had argued in the state legislature that Oxford, because it was too far removed from most of the state's main population centers, would not be a suitable location for the state university. Perhaps because he was still of the same opinion, after several months of apparent indecision, he had still not accepted their offer. In October 1866, therefore, the board, in desperation, asked Lamar to take up the law professor's duties in addition to those he already had as professor of ethics. As of January 1, 1867, he turned over the chair of ethics to a colleague and became solely the professor of law. It is perhaps not surprising therefore, that, though there was an 1866–67 senior law class, its only graduating member was Oxonian Charles Howry.[65]

Lamar, Charles Howry recalled decades later, was really not much interested in the practice of law and not very much concerned about money matters. But he loved the science of jurisprudence, loved teaching, and was a wonderful friend to his students. In the summer of 1866, he was of great assistance to Howry personally. The young Confederate veteran needed a temporary license to practice law that summer and to obtain it would have to pass an examination administered by former board chairman Alexander Clayton, who was now the local circuit judge. Judge Clayton's special area of interest and main field of legal expertise, Lamar confided to him, was "Limitation of Estates." So Howry made sure he knew all about that topic, and indeed the exam turned out to be "largely confined to the subject mentioned" by Lamar. Like Howry, about a third of the fifty-four students who were enrolled in the law program during Lamar's tenure as professor were Confederate army or navy veterans desperately trying, at the same time, both to earn a living and to support their impoverished families. Many of them, including future Mississippi Congressman "Private John Allen," "Colonel Lamar" (as everyone called him now) excused from paying the fifty-dollar "tuition fee," which law students alone now were required to pay and would have gone directly into his own pocket.[66]

Furthermore, according to Edward Mayes, another one of his students, his future son-in-law, and the university's future chancellor, Lamar had "the happy faculty of being able to explain clearly and succinctly the great principles of jurisprudence so that the dullest intellect [would] comprehend them." The law curriculum during those immediate postwar years, meanwhile, was generally very little changed from what it had been a decade earlier. The prescribed textbooks were the same ones that had been listed in the 1858 *Catalogue* and basically the same ones that were being used, around that same time, in the law programs at the University of Virginia, the University of North Carolina, and even Harvard. Although no evidence supports the assertion sometimes made that he pioneered the use of case law in teaching his classes, Lamar did, in addition to lecturing on the texts and giving regular oral examinations, introduce the practice of designating at the end of each day's lecture, one student to summarize the lecture's substance at the beginning of the next class meeting and lead a brief class discussion of it. His other innovation was having, some weeks, federal moot courts instead of the customary state-level ones. In either case, he presided as judge while the students served as attorneys, court clerks, or officers of the law.[67]

Fortunately, the law library, which the board of trustees had ordered left housed in the premises on the Courthouse Square leased from banker Avent in 1861, had somehow survived the war. Someone had evidently moved it back onto the campus sometime before the Square was burned by General A. J. "Whiskey" Smith in August 1864, for according to the 1866 *Catalogue*, it contained then "upwards of a thousand well selected volumes." At a time when the volumes of Mississippi Reports numbered only forty-one, *The United States*

Statutes at Large only fifteen, and law journals were not yet in existence, that was a very respectable total. And things soon got even better. In 1868, in response to a request from the board of trustees, the legislature committed itself to furnishing at least ten copies of each new volume of the *Mississippi Reports* for the law library and also a complete bound set of the journals of both its houses each year. And around that same time the board itself came up with five hundred dollars to purchase *The United States Supreme Court Reports* plus any "standard elementary law works" that Lamar felt were needed.[68]

Presumably, the law library was now housed once again in the Lyceum, and the law classes were conducted there also. Though Howry was the only 1867 law graduate—another attempt by the university faculty, that year, to confer an honorary LL.D. on Jefferson Davis was again vetoed by the trustees—the class of 1868 had twelve graduates (including three Tennesseans and one Texan); the 1869 class had ten, and the 1870 class had fifteen (including, again, four from out of state). Sixteen more students, who for one reason or another never did graduate, were enrolled in Lamar's classes at one time or another.[69] To give the commencement address to the 1869 law graduating class, on June 23 of that year, Lamar invited his long time friend, Wiley P. Harris, one of mid-nineteenth century Mississippi's most eminent legislators and jurists. "The profession of Law is not the easiest, nor the shortest road to wealth or fame," Harris cautioned them, though "it is, in America, a highly respectable calling." Unfortunately, however, admission to its ranks was becoming rather too "easy." It had always to be remembered that, remarked Harris, "One of the three great Departments into which the supreme government is divided by the constitutions of all the states and of the United States is confided to the legal profession exclusively." They had had the good luck to be given a "systematic and comprehensive legal education." Now they were ready to offer their services as "the future Judges of great Commonwealths, and the advisers of Judges." If they wished for success in those capacities, they must always remember that "What constitutes force in writing and speaking consists in forming an idea complete and perfect in itself in our own minds, and the employment of the plainest words to convey it to the minds of others as it exists in our own." He advised, "You will find that you begin to exert influence with Judges when you are known to be accurate, and when you have come to be clear. For a clear comprehension of legal doctrines—simplicity and clearness of statement, combined with a respectful demeanor to the court, and a courteous bearing to counsel, are the sure guarantees of influence." He would, he assured them, watch their careers "with more than ordinary interest."[70]

In the aftermath of the Civil War, meanwhile, Professor Lamar was a rising star in Mississippi politics. Back in the fall of 1866 his faculty colleagues had elected him to be their "historian." But over the next few years he very rarely attended the faculty meetings chaired by Chancellor Waddel and was frequently out of town. In 1867, he was elected to the board of directors of the Mississippi Central Railroad, which met regularly in Water Valley. He very frequently attended and spoke at Confederate veteran reunions. He also spoke, on occasion, at ladies' literary club meetings, and in the spring of 1869 he told the faculty and students at the Female Institute in Jackson, Tennessee, that he saw "no generic difference between the mind of man and woman." In fact, he told them, "education for women should be put on the same level as education for men." By the spring of 1868, he had opened up a law office on the Square in Oxford and soon was representing clients in both the circuit court and in the newly established United States federal court in Oxford. Around that same time, he also began to be very active again in Democratic party politics, and in the spring of 1869, made an hour-long welcoming address to former Confederate Jacob Thompson when he was finally allowed to return home from foreign exile.[71]

In October, 1869, the office of faculty historian was formally terminated. By then, Lamar's practice was bringing in enough income to enable him to support his family without a university salary. And at the university itself things were changing. In Jackson, where a new "Reconstruction" constitution for the state was being put into place, the university's existing board of trustees was replaced by a new one appointed by Governor James L. Alcorn. By the spring of 1870, there were rumors circulating that Negroes would soon be admitted to the university. At the end of that academic year, in June, Lamar tendered his resignation. His students presented him with "a fine divan" as a parting gift. And he, in his farewell address to them at the June Commencement, wished them all happiness and prosperity throughout their lives, though "with just enough of sorrow to remind you that this earth is not your home." Two years later, in 1872, taking advantage of the federal Amnesty Act passed that spring, he was reelected to Congress. In 1876, he was elected one of Mississippi's two senators; in 1885, President Cleveland would appoint him secretary of the interior in the first Democratic administration since before the Civil War, and in 1887 he would become the first former university law professor ever to be appointed to the United States Supreme Court.[72]

But, while Lamar's career was in its ascendancy, the university was going through a time of depression. Undergraduate enrollment generally lagged below three hundred and, between 1870 and 1874, the total law student enrollment was only nineteen. A suggestion by the new board of trustees, in 1872, that the legislature should perhaps amend the university's constitution so as to move the law department to Jackson did not help the situation. Nor did a bill passed by the legislature in 1873 that authorized (though it did not order), the newly endowed college for black students, Alcorn A&M, and the university to establish and operate jointly a law school in Jackson—though that never actually happened, both because no funding was ever provided for the project and because neither of the two institutions involved were very interested in the idea.[73] Meanwhile, faced with Lamar's resignation in the spring of 1870, the trustees had invited Judge J. A. P. Campbell to take his place. But the judge (who would later serve on the state's supreme court and be granted an honorary LL.D. by the university in 1883) declined the offer. So apparently did Henry Craft of the Memphis bar, who was elected next. Though Craft was listed as the "Titular Professor of Law" for the 1870–71 academic year, the actual teaching of the seven law students enrolled that year was done by Colonel Jordan M. Phipps, a Lafayette County native who had earned a B.A. in mathematics from the University in 1851 and had then become the "Acting Adjunct Professor of Law." It was a second-time experience for Phipps, who, back in 1852, after Lamar's first departure from campus had succeeded him as the "Adjunct Professor of Mathematics." After him, another alumnus of the university, Thomas J. Walton, who had earned a B.A. (with honors) in 1854 and an LL.B. in 1857, filled the law chair from 1871 to 1874. In 1874, he was appointed chancery court judge for the Twelfth District and, for the next three years, the law program at the university was suspended.[74]

CHAPTER 2

Up Again and Going Strong
(1877–1911)

By 1877, the political climate of the state was much changed from what it had been just three years earlier. A sweeping Democratic victory in the state election of 1875 had put an end to "Reconstruction." A new board of trustees had been created whose fifteen members, at least five of whom had to be alumni of the university, were appointed to serve six-year, staggered terms by the new Democratic governor, who also served as their ex-officio chairman. The university also had a new chancellor, Alexander "Old Straight" Stewart, a highly respected Confederate Army general. Working closely with the new board members, Chancellor Stewart raised the university's student enrollment back up to nearly five hundred, and on June 28, 1877, the board voted to revive the university's law program.[1]

Their first choice to serve as law professor, Circuit Court Judge James S. Hamm of Meridian, evidently refused their offer. They next offered the position to Edward Mayes, who accepted. A native of Hinds County, Mayes, while still in his teens, had experienced combat in a Confederate cavalry unit during the last year of the Civil War and, in the autumn of 1865, had been the first nonresident of Oxford to enroll in the university as an undergraduate. Awarded a B.A. degree in 1868, he had, just a year later, on May 11, 1869, married Law Professor L. Q. C. Lamar's daughter (and former university president "judge" Longstreet's granddaughter), Francis Eliza Lamar. By 1870, he had earned an LL.B. degree. After spending another year on campus working both as a tutor in English and as the manager of the library, he had followed his father-in-law's example from five years earlier and moved with his family to Coffeeville and established a law practice there. Then, when Lamar left Oxford in 1872 to serve in the House of Representatives in Washington, Mayes came back to Oxford to take his place and soon had a flourishing practice on the Square.[2]

No doubt his family connections helped Mayes get the professorial appointment, but once appointed he began proving he deserved it. C. B. Howry remembered him as having been "very learned in the law" and remarked, "I never knew a man his equal except perhaps Attorney General [Augustus H.] Garland of the Cleveland administration." An article in the March 1880 issue of the *University Magazine,* an on-campus student publication, on "The Law School" reported proudly with regard to the professor: "Mr. Mayes is ranked among the most learned lawyers in the state, and by his indefatigable energy, determined purpose and high reputation, has caused a large number of young men to attend the law lectures here."

Five years earlier, in 1872, as part of the desperate campaign to save the law program from extinction, the curriculum for the LL.B. degree had been cut down from two to just one year of course work, and Mayes did not change it. Presumably because of the three-year closedown that was just ending, a record total of thirty-six students enrolled in the 1877–78 law class, and twenty-nine of them would graduate at the end of that academic year. Altogether, during the four-year period beginning in September 1877 and ending in July 1881, although law students still had to pay a tuition fee of fifty dollars in addition to their other expenses, which undergraduates did not (except for students from out of state, who had to pay thirty dollars), a total of ninety-one students enrolled in the law program under the new professor. And seventy-seven of them would graduate.[3]

The *University Magazine* article reported further that "A Chancellor, one Professor, and five Lecturers constitute the Law Faculty." Chancellor Stewart was, of course, an honorary member. As for the "five Lecturers," a note inside the back cover of the same issue reported that during that year "courses of lectures were delivered before the Law Class" by six notable members of the legal profession in the Oxford area. They were Chief Justice Horatio F. Simrall (who fourteen years earlier had declined an offer of appointment to the law professorship), Associate Justice Hamilton H. Chalmers, U.S. District Judge Robert A. Hill, the Honorable Jehu A. Orr, the Honorable Hugh A. Barr, and the Honorable Harvey W. Walter. The new curriculum was essentially an abridged version of the two-year program that Professor Stearns had taught two decades earlier. Blackstone's four-volume *Commentaries* was still the basic foundation text. Stephen on *Pleading,* the first volume of Greenleaf's *Evidence,* the three volumes of Kent's *Commentaries,* Adams's *Equity* and Smith on *Contracts* were all still required reading. The addition of the abridged Harvard edition of Addison on *Torts* brought the total number of required texts to twelve, which meant that students had to read and master a little more than one of them in each month of the academic year. The one-year course was not a light workload.[4]

Moot court trials were still a part of the curriculum also, and the same *University Magazine* article reported on three that were to be held in that spring 1880, with "Judge Hill" presiding:

No. 3.
On the first day of January, 1880, the south-bound passenger train of the Chicago, St. Louis and New Orleans R. R. Co., ran against and instantly killed a bay mare, the property of Henry Tyler, worth $200. Henry Tyler lived in Oxford, and a corporate ordinance required all cattle, horses, &c., to be kept up by the owners, and if permitted to run at large, there was a fine of $10 for each violation of the ordinance. The mare was estray, Tyler's gates having been left open by his servant; and the killing was done in the corporate limits while the train was running twelve miles an hour. The bell was rung and whistle sounded, and brakes put on by Company's servants.

Hendrick & McDonald for Plaintiff
Millsaps & Pegues, for Defendant"

No. 6.
On the first day of January, 1876, Harrison Taylor bought lot 116 in the town of Oxford, Miss., for the purpose of building a residence on it, he being a man of family. He commenced building a dwelling, and necessary outhouses immediately. On the first of March, the house being nearly completed, he gave a mortgage on the property to George Askew. Taylor's wife did not join in the mortgage deed. On the first of April, he moved on the premises, and from that day has occupied it as a residence. On the third of June, 1879, the debt not being paid, the trustee in the mortgage put up the property and sold it. The sale was regularly made, and Askew bought it in for his debt and wants to have possession, but Taylor will not vacate, claiming that the mortgage was void. The trustee has executed a proper deed to Askew.

Downing & Grimes for Plaintiff.
Dyer & Harrison for Defendant."

No. 5.
George Peabody drew the following check:
$800.00. OXFORD, Miss., January 1, 1880.
At sight, pay to the order of Geo. Blair, the sum of eight hundred dollars, and charge to the account of Geo. Peabody.
This check Blair altered by inserting *one* before eight hundred, *een* after the word eight, so as to make it read a check for eighteen hundred dollars. He then offered to sell it to Fletcher Jones. Jones went to West, cashier of the bank, after bank hours, showed him the check and asked him if it was good. West replied that he would pay it in business hours. Thereupon, Jones bought the check, and the next day it was paid by the bank. A few days afterwards, the bank discovered the alteration. And now desires to make Jones pay back to them one thousand dollars.
Buford & Stokes for Plaintiff
Buntin & Wheat for Defendant."[5]

The one-year law program was replaced in June 1881, with board approval, by a two-year curriculum scheduled to commence in the 1882 academic year. The first year reading load now comprised eleven textbooks, including the first three volumes of Blackstone, Stephens, Greenleaf, volumes II and III of Kent, plus Bishop's three volumes on criminal law (all of which had been used by both Stearns and Lamar), and Bigelow on *Torts* (published in 1882), which replaced Addison. The second year reading load included eight textbooks: Adams, Blackstone's fourth volume (*Of Public Wrongs*), and volume I of Kent, plus Bispham's *Principles of Equity Jurisprudence,* Cooley's *Constitutional Limitations,* Desty's *Federal Procedure,* May on *Insurance,* Pierce on *Railroads,* and also the Mississippi Code and the United States and Mississippi Constitutions. Over the next decade, Davis on *International Law* replaced volume I and Brooms' *Commentaries on the Common Law* replaced volumes II and III of Kent; Curtis's *Lectures on Federal Law* replaced Desty, and Teleman on *Real Property* replaced May.[6]

The curriculum was very much in accord with prevailing national standards. An 1892 ABA Committee on Legal Education report indicates that those same textbooks were being used generally in law school programs nationwide. And although a handful of universities, including the University of Maryland and the University of Pennsylvania, had three-year programs and some, including the University of Georgia, Emory College, and Tulane University, still had only one-year programs, a two-year program was the national norm.[7]

Over the first decade of the restored two-year program at the University of Mississippi, under Mayes's leadership the total number of students enrolled in the program nearly doubled from just twelve in 1881–82 to twenty-two in 1890–91. Out of a total of 145 students (and, although the university became co-educational in 1882, all of them male) enrolled over the decade, eighty-two achieved "senior" status, and seventy-eight graduated with LL.B. degrees. And, thanks to Mayes and their other instructors, according to one of the graduates, University of Mississippi–trained lawyers went out into the world persuaded that "the common law possesses the unapproached vigor of ideal beauty, clothed with the attributes of wisdom" and that it gave "expression to the deep feelings of the human heart, rolling in cadence with the echoes of morality and religion."[8]

As law professor, unlike the university's other professors, Mayes was not required to attend daily chapel, but he was a very active member of the university faculty. His colleagues' high regard for him was demonstrated in July 1886, when the board of trustees abolished the office of chancellor and instead directed the faculty to elect a chairman. The faculty members voted unanimously for Mayes to fill that office. A year later, after drawing their attention to the fact that the board had set no fixed time period for their chairman to serve, Mayes asked them to vote again. They did so and again elected him unanimously, as they did for the two years that followed.[9]

In his capacity as their chairman, Mayes successfully combated a campaign by State Senator J. Z. George, in 1886–87, to get the legislature to make the university share a portion of its special annual appropriation with the newly endowed Mississippi A&M College in Starkville. In 1888–89, he presided over a major redrafting of the university's undergraduate curriculum whereby a total of nineteen "schools" would now offer a wide variety of majors and elective courses for students working for B.A., B.S., or B.P. degrees. In the summer of 1889, he traveled the state telling audiences at public meetings in all of the major cities about the programs that the university had to offer their sons and daughters The result was a 36 percent increase (from 160 to 218) in its undergraduate enrollment for the 1889–90 academic year.[10]

In their June 1889 meeting, the board of trustees rewarded Mayes for his efforts, first by dismissing five of the university's eight professors who, he had suggested, were no longer pulling their full weight, and second by restoring the office of chancellor of the university and appointing him to fill it. Thus he became the first professor of law in the history of the university to hold the office of chancellor—although he would not be the last. His two and a half years in that dual capacity were probably the most productive of his professional career. On campus, in addition to conducting his law classes, he was responsible for providing the university with its first library building. At that same portentous June 1889 meeting the trustees had allocated ten thousand dollars to build a library. Two years (and twelve thousand dollars) later, a two-story red brick "neo-Gothic" structure with a round tower and spire roof had been built on the campus just to the east of the antebellum Chapel. Known today as "Ventress Hall", it was destined just two decades later to be the first building on the campus to be named "Lamar Hall." The twelve thousand volumes that constituted the university's general library were moved into it out of the Lyceum. The law library, however, by then consisting of fifteen hundred volumes, continued for the time being to be housed in the Lyceum.[11]

Off campus, in addition to recruiting vigorously for the university, Mayes was also active in the statewide legal profession. Encouraged and inspired by the founding of the American Bar Association in Saratoga Springs, New York, in 1878, Mississippi's second statewide bar association—the first had operated 1821–25 in Natchez—was organized in a meeting held in Jackson on January 4, 1886. Those present began by electing as their first president the university law program's founding father and longtime guardian, patron, and sponsor, Judge Andrew M. Clayton. They concluded their proceedings that evening with a speech delivered by Professor Mayes on some aspects of his specialty, property law. The following year, he was elected chairman of the association's newly created committee on legal education, and his lectures on property law became a staple of their annual meetings. During the six years that the association remained active, it played the leading role in organizing the state constitutional convention of 1890, in which the constitution by which the state continues to be governed to this day was drafted. In the convention Mayes both served on the education committee and chaired the committee on the bill of rights and general provisions.[12]

Mayes also, in 1890, played a leading role in the revival of the Mississippi Historical Society and served as its first president. Volume I of *The Biographical and Historical Memoirs of Mississippi,* published by the Godspeed Publishing Company of Chicago in 1891, contained an article by him on the state's

"Legal and Judicial History", and volume II contained another by him on its "Educational History." The United States Department of Education commissioned him to write a *History of Education in Mississippi,* which he completed and submitted in 1891, though it was not published until 1899.[13]

All of these outside activities, in addition to his everyday, on-campus responsibilities as law professor and chancellor, must have kept Edward Mayes exceedingly busy. On June 23, 1891, he told the university trustees that he wished to be relieved of those responsibilities as soon as possible. "I am convinced," he told them, "that I have come to the parting of the ways. I must choose between the office of Chancellor and my profession as a lawyer. I cannot attend to the latter, and at the same time to the former . . . [and] as things are now, I prefer the law."[14]

In fact, Mayes did not even remain on campus through the next academic year. Offered a position in a prominent Jackson law firm in December 1891, he formally resigned both of his positions and in January 1892 moved to the state capital. There, over the next few years he built up a flourishing practice, serving, among others, the Illinois Central Railroad and the Yazoo and Mississippi Valley Railroad and trying several cases before the United States Supreme Court. But he must soon have discovered that the field of legal education was not an area of activity he could distance himself from for very long. In 1895, he accepted the deanship of the newly established law faculty at Millsaps College and remained in that office until his death in 1917.

In the mid-1880s, Mayes had been awarded an honorary LL.D. degree (one of several that he was honored with during his long career) by Mississippi College in Clinton. In 1918, the departure of most of Millsaps's law students to take part in World War I would cause the law program there to be discontinued permanently. In 1930, however, a group of Jackson lawyers, some of them former Millsaps law faculty, organized an unaccredited, private law night school called the Jackson School of Law that held night classes on the Millsaps campus. In 1972, Mississippi College bought out the Jackson School of Law and quickly developed it into a fully-accredited institution known as the Mississippi College School of Law. Thus it may be said of Edward Mayes that he is part of the history of every law school that has existed to this day in Mississippi.[15]

The University of Mississippi Board of Trustees, faced with Mayes's sudden departure in the middle of the 1891–92 academic year, appointed Robert Fulton, the professor of physics and astronomy, to serve as the vice chancellor for its remaining six months and then in June 1892 elected him chancellor, in which position he served until 1906. To fill the law professor position, in January 1892 they chose one of their own members, the Honorable Albert Hall Whitfield, who had been appointed to the board by Governor Robert Lowery in 1889. As were Mayes and Fulton, Whitfield was both a native Mississippian and an alumnus of the university. Born on his father's plantation near Aberdeen in Monroe County in 1849, he had enrolled on the Oxford campus in 1868 and earned his B.A., with first honors, in 1871. Then, over the next three years, he had served on the faculty as an adjunct professor of Greek and also as a teacher of Latin, English, and history, while earning an M.A. in 1873 and his LL.B. in the tiny law class of 1874. In 1875, he had returned home briefly to Aberdeen and practiced law there for about a year before moving on to Grenada. By 1880, he was back in Oxford practicing law in partnership with future United States Senator W. V. Sullivan and enjoying a professional relationship with, among others, Edward Mayes and Charles B. Howry. In the courtroom, Howry later recalled (quoting the English historian, Hallam, with regard to a pillar of the English bar): "He scattered the flowers of polite literature over the thorny brakes of jurisprudence."[16]

Whitfield's tenure as law professor was brilliant but brief. In the summer of 1894 Governor John M. Stone appointed him an associate justice of the state supreme court. From 1900 to 1908 he would serve as the supreme court's chief justice. From 1896 to 1904, he would serve again on the university's board of trustees. Most of the board members would have known him well. In 1893, he had negotiated an agreement on their behalf with the Illinois Central Railroad with regard to the land immediately to the east of their tracks bordering on the campus that is, today, occupied by the Gertrude Castellow Ford Theater, the Richard and Diane Scruggs Hall, and the baseball stadium. During his two and a half years in the law chair, a total of thirty-eight students had earned an LL.B. degree, fifteen of them "with special distinction," including Stone Deavours of Laurel, who would later serve both as president of the state bar association (1924–25) and dean of the law school (1930–32), and nine others "with distinction." By 1895, of those thirty-eight, twenty-five were engaged in the practice of law in Mississippi; two in Kansas City, Missouri; two in Arizona; one in Texas; one in New Mexico; one in Arizona; one in California; one in Atlanta, Georgia; and one in New York City. Two had opted out of the legal profession—one to become a Methodist minister and the other to become a school teacher—and one had died. Four of them had been elected to the lower house of the state legislature, and one was a member of the state senate. As a departing gift, Whitfield himself was awarded an honorary LL.D. by the university in the 1894 commencement ceremonies.[17]

Whitfield's successor, Garvin D. Shands, was another well known Mississippi figure, having served as the state's lieutenant governor from 1882 to 1890. He was, however, by birth and upbringing, a South Carolinian and had received his undergraduate education at Wofford College in that state. During the Civil War, he served successively in two South Carolina units of the Confederate army. After the war, he eventually settled in Panola County, Mississippi, where he both taught school and read law for two years before earning a law degree at the University of Kentucky in 1870. Returning then to Mississippi, he began practicing law in Senatobia in Tate County, where he quickly came to be regarded—C. B. Howry recalled decades later—as "a leading lawyer in northwest Mississippi." Prior to his election as lieutenant governor, he had served a term (1876–80) in the lower house of the state legislature. In 1892, several of the university trustees had wanted to see him succeed Mayes as chancellor, but he lost to Fulton by a vote of five to four.[18]

Just as " Governor Shands" (as he was commonly called on campus) was taking over control of the university's law program, it was again moved out of the Lyceum. The October 1894 issue of the *University Magazine* reported that the "Elocution and Law classes" were being moved into the old "northwest dormitory." Their new home would be in Jefferson Hall, located immediately to the northeast of the Lyceum, approximately where Peabody Hall stands today. It was at the west end of the men's dormitory building, originally built in 1848. The middle portion of the building was called Lafayette Hall and its eastern portion Rittenhouse Hall. The building, which had three floors with a balcony running along the outside front of each floor was surrounded by tall shade trees and had been "nicely refurbished." So the move would "put these important departments of the University upon a progressive and efficient basis." They would have their offices and lecture rooms there, and the YMCA was going to be "provided with a commodious and elegant room in the same building."[19]

The *University Magazine*'s editors also remarked that "we congratulate ourselves in having the law chair filled by that cultured and affable gentleman, Governor G. D. Shands." "The Governor," Howry later on remembered, quickly brought about "an increased attendance and an extended scope of instruction" in the law program and soon became a very popular man on campus, "not only with his classes but with all around him." The number of law graduates, just a year later, in the summer of 1895, was up to twenty. Just four years later, the 1898–99 law class included a record total of fifty-eight students. In the mid-1890s, former chief justice Horatio F. Simrall, Judge Robert A. Hill, Jehu A. Orr, and Hugh A. Barr were still coming in from outside to lecture the law classes, just as they had been doing fourteen years earlier By 1897, however, the board of trustees, could not help realizing that more full-time help was needed. That year they voted to revive the second law professorship that had been created back in 1859 but unfilled since 1861 and appointed the Honorable Thomas H. Somerville of the Winona Bar to fill it. At the same time, they voted to elevate Professor Shand's position to that of "Dean of the Law Department."[20]

The law students, meanwhile, were organizing themselves. Since 1849, the university's undergraduate students had been required to belong to one of its two "literary societies," either Phi Sigma or the Hermean Society. Both of those societies had a campus office in the Chapel, elected officers, elected the honors speakers for the annual commencement ceremonies, and appointed the editors of the *University Magazine* and other student publications. Any law student who wanted to could also belong to one of the societies and, probably by the early 1890s, the law students, being generally older than the undergraduates and more numerous than they had been in earlier decades, were coming to dominate them. So the board of trustees, in their 1894 annual meeting in the spring of that year, ruled that, thenceforth, no law student would be eligible for any honor offered by either of the two societies.[21]

The law students' response to that ruling was reported in the *University Magazine*'s October 1894 issue: "The promising young disciples of Blackstone" had "organized themselves into a society similar to the literary societies." Called the Blackstone Society, it had "met the approbation of each and every member of both the Literary and Law Department" and it was hoped that "opportunities for more honors in the University [would] be given by this young Hercules of eloquence and knowledge." Meanwhile, "as a part of the student body of the university," they were certainly "entitled to representation on the staff of the University magazine. Accordingly Hermean and Phi Sigma [would] have fewer representatives on the staff by one each, these two places being filled by students from the law society." According to the 1895–96 university *Catalogue,* the club, "composed exclusively of members of the law classes," held "weekly meetings for mutual improvement in the forensic arts and for the study and discussion of legal and politico-legal subjects." "This branch of the law school work," it was believed, would "be a valuable auxiliary in the acquisition of ready learning for practical use." Also, it soon became the custom to hold an "Anniversarian Contest" every year on the evening of the first Friday in April. The contest was an oratorical competition, the winner of which would make the valedictorian speech on behalf of his fellow members of the graduating law class during the June commencement ceremonies a few weeks later.[22]

The law curriculum in 1895–96 was essentially the same as it had been fifteen years earlier. The nine-month academic year was divided up into a first term (September–January) and a second term (January–June). The curriculum for the junior class included:

FIRST TERM
The Political and Legal Constitution of England
The Public and Domestic Relations of Individuals
The Law of Real Estate and Conveyance Thereof
The Laws of Personal Property and Transfers Thereof
The Organization and Jurisdiction of Courts
Pleading and Practice
The Law of Evidence

SECOND TERM
Bills of Exchange and Promissory Notes
Principal and Agent
Partnership
Principal and Surety
Bailments
Insurance
Corporations
Criminal Law, Common Law, and Statutory
Criminal Pleading and Practice

The curriculum for the senior class included:

FIRST TERM
Contracts: A Brief Review
Torts: A Brief Review
Equity Jurisprudence, Including Testaments and Administration
Equity Pleading and Practice, Including Probate and Minors' Business

SECOND TERM
Public International Law
Special Reference to the Federal Jurisprudence and Procedure
Railways and Common Carriers
Real Estate: A Review, with American Systems
Code Study: Mississippi Code of 1892, Annotated

The required textbooks were still mostly the same ones that had been used fifteen years earlier. First-year students were expected to master twelve volumes, and second-year students a total of eleven plus the 1892 Mississippi Code and both the United States and the Mississippi Constitutions.[23]

Moot courts were "held from time to time during the term" for the purpose of making the students into "not merely theoretical but practical lawyers. They were presided over by the professor who would conclude each of them by reviewing the arguments offered and giving his decisions upon them. Every student was "required not only to frame pleadings for circuit and chancery court cases, but [also] to take cases supposed to have been decided in the court below and prepare them for the supreme court, giving careful attention to every detail." That was to say that the student would be "required to prepare a petition for appeal, an appeal bond, a transcript of the record, a bill of exceptions, an assignment of errors, an abstract of the case, and a written brief." All of the senior students could also expect to be afforded an opportunity "to participate in the actual management" of moot court cases. Also, written examinations were held each year in each class, and before graduation each student was required to submit to the law faculty "a thesis on some legal topic selected by himself."[24]

A section in the law school portion of the 1895–96 *Catalogue* titled "Why a Mississippian should Study Law at Oxford" repeated essentially the same arguments that Professor Stearns had used in his circular sent around the state forty years earlier. One got a much better legal education than one could by going through an apprenticeship in a law office. One got to know and make friends with the other up and coming young men of the state in one's own age group. One had access to all of the various services and benefits offered by the university, including taking optional courses in other fields of study and the use of the libraries, reading rooms, and gymnasium. Finally, and most important, one's diploma, once earned, secured one a license to practice law in any court in the state. The cost of doing so, furthermore, was "exceedingly small." The annual tuition fee for law students was still fifty dollars. And the cost of buying the required textbooks was "sixty dollars for the junior course and about fifty dollars for the senior." Most students, however, borrowed at least some copies of the required texts from their friends. So the going overall expense rate per student was, in fact, around seventy-five to one hundred dollars per year.[25]

It was still possible, in 1895–96, to meet all of the diploma requirements, including "recitations, lectures and examinations" of both the junior and the senior courses over the course of a single academic year. A few students could, and did, economize by doing so. The 1895–96 *Catalogue* warned, however, that "The list of subjects studied is being added to yearly, and whatever other students may have accomplished in the past in the way of double work, future students are warned that, only with great difficulty, will they be able to compass the whole course in one year." Another alternative for "young men who [found] themselves unable to spend more than one year at a law school" was to enroll for just the junior course. There had never been a case where any student who had done so had failed to secure admission to the bar by the alternative method, still in place, of applying to any one of the state's chancellors (chancery court judges) and passing the tests that they routinely gave. Another available alternative was to take the two years of law classes but not the examinations, and then apply, with confidence, to one of the chancellors.[26] At the other extreme, at least one student, James E. Edmonds of Bolivar County, demonstrated that it was possible (by working diligently) to earn both a B.A. degree and an LL.B. degree in just four years (1896–1900) on campus. And, beginning in 1898, the handful of students who earned an LL.B. with either "distinction" (a 90 to 94 percent overall grade average) or with "special distinction" (95 to 100 percent) became entitled to compete with one another for a prize given by the Edward Thompson Company, Law Book Publishers, of Northport, Long Island,

New York. The prizewinner could choose to be given "a complete set either of the Encyclopedia of Pleading and Practice or . . . of the new American and English Encyclopedia of Law," both of which were worth approximately two hundred dollars each.[27]

Also, by 1898, the increased student enrollment meant that yet another distinguished member of the Oxford area bar had been hired to serve as a part-time member of the law school faculty. The man who joined J. A. Orr and H. A. Barr as a third "Lecturer on Common and Statute Law" was Colonel J. W. T. Falkner (the grandfather of 1949 Nobel Prize winner William Faulkner). One of L. Q. C. Lamar's students, Falkner had earned his law degree at the university in 1869. Then, over the next two decades, he had been in partnership with C. B. Howry, served as an assistant United States district attorney, occupied a seat in the lower house of the state legislature (1892–94), and been elected to the state senate in 1895. That same year he was appointed to serve on the university's board of trustees and would do so until 1908.[28]

In addition to what they learned in class from their professors and from Colonel Falkner and the other regularly scheduled lecturers, the law students of this period, as did their predecessors as well as those who would follow them on down to the present, also learned a lot that was interesting from occasional, visiting distinguished speakers. On June 5, 1900, the graduating law class heard a commencement speech delivered by a man whom Mississippi historian Dunbar Rowland would later come to regard as "one of the truly great lawyers of the state" and upon whom, that same day, the university conferred an LL.D. degree, Supreme Court Justice C. H. Alexander of Jackson. Mississippians, he told them, must regret the fact that they and their fellow southerners lived in a region where mob violence continued to be a very serious legal problem. But, though they should try to limit it in every way they could, its prevalence was not their fault. To understand its existence one only had to look back to the time, three decades earlier, when the champions of Reconstruction ruled over their region. Who could wonder that a white Mississippian, "when he saw his former slave, protected by Federal bayonets, in the seat of magistracy, above a code he could not read" soon concluded that "force and intimidation brought surer and quicker protection for . . . persons and property than the mockery of an appeal to such magistrates." Furthermore, English legal history offered some venerable precedents for both the exercise of private justice and law enforcement by mob violence: Back in the days of the Anglo-Saxons, "the punishment of one crime was left to the family of the injured one" and "the hue and cry was raised and the murderer pursued by an unofficered mob and speedily tried, and the jurors were taken from those who knew most of the crime." Lynching was indeed unlawful, but it was "not always unnatural." And, as the Duke of Wellington had once remarked: "Talk of punishment being inhuman! There is nothing so inhuman as impunity." Fortunately for Mississippians, the Supreme Court of the United States had generally been protective of the rights of southern whites. It had been the court, thank goodness, that had "affirmed the right of Mississippi to separate the races on the highways of travel and also her right, by limitation of suffrage, to exclude ignorance from the polls, and thus to perpetuate the rule of intelligence, which means white supremacy."[29]

Another speaker, a few years earlier, J. R. Yerger of Rosedale, "one of the most prominent legal lights of Coahoma County," had shared with the law student body thirteen points he called "Some Practical Advice to a Young Lawyer." First, he had cautioned them that they should never forget that "the Law is a jealous mistress" and that "unflagging industry" was "the most important element of success at the bar." Second, he advised that they should avoid making the all-too-common mistake of trying to launch both a professional career and a political career simultaneously. A young lawyer who did so would "only discover when it is too late to rectify the fatal error that he has committed professional suicide." Third, while it might be a good idea to begin ones' career in a frontier area where there were not too many established lawyers already in place, one must be sure to do so somewhere where a lot of settlers were pouring in. Fourth, however, all other things being equal and because low professional standards would discourage striving for excellence, he "would strongly advise a location at a point where the bar is strong." Fifth, although "partnerships with a lawyer of experience" were "often valuable to the young practitioner," they should not be continued for too long. One needed to learn to be one's own boss. Six, a young lawyer should always be in his office. "Except in large cities . . . regular business hours were "not anywhere observed in this region," and clients came seeking counsel "at all hours of the day." Seventh, "punctuality in correspondence" was "a professional duty that can never be violated with impunity." As a general rule, "Any business letter should be answered no later than the day after it is received." Eighth, one must be careful to always maintain accurate, alphabetized correspondence files, and "a copying press, costing but a few dollars," would enable them "with very little trouble to take copies of all of your own letters." Ninth, one must keep accurate and detailed records of one's clients' cases and see that court officials do what they are supposed to do when they are supposed to do it. If they do not, then one should complain to a higher court and demand compensation. Tenth, one must always remember that "the client is always in danger whose lawyer does his writing first and his reading afterwards." Eleventh, keep carefully detailed written records of clients' cases. Twelfth, always write clearly and legibly. Thirteenth, and lastly, always keep up-to-date with knowledge of the law and keep on expanding jurisprudential horizons.[30]

Some glimpses of just what a law student's everyday life was like around 1900 are provided in the letters that law and literature student James Edmonds sent home to his parents in Bolivar County in the spring of that year. His "double role of literary student and law both" could be "slightly embarrassing at times," he wrote. For instance, he belonged to both the Blackstone Society and the Hermean Literary Society, which was, strictly speaking, illegal, and they both met at the same time on the same day. "It is all my friends can do to keep me in both," he reported. But on one occasion, when members of the Hermean Society were going to "try" him "because of failure to pay some fines," he was able to put his legal training to good use: "I had my case thrown out of court and wound up by having the officers of the society impeached for malfeasance in office. And all my success was founded on one or two simple law facts my prosecutors and those who brought the charges had failed to remember." In his February 26 letter, he enquired: "Have you a Chase's Blackstone." In addition to the thirty-dollar law tuition fee he had to pay each of his last two years, he estimated that law textbooks, room and board, laundry bills, and barbers' bills cost him around twenty dollars per month. Sword or pistol duels were no longer a part of student life, but formal boxing matches were. In that same February 26 letter he reported: "I had a fight the other day. A regular affair with seconds, referee and time-keeper. It was in a closed room with no spectators. It lasted three rounds and a half under Queensberry rules. And ended by my opponent giving up the fight. He insulted a girl with whom I had an engagement and did not apologize. . . . I had the pleasure of seeing him wear two black eyes and an enlarged nose for three or four days."[31]

Although his "law books cost like everything," he wrote, including "one the other day that cost thirty cents a lesson," Edmonds found his second-year classes, generally speaking, to be "much easier" than his first-year ones. All of the

classes taught by Governor Shands were "informative, profound and awe-inspir-
ing." The Dean had "the most inexhaustible supply of words" he had "ever heard
from a man's mouth." He knew the Mississippi Reports "by heart" and could
"tell you the page, paragraphs and report numbers of every suit . . . brought since
the lines of the state were run." When he was out of town the last week of March
1900, "old Judge Orr" came up from Columbus to lecture on criminal law. The
textbooks were mostly all right, but Hale on *Damages* was referred to by the students as "Hell and Damnation."[32]

In addition to all of his other talents, Edmonds was a skilled sketch artist.
His letters home to his parents often contain one or more amusing drawings.
Several of his drawings can also be seen in volume I of the *Ole Miss* yearbook,
which was published in 1896–97. Volume II (1897–98) opens with a tribute
to the life and achievements of L. Q. C. Lamar—"Educator, Orator, Jurist,
Statesman, Patriot"—who had died in Macon, Georgia, in January 1893 and
tells us that, in October 1894 his body had been brought to Oxford and rebur-
ied in St. Peter's Cemetery close to his old home off North Lamar. Volume II
also included a section several pages in length on the law department. From it
and from those that were included in successive *Ole Miss* volumes, we can learn
a lot of detailed information about the lives, activities, and achievements of successive generations of law students.[33]

The section in volume II indicates that that the forty-three-member
Blackstone Society had elected for each academic year eight officers: a president, vice-president, secretary, treasurer, chaplain, censor, sheriff, and door
keeper. And we also learn that, of the thirty members of the 1898 law graduating class, only seventeen had already been on campus in the fall of 1896. Now,
they were very proud of the fact that they had been "the first class in a life of
five decades to effect a *bona fide* organization, an example which '99 soon followed, and a precedent among many other wise ones, which succeeding classes, noting the doctrine of *stare decisis*, must regard." They had elected four class
officers: a president, a vice-president, a secretary and treasurer, and a historian.
Their president was Dean Shands's son, Audley W. Shands, a future two-time
vice-president of the state bar association (1912–13, 1927–28). The junior law
class that year included "more than a score of members," of whom "fully one-
third" were "graduates of this or some other institution." More than a quarter of
them had taught school, and all of them were "of such an age and deportment
as bespeak a reasonable familiarity with the ways of the world." Although none

of them had, as yet, appeared as "attorneys" in the class moot courts, that privilege being limited to seniors, they had, "however, done faithful service as jurymen and chaplains." The accompanying photographs of the two classes show most of them in dark suits and bow ties, though a few are wearing what appear to be gray suits or black jackets with gray pants, and a few have full-length ties. About half are carrying or wearing hats, mostly black bowlers.[34]

Although the 1897 *Ole Miss* did not have a separate section on the law department, it did devote one page to a description of the Stag Club. Founded in 1895, the club was "restricted to the Law Department" and was "composed of fraternity men entirely, active membership being limited to seven." Its object was to "promote a stronger feeling of brotherly love between members" of the department, "to raise them to a higher plane of social enjoyment and let it be known that the Epicurean tastes of its members are not forgotten." Every year its members hosted an annual banquet, a "feast for the gods," which "many a distinguished man" attended and bowed his head "in homage to our venerable stag."[35]

Generally, down through the last years of the nineteenth century and into the first few years of the twentieth, the law department continued to flourish. The number of graduating law seniors ranged from twenty to thirty per year. Though two of them were from Tennessee, one from New York, and one from Virginia, the overwhelming majority were Mississippians. In 1897, an honorary LL.D. was conferred on alumnus C. B. Howry, "formerly Assistant Attorney General, now Justice, Court of Claims, Washington, D.C." Another LL.D. recipient, in 1906, was Dunbar Rowland, the first director of Mississippi's State Department of Archives and History and future author of *Courts, Judges and Lawyers of Mississippi, 1798–1935.*

Rowland, who had earned an LL.B. in 1898, at the annual meeting of the University's alumni on June 3, 1902, had treated attendees to "an exhaustive treatise on the race question." By 1902, the law library contained some seventeen hundred volumes, and it had become customary to appoint and pay a member of the senior law class as the "Law Librarian." The first separate *Bulletin* for the *Law School of the University of Mississippi* was printed up by the Mississippi Stationery Company of Yazoo City in 1901. It only contained the same material on the law program that was also included in the University's *Catalogue* for 1901–02, however, and it would be several decades before another separate law school bulletin would be published.[36]

Meanwhile, the 1895–96 *Catalogue* described, for the first time, the university as being made up of two "Departments " One was the "Department of Science, Literature and the Arts," which included twenty-one "schools" of literature, humanities, arts and sciences. The other was the "Department of Professional Education," which consisted of only one school, the "School of Law," which was "presided over by one 'professor,' assisted by 'several competent lecturers.'" But, the *Catalogue* reported, it was expected that schools of medicine, pharmacy, and engineering would be established "in the near future." As things turned out, a School of Engineering was established in 1900. In 1903, both a School of Education and a two-year College of Medicine came into being on the campus, and a Pharmacy School opened up in 1908. In the 1905–06 *Catalogue*, although the "School of Law" was listed as part of the "Department of Professional Education," along with Engineering, Education, and Medicine, Garvin Shands was still listed as "Dean of the Department of Law." His colleague, Thomas Somerville, "Professor of Law," was also listed among the medical faculty as the "Professor of Medical Jurisprudence."[37]

By then, trouble was brewing for Dean Shands. As most of the leadership elite of the Mississippi bar did, he strongly disapproved of Mississippi's then "populist" and "redneck" governor, James K. Vardaman (1904–08). On January 4, 1906, lawyer members of the state legislature meeting in the Hall of the House of Representatives in the New Capitol passed a motion calling for the formation of "a Bar Association of the State of Mississippi." Three weeks later, some three hundred lawyers from around the state gathered in the same room. After hearing an "eloquent and forcible speech" from Dean Shands, followed by another address from Professor Somerville, both of whom stressed the urgent need, given the prevailing political climate, to create and enforce a code that embodied the very highest standards of professional ethics, they voted to create the "Mississippi State Bar Association." A few minutes later, they elected Garvin D. Shands to serve as the association's first president.[38]

That same month, a 1905 graduate of the law school, Duncan H. Chamberlain, published a pamphlet entitled *The Facts About the Troubles of the University of Mississippi: The Jim Crow Laws Against Whites at the University*. In it he accused Chancellor Fulton and the other members of the university faculty of blatant favoritism toward the "so-called upper classes," the young scions of the state's well-to-do families who made up the membership of the Greek fraternities on campus. They were allowed, Chamberlain alleged, to get away with virtually any offence short of murder while the non-Greeks were subjected to a strict and severe code of discipline. Both a committee of members of both houses of the legislature and also the board of trustees, in a called meeting held on April 3, 1906, dismissed the accusations against Fulton and his colleagues. But, by the time the board held their regular annual meeting in June, its membership included three new Vardaman nominees. All of them were out to get Chancellor Fulton, and one of them, Judge Robert Powell, was also gunning for Shands[39]

Judge Powell, a Canton resident, had himself graduated from the university with a B.A. in 1870. His son, Robert Powell Jr., had earned a B.Phil. in 1904 and was then a member of the graduating senior law class. A year earlier, however, he had been one of seven students who were temporarily suspended by the faculty for violating fraternity rules, and the judge blamed Dean Shands personally for that humiliation. When the board met in June 1906 he was able to persuade his colleagues, soon after they had pressured Fulton into resigning the chancellorship, to vote to lower Shands's annual salary by four hundred dollars. A couple of months later, on August 23, Shands, whose term as president of the new state bar association had ended already in June announced that he, too, "found it in his interest" to tender his own resignation and to accept the offer of a position at the law school of Tulane University in New Orleans.[40]

Shands's departure meant that Thomas Somerville became the university's new dean of the law department in the autumn of 1906. He was to hold the position and to continue serving as the professor of medical jurisprudence for the next seven years. Meanwhile, at their organizational meeting in Jackson, back on January 25, 1906, his colleagues in the new state bar association had elected him to serve as one of their three delegates to the annual meeting of the American Bar Association. And a few weeks later, then State Bar Association President Shands had appointed him to serve as the first chairman of the association's committee on legal education and admission to the bar. The person chosen to replace Somerville as the university's professor of law was Clarence L. Sivley, who had earned his LL.B. at the university in 1893. Obviously greatly respected by his colleagues, Sivley had been one of those elected to the new association's fifteen-man board of directors in the meeting in Jackson back in January, and, at its first annual meeting five months later, in Gulfport, had been elected chairman of that board. In fact it soon turned out that his reputation was too great. Early in the spring of 1907, he would tender his resignation from the faculty and move to Memphis to accept appointment to the highly prestigious position of general counsel to both the Illinois Central Railroad and the Mississippi Valley Railroad.[41] Immediately that same spring the board chose John Elmore Holmes to succeed Sivley as the professor of law. A native of DeSoto County who had served as the oratorian of the 1899 graduating law class, Holmes served in that capacity until 1910. Then he too, as did Sivley before him, left to commence a prestigious career as a member of the Memphis bar.[42]

The professor appointed as Holmes's successor in the summer of 1910 brought to the University of Mississippi campus in general, and to the law program in particular, a name that would be highly honored for the next fifty years and is still remembered with both affection and respect today. Leonard J. Farley, like his predecessor, was a DeSoto County man. His father had been killed fighting for the Confederate cause at Gettysburg, and he had attended the university as an undergraduate on one of the very first LaBauve scholarships, founded in 1882 to provide scholarships for DeSoto County orphans. Graduating in 1884 with a B.S. degree, he had worked for a while as a teacher while studying law under Judge Sam Powell. In 1890, he had been admitted to the bar. From 1892 to 1896, he had served as DeSoto County's superintendent of education, and from 1901 to 1909 represented DeSoto County in the state senate. He would serve on the law faculty for the next eleven years.[43]

Besides Dean Somerville and Professor Farley, the law faculty listed in the 1910–11 *Catalogue* included the usual list of additional "Lecturers." Walter H. Drane, M.A.,the University's Professor of Civil and Municipal Engineering, was listed as the "Lecturer on Land Law." The "Lecturers on Common and Statute Law" were Colonel J. W. T. Falkner; former professor Holmes, who apparently was still retaining some connection with the program; Justice C. H. Alexander from Jackson, the 1900 Commencement Speaker and LL.D. recipient who had served as president of the state bar association in 1907 and was now apparently a regular visitor to the campus; and Oxford attorney Duke McDonald Kimbrough. An Oxford native, Kimbrough had entered the university as a freshman in 1892, had been initiated into the Sigma Chi Fraternity, had earned the medal for being top of the sophomore class in 1892, and had graduated with a B.A. in 1896. By 1897–98 he was enrolled in the law program and serving as an associate editor of the *University Record.* After graduating in the 1899 senior law class along with J. E. Holmes, he had not left the campus but stayed on, as "Director of the Gymnasium" until 1902. By then he had an established law practice in Oxford. In 1908, in addition to being listed for the first time as one of the law department's guest "Lecturers," Kimbrough was appointed by the state's new governor, Edmond F. Noel, to a seat on the university board of trustees.[44]

During the 1910–11 academic year, the law program continued to flourish. Hundreds of its alumni were by then practicing law everywhere around Mississippi, and more than a hundred were practicing elsewhere. Not surprising, the largest contingents of its out-of-state alumni were to be found in Tennessee and Texas, but one or more were also to be found practicing in Alabama, Arkansas, Colorado, Florida, Hawaii, Illinois, Kentucky, Louisiana, Missouri, New York City, New York State, Oklahoma, Utah, Virginia, Washington, D.C., and Washington State, as well as in Cuba and the Philippines.[45] Student enrollment in the program continued at the level of forty to fifty. But student costs were rising. The annual tuition fee was up to seventy-five dollars per academic year, payable in advance, and every student also had to pay both a five-dollar "incidental fee" and a five-dollar "hospital fee." The board, lodging, and utilities fees in the dormitories were by that time approximately $160. Board and lodging with a private family off-campus varied from around $160 to approximately $225. Though the law students were once again "controlled by the same faculty, and . . . subject to the same laws and discipline as the students in the Department of Arts and Sciences," they had "also, and without extra charge the same privileges—access to the reading room, the libraries, gymnasium, the literary association, etc." The law library now contained approximately two thousand volumes and was steadily increasing its holdings. In addition to the Thompson Publishing Company annual prize of "a complete new set of the American and English Encyclopedia of Law" for "the best discourse on a legal topic to be selected by the faculty," the Bobbs-Merrill Company of Indianapolis was contributing each year a copy of Elliott's *General Practice* as an award "for such merit and on such terms as the faculty may prescribe."[46]

But everything was not perfect. On May 31, 1910, Mr. I. T. Gilmer read to the annual meeting of the university alumni association "a very excellent paper on the needs of the Law Department." What they needed most, he told them, was a better on-campus home. Jefferson Hall, into which they had moved so proudly and happily back in 1894, was by then in a sad state of disrepair. A few days later the board of trustees, in their annual meeting, would be told by Chancellor Kincannon:

The building has . . . become both uncomfortable and unsafe. A large
section of the rear wall fell out of place several years ago; there are
large cracks in the wall; the window frames are no longer plumb. I am
informed that . . . the architect has condemned the structure as unsafe.
The roof, especially that part over the Library, is practically worthless;
the rain comes through with the pitch which has been used to stop it.
The only protection for the books is that afforded by the cases in which
they are kept. The lighting system is inefficient. The appliances for heat-
ing the rooms are practically worthless. In cold weather, it will be dan-
gerous for students and teachers to remain there. The old floor covering
contains an accumulation of dust and dirt, and conditions are not sani-
tary. The chairs and other furniture are old, meager and rude.[47]

Fortunately, an easy solution was at hand. In January 1909, Chancellor
Kincannon had persuaded the trustees to accept an offer from the Carnegie
Foundation of New York of a matching grant to build a new library building
on the campus. The new, sixty-thousand-dollar structure (now "Bryant Hall")
was finished by the spring of 1911, and that summer the thirty-two-thousand-
volume main library of the university was transferred into it. That left the old
red brick gothic library building with the tower and spire, built back in 1889
under Chancellor Mayes, totally empty. In the "Department of Law" section
of the 1910–11 University *Catalogue* it was announced that "The old library
building of the University will be devoted exclusively to the department of law
and will be thoroughly furnished and equipped for the comfort and conve-
nience of students and teachers."[48]

CHAPTER 3

THE VENTRESS HALL YEARS
(1911–1930)

At first, life in the law program's new home was not very different from what it had been during the previous decade and a half in Jefferson Hall. The old library had been formally renamed "Lamar Hall" but was usually referred to as the "law building." The law library and a classroom were on its ground floor, and the upper floor provided office space for the faculty. The full-time faculty members were still Dean Somerville, Professor Farley, and Colonel Falkner. The same outsiders were still coming in to assist as "lecturers." Professor Drane from engineering, however, was no longer serving as a "Lecturer on Land Law." The number of students enrolled continued at around forty to fifty, and the law school degree program was still a two-year one. Each academic year was now divided up into three "terms," with the first term running from mid-September to Christmas, the second term from January to mid-March, and the third term from late March to early June.[1]

A close-up view of student life during the first two years in the original "Lamar Hall" is provided by a collection of letters written approximately once a week during term time by Charles Ferriday Byrnes to his girlfriend, Roane Fleming, back home in Natchez. Through his junior year (1911–12), he and his classmates were directed and supervised in their studies by the "Law Professor," Leonard J. Farley. Their class work began with an in-depth study of Blackstone's *Commentaries* that often required reading—and becoming totally familiar with—as many as seventy pages a day. On October 30, they were examined on the first three hundred pages of Blackstone, and the Blackstone final was given on December 18. Final exams on two other texts were scheduled three days after that.[2]

On January 4, 1912, Charles was proud to be able to report to Roane that "I came out with a very nice grade in everything, only a few failed in the class but a good many just got over the line." Even though each exam began at eight in the morning and lasted until five in the afternoon, he did even better in the second term finals, taken in mid-March, and got a "terrific grade." In the last week in April, moot court trials for the seniors were held, in which the junior class men were expected to participate "as witnesses, etc." Finding himself cast as the victim's widow in a murder case, Byrnes decided it would not be proper (Roane, presumably, was pleased to read) to attend a student dance scheduled the night before the trial and thought that he might just "keep on studying law until I become a suffragette." Two weeks later, he was faced with reviewing "something like three thousand pages read this term" in preparation for the year's final exams that would be given at the end of May.[3]

Two of Byrnes's classmates in the 1912–13 senior class bore names that are still remembered affectionately by everyone in north Mississippi and its surrounding area who is fond of outdoor sports and recreation. Future United States Senator Wall Doxey from Holly Springs earned a B.A. degree that year, but he must have also taken some law classes for he was a member of the Blackstone Club. Future Mississippi State Senator John W. Kyle from Batesville was not only a law student but also president of the Blackstone Club in the first term of that year.[4]

The academic work of the senior class was directed by the law dean, Doctor Somerville. Now number four in seniority on the university faculty, "Uncle Tommy," as the students referred to him among themselves, was not without a sense of humor. A student who submitted a poorly written paper to him was likely to get it back inscribed with the terrible warning given the wicked Babylonian king Belshazzar in his dining hall: "Mene, Mene, Tekel Upharsin" ["You have been tried in the balance and found wanting"]. And on the evening of January 31, 1913, he hosted the traditional dean's dinner party for the senior class, which was also attended by Chancellor Kincannon, Professor Farley, and other "honored guests." The "old gentleman," Byrnes reported, feasted them all "quite elaborately" and, at the end of the meal, handed out fancy "ten-cent cigars," which the students all solemnly puffed on as they listened, with great interest, to the "old Profs" who told of "the different careers of famous men who in years gone by had graduated" from the university and now were "scattered all over the universe."[5]

But, Byrnes nervously noted early in the 1912–13 academic year, as law professors went, Thomas Somerville was reputed to be "the strictest and hardest in the south." And perhaps he had, by then, done all the teaching he could handle. When the eighteen students in the senior law class returned to campus after the Christmas break and learned the results of their first term final exams, they were appalled. "Old doctor Somerville" Byrnes wrote to Roane on January 7, 1913, "has simply wrecked our class, he failed exactly fifty percent of it, and . . . the majority of the ones that failed were good students." Though he himself had passed, he continued to worry. On February 1, he wrote: "old 'Uncle Tom' is growing more *unreasonable* all the time." And, three weeks later, he observed that the dean was "the most unreasonable of all people about some things." By the beginning of the third term, only eight (including Byrnes and Kyle) out of the original eighteen class members were still in the running for the LL.B. degree. In their finals, all of those survivors qualified for their diplomas and, on May 30, were admitted to the state bar by the local chancery court judge, Donald M. Kimbrough. Over the next seven days, waiting for commencement, they celebrated with "a lot of dances and banquets."[6]

Meanwhile, in late February of that year, the members of the junior law class, Byrnes reported, had been "tickled to death" by the news that "Uncle Tommy" was going to retire at the end of it. And, indeed, he did so, and went into private practice in Oxford. The *University Catalogue* for 1913–14 was the first one to include a list of "emeritus" faculty, including T. H. Somerville as the "Dean Emeritus School of Law." Its "Law Department" section now listed Leonard J. Farley as the "Law Dean," and the new "Law Professor" was former judge D. M. Kimbrough. The only two "Lecturers" still listed then were Colonel Falkner and J. E. Holmes.[7]

A year later, World War I began in Europe, and one of its consequences was to accelerate throughout the western world a trend, one that had begun a decade or so earlier, for women to move into some areas of activity that had previously been regarded as being for men only. One such area was the practice of law. In the 1915 Mississippi Bar Directory a Mrs. Lucy H. Greaves is listed as a member of the bar in Gulfport. The university *Catalogue* for 1914–15 includes in its list of law students a Ruth Watkins from Newton in the junior class and a Bessie Young from Grenada in the senior class. Young was one of the twenty students who received an LL.B in the 1915 commencement. Her class historian reported in the 1915 *Ole Miss* yearbook: "certainly the senior class is proud of its only Co-ed. Her cheerful smile and kindly spirit . . . and her thorough preparedness for recitations will always be an inspiration to, and command the respect of the entire class." In 1916, Linda Reaves Brown of Meridian was an honors graduate in law. "[8]

One of Brown's fellow law graduates in 1916 was Phil Stone of Oxford, the life-long friend of novelist William Faulkner and generally considered to be the main model for lawyer Gavin Stevens, a leading member of the bar in Faulkner's fictional city of Jefferson in Yoknapatawpha County.[9]

By 1916, the law student enrollment had risen to eighty-eight. So Dean Farley and Professor Kimbrough, called "the Duke," by the students, needed some help. In 1915, Tom C. Kimbrough (apparently no relation to "the Duke") was employed as an "Acting Professor of Senior Law." After earning a B.Ph. at the university in 1895 and an LL.B. at Millsaps College in 1898, this Kimbrough had practiced law in his hometown of West Point for thirteen years and had served as clerk of the Mississippi railroad commission before becoming a circuit judge in the 16th circuit in 1911. Although his future impact on both the university's law school and on the legal profession as a whole in Mississippi was going to be tremendous, he only served, at that time, one year on the law faculty. For the 1916–17 academic year Dean Farley and "the Duke" had to help them with their heavy teaching load one of their own alumni, Assistant Professor of Law Harry Meredith from Seneca, South Carolina, who had graduated from the U.M. law program with top honors in 1916.[10]

America's entry into the war quickly reversed the enrollment situation. Thirty-six graduates, including the later celebrated judge and law professor Noah S ["Soggy"] Sweat, were granted LL.B.s in the spring of 1917. No formal commencement ceremonies were held for them, however. During the 1917–18 academic year only thirty-nine students were enrolled in the law classes, and only twenty-one were enrolled in 1918–19. During that academic year the law faculty consisted solely of Dean Farley (assisted by James T. Crawley, a "Student Assistant in Law") for, by the summer of 1918, Donald Kimbrough was enrolled in the Y.M.C.A. corps serving American troops overseas in France. He did not return home to Oxford until February 12, 1919, and did not resume teaching law classes until the fall.[11]

In fact, only two LL.B.s were awarded in the 1919 commencement. One of the very few B.A.s awarded went to Dean Leonard Farley's son, Robert J. Farley, who, in his senior year, had served as president of the Hermean Society, president of the Scribblers Club, editor-in-chief of the *Ole Miss* yearbook and president of the senior class. In the 1919–20 academic year, however, things were about back to normal. Sixty-two law students were enrolled, and their classes were taught by Dean Farley and "Duke" Kimbrough. Twenty-six LL.B.s were awarded in the 1920 commencement, all of them to men.[12]

Things were about to change again, however. Soon after the 1920 spring commencement, "the Duke" decided to retire and took off to "engage in a lucrative practice of law in Boulder, Colorado." To replace him as the professor of law the board elected his namesake, Judge T. C. Kimbrough. Although the law student enrollment for 1920–21 was about the same as the previous year, seventy-four, it now included four women, one of whom was Dean Emeritus Somerville's cousin, Lucy Somerville. Another of the four was a second-year law student named Isabel Peebles, from Philadelphia, whom Dean Farley and Professor Kimbrough chose to work for them as their "Student Assistant," thus making her the first woman ever to be included on the law school's professional payroll. At the 1921 commencement she received one of the thirty-three LL.B.s awarded, graduating "with distinction."[13]

A little later that summer of 1921, Dean Leonard Farley died, and the board of trustees elected Professor T. C. Kimbrough as his successor. For most of the next two and a half decades, Kimbrough was to be dean of what was now being called the university's "School of Law." During, most of his deanship, the school expanded its enrollment, improved in quality and rose in national status. The first major change he made was to expand the degree program from a two-year to a three-year one. Although only sixty-four law students were enrolled for 1921–22, he was also able to persuade the trustees that the expanded curriculum required an expanded faculty. To fill his now vacated position as professor of law the board appointed William Hemingway, a Jackson lawyer who had earned a B.Ph. at the university before embarking on reading law on his own and gaining admittance to the bar by examination. He had very soon become a highly respected member of the legal profession in the state and had served a term as Jackson's mayor. In 1916, he had been appointed by his colleagues in the state bar to draft an updated code of Mississippi's laws, and the first edition of Hemingway's *Mississippi Code* was published in 1917. A very keen supporter of the university's football program, he soon was serving, along with Kimbrough (who, during his undergraduate career, had been a member of the University of Mississippi's first-ever football team in the autumn of 1893) on the faculty athletic committee and quickly became its chairman. The 1924 *Ole Miss* yearbook saluted him as the "Most Popular Professor." To this day, his memory is kept very much alive on campus by the existence of the much-hallowed Vaught-Hemingway Stadium. Meanwhile, in 1922 the board appointed former Chancery Court Judge Dan M. Russell of Gulfport to serve as the second professor of law. He would serve in that position for four years before resigning to return to private practice.[14]

The sixty-one male and three female law students enrolled for the 1921–22 academic year had to pay a total of $201 to the university for fees and tuition (sixty dollars), plus accommodation and service charges. In addition, "books, stationery and incidentals," it was calculated, would cost a student approximately sixty dollars. But it was an exciting year to be at the law school. There were now more than five thousand volumes in the law library on the ground floor of Lamar Hall, and a new, expanded curriculum was being taught. "Patterned after that of the other great schools of the country, being especially in line with that of Vanderbilt and the University of Virginia," it consisted of a course of study designed "to afford such training in the fundamental principles of English and American Law" as would "constitute the best preparation for the practice of [law]." The faculty's aim had been "to make the program practical." Blackstone's *Commentaries* (published a century and a half earlier on the other side of the Atlantic) were no longer part of it. Portions of Hemingway's 1917 *Mississippi Code*, however, were required reading in nineteen of the thirty-four required courses offered.[15]

The courses were:

FIRST YEAR
First Semester:
Contracts
Torts
Domestic Relations
Criminal Law and Procedure
Evidence
Mississippi Code
Second Semester:
Agency
Bailments and Carriers
Common Law Pleading and Practice
Code Pleading and Practice
Partnership

SECOND YEAR
First Semester:
Briefs: Legal Bibliography-Statutes
Insurance
Negotiable Instruments
Sales
Judgments
Legal Ethics
Practice Court
Second Semester:
Real Property
Private Corporations
Equity Jurisprudence
Equity Pleading
Admiralty
Practice Court

THIRD YEAR
First Semester:
Constitutional Law
Wills and Administration
Bankruptcy
Taxation
Public Service Companies
Personal property
Practice Court
Second Semester:
Federal Jurisdiction and Procedure
Conflict of Laws and Jurisdiction
Damages
Trusts
Municipal Corporations
Land Abstracts
Practice Court

Written tests upon the subject matter of each course were administered either at the conclusion of the course or at the end of the semester. Furthermore, the old moot court requirement for students at the end of their senior year had been replaced by a system of "practice courts," conducted at the end of each semester in the second and third years, in which the emphasis would be very much on the practical technicalities of courtroom procedure rather than on the philosophical aspects of litigation. Regular attendance at all classes was a firm requirement, and only the dean could excuse an absence.[16]

The mostly bright and enthusiastic young men and women enrolled could handle all of that and more besides. At their annual meeting, held in Vicksburg the last week in April 1922, members of the state bar association entertained a proposal made by John Edward McCall, the first law student ever invited to address that prestigious body. He and his fellow students, he told them, would like to establish, under the auspices of their honor society, the Blackstone Club, a "Mississippi Law Review" similar to the law reviews published by Harvard and other prestigious law schools around the country. To do so they would need the association's help. They hoped that every member would take out a two-dollar annual subscription to it and that some would also be willing to submit articles for publication in it. By the early fall of that same year, he assured them, letters would be going out to every lawyer in the state soliciting their support for it. In fact, by early October, one hundred and forty subscriptions had come in, and over three hundred dollars of advertising space had been sold to such firms as the West Publishing Company of Minneapolis. "I have carefully gone over the proposed plan . . . for the publication of a periodical to be known as the Mississippi Law Review," Dean Kimbrough told the university student newspaper, the *Mississippian*, and "most heartily approve the same."[17]

At a business meeting of the Blackstone Club held the previous spring, Addie M. McCain, vice-president of the first-year law class, had been elected chief editor of the proposed *Review* by acclamation. And Joseph M. Howorth of Cleveland (a World War I Marine Corps veteran) had, by a narrow margin in a hotly contested election, been selected over Levi M. Pettis of College Hill to serve as its business manager. As things turned out, however, McCain did not come back to school that next fall, so Howorth was elected editor and Pettis as business manager. Selected to assist Howorth as "associate editors" were L. C. Corban, A. H. Bell, J. C. Hathorn, F. B. Jackson. D. R. Stump, and a future dean of the law school, R. J. Farley. And through the 1922–23 school year, though it was not published quite so frequently as "monthly November to June," as its founders had intended, the new publication flourished. Thanks to Louis M. Jiggitts of Canton, a recent graduate of the university who had gone over to Oxford, England, as a Rhodes Scholar, its February 1923 number included an article titled "Charles Viner and the *Abridgments of English Law*" written by Oxford University's celebrated Vinerian Professor of English Law, W. S. Holdsworth.[18]

All of these improvements—the larger faculty, the five thousand-plus-volume law library, the expanded and revised curriculum, the launching of the *Law Review*—had one very important consequence in December 1922. The Association of American Law Schools, at its annual meeting in Chicago, formally recognized the University of Mississippi's law school as "one of the standard A-grade schools of the country." A year later, in the fall of 1923, the completion of at least one year of undergraduate work, "or such work as would admit one to Sophomore in the College of Liberal Arts in any of the leading Colleges or Universities of the country," was required for the first time for admission to the law program. In 1924, the requirement was raised to two years. Also, the Ole Miss law school now would accept transfer law credits only from an AALS-recognized law school.[19]

Meanwhile, in the 1922 commencement, the last class to graduate under the old rules earned a total of twenty-four LL.B. degrees. One of their number was Lucy Somerville. She had earned an A.B. degree in 1916 from Randolph Macon Women's College in Lynchburg, Virginia, and had done some graduate work at Columbia University. She now earned her LL.B. "with special Distinction" and also won the Bobbs-Merill book prize and delivered the valedictory address. Within a few months, she was practicing law in both her hometown of Cleveland and also in Greenville, and, in 1923, she became only the third woman ever to be admitted to membership in Mississippi's state bar association. In January 1924, her mother, Nellie Nugent Somerville, took her seat as the first-ever woman member of the Mississippi legislature. A few months after that, Lucy herself became the first woman ever to make a formal presentation at a bar association meeting, giving a talk on "Laws about Lawyers." Later that year, she was one of the Mississippi association's three official delegates to the annual meeting of the American Bar Association in Philadelphia, Pennsylvania.[20]

Because of the expansion of the curriculum to three years, only five LL.B.s were awarded in 1923. None of them were awarded "with distinction," and no publishers' prizes were won. Five numbers of the *Law Review* had been published by April 1923, however. And that month's issue opened with an article by Lucy Somerville entitled "A Constructive Proposal," describing and supporting the AALS's proposal for the creation of an American Law Institute. It also included a farewell editorial article by Joseph Howorth, wishing the very best to his expected successors and apologizing for being already in Jackson working for a law firm. Five years later, having married Lucy Somerville in February 1928, he would be practicing law with her in the Howorth and Howorth law firm in Cleveland, Greenville, and Jackson.[21]

Meanwhile, back in May 1923, the Blackstone Club had met and elected L. C. Corban to succeed Joseph Howorth as editor of the *Review* and D. R. Stump to be its business manager, through 1923–24. Apparently, however, no further issues of it were ever published. After the state legislature had sharply reduced the budgets of all of the institutions of higher learning early in 1924, the law faculty voted to cut the *Review* out of the school's budget. And, although volume I had been financed, in part, by advertisements, some from major law publishers such as the West Publishing Company and Bobbs-Merrill and some from such local businesses as the Bank of Oxford, the J. E. Neilson Company and "The Shack," ads apparently did not bring in enough to keep the publication going. A few years later, nearly everyone had forgotten that it had ever existed.[22]

In June 1924, twenty-seven students, all of whom were male, successfully completed the new three-year curriculum (five with distinction). Two of the twenty-seven were Louis M. Jiggitts and Robert J. Farley. Perhaps because they had both been very busy with out-of-class activities, neither of them earned distinction, but both of them had distinguished themselves by the honors they had already earned, and both would earn much distinction in future years. Of Jiggitts, the former Rhodes Scholar, with an honors B.A. in jurisprudence from Oxford University, the 1924 yearbook editors would say: "Returning to us after three years of absence in . . . England, where his name became known to periodicals, both at home and abroad, he has achieved a record that would make the most vain of us jealous. He has indeed come up to our expectations, and his last year in the university has been marked by great influence and popularity." In 1924, in fact, he was the first winner of a newly instituted medal awarded by the state bar association for the best paper written by a law student on a legal ethics topic. From 1928 to 1933 he would serve as secretary-treasurer of the state bar association (after 1932, called "the State Bar"), and generally he was to have an influence on the development of the legal profession in Mississippi in the interwar period second only to that of Dean Thomas Kimbrough.[23]

Jiggitts's classmate, Robert Farley, after earning a B.A. (with distinction) at the university in Oxford, Mississippi, at the age of twenty, had served as principal of the high school in Canton for the 1919–20 school year and then was principal of the high school in Natchez for 1920–21. In 1923, during his senior year in law school, he was elected mayor of his hometown of Oxford, and the yearbook editors said of him: "The 'Lord Mayor of Oxford' will never be forgotten. His genial personality endeared him to both the men and the co-eds alike. While he was never known to seek campus position, yet offices just seemed to heap themselves upon him." In 1924, after graduating, he began practicing law in Oxford in partnership with law school Dean Emeritus Thomas Somerville in offices located on the east side of the Square immediately next door to the Federal Building (now City Hall). In 1926, he would begin teaching part time in the law school as an assistant professor.[24]

Shortly before they graduated, the 1924 senior law class were lectured on legal ethics by Judge Robert H. Thompson of Brookhaven, the 1923–24 president of the state bar association. Dean Kimbrough was firmly of the opinion that the best time for lawyers to learn the accepted ethics of their profession was while they were still in school. Two years earlier, the dean had told the 1922 meeting of the bar association, in Vicksburg, how much he had appreciated the fact that their then outgoing president, George J. Leftwich, had twice traveled to Oxford from his home in Aberdeen to lecture law classes on "The Ethics of the Legal Profession." He hoped, he added, that it would become customary for future presidents to do the same; and, indeed, it did.[25]

Judge Thompson, originally from Jackson, had earned a B.A. from the university in 1869 and then enrolled in the 1869–70 junior law class. Because of the 1870 suspension of the law program, however, he had gained admission to the legal profession by taking a bar exam. Almost a quarter of a century later, in 1893, by which time he was serving as a member of the state's law code commission and also (since 1890) as a member of the university's board of trustees, the university made that up to him (perhaps) by granting him an honorary LL.D. And, just a year later, on June 5, 1894, he was elected president of its alumni association.[26] During his few months as a law student, under the tutelage of L. Q. C. Lamar, he told the 1924 law class, "the only book I studied . . . was Blackstone's Commentaries." "And," he added (causing Dean Kimbrough some embarrassment perhaps), "I cannot but regret that it is not now used as a textbook in this law school." But "the two indispensable essentials to a lawyer's success" were, first of all, "Integrity of Character, Absolute Honesty. The lawyer must be honest with himself, with his clients, with his adversaries, with the juries and courts before whom he practices his profession; his honesty must be absolute and true." And, second, "a lawyer's work must be accurately performed; unless so performed it is likely to prove ineffectual."[27]

At the time of Thompson's address, the moral and ethical standards of the law students were elevated, perhaps, by the continuing requirement of compulsory chapel attendance on campus at least one day a week. Failure to do so just two weeks in one semester could cause one to forfeit all academic credit for that entire semester. Both law and engineering students were scheduled to attend chapel each Thursday, and it was also hoped and expected that on Sundays they would attend the church of their choice in Oxford. By 1926–27, the "chapel" services were being held in Fulton Chapel rather than in the "Old Chapel," which was coming to be known as the "Y Building," because the campus Y.M.C.A. organization had their offices in it). Beginning in 1928–29, chapel attendance was no longer required.[28]

Through the decade of the 1920s, the enrollment each year in the law school was slightly over ninety students—about 10 percent of the overall student enrollment in the university—and usually included one or two women. The number of LL.B.s conferred at commencement each year was around two dozen.[29] The annual tuition fee was by then seventy dollars, but two students each year now could get financial assistance by working as "attendants" in the Law Library which, by 1925, reportedly contained six thousand volumes. The student attendants for 1925–26 were two men destined to play important roles in the future history of the university: Ross R. Barnett and M. M. Roberts. In 1925, law classes were included in the university's summer schedule for the first time. In the summer of 1930, Dean Kimbrough and Professor Roberds offered courses in Personal Property, Agency, Sales, Legal Bibliography, Conflict of Laws, Bankruptcy, Negotiable Instruments, Mississippi Pleading, Criminal Law, and Federal Procedure. The tuition fee for summer work was forty dollars.[30]

The 1925 graduating class, at the invitation of the state bar association's then president, Stone Deavours, attended the association's annual meeting, held that year in Deavours's hometown of Laurel. At the meeting, they heard a report given by George J. Leftwich of Aberdeen on behalf of the association's legal education committee. Members of the committee, he said, were very proud that the university's law school now met the ABA standards with regard to admission requirements, faculty size, curriculum, and library holdings and that it was now AALS associated, with a Grade A rating. They did think, however, that courses in bookkeeping, English and American history, and economics ought to be added to the curriculum. And, much more important, they were very strongly of the opinion that the Lamar Hall law building was "entirely inadequate" to meet the law school's needs. To provide its faculty and students with adequate office, classroom, and library space. A new, larger building was urgently needed. The association's members responded by passing a resolution calling upon the state legislature, at its next meeting, to provide funding for a "more suitable" law school.[31]

The 1926 session of the legislature, however, failed to appropriate the money. And at the 1927 state bar association meeting in Jackson, the members heard disturbing news from Dean Kimbrough. In November 1926, an AALS inspector had visited the law school, and his report to its executive committee had not been a favorable one. For one thing, the AALS's minimum library size requirement was now seventy-five hundred volumes. Although the University of Mississippi claimed to have six thousand, it could only show fifty-five hundred, and its law library budget of only five hundred dollars per year was regarded by the association as pathetically inadequate. Other shortcomings reported included a finding that many of the library's books were shelved where it was very difficult to access them. Also, because the library had to be also used as a classroom, access to it during the daytime was limited, and since there was only one other classroom, all classes could not be held—as the AALS said they should be—during the morning hours. The faculty—consisting only of Dean Kimbrough, Professors Hemingway and Roberds, and Assistant Professor Farley (only part-time)—was smaller than required, and, except for the dean, none of the faculty members had offices in the law school building. There were four lists of the students supposedly enrolled in the school, no two of which were exactly the same. Finally, some of the students confessed that they, in fact, did not have the fifty hours of prior freshman and sophomore college work that the association required. The result was that the AALS, at its 1926 annual meeting in Chicago just after Christmas, placed the University of Mississippi law school on probation and indicated that, if something was not done soon, the law school would lose its accreditation altogether.[32]

Both Dean Kimbrough and Chancellor Alfred Hume pleaded for the association's support, and they got it. In accordance with the membership's instructions, the association's new president, R. E. Wilbourn of Meridian appointed a committee, chaired by the association's outgoing president, D. W. Houston, and including a least one member from each of the state's congressional districts, to lobby the legislature on the law school's behalf. On Homecoming Day, November 5, 1927, all of the committee members and Wilbourn came to the campus and inspected the law building for themselves. Then they sat down together and drafted a memorial to the legislature, which was also enthusiastically endorsed by the university's alumni association, stressing the urgent need to do something to address its deficiencies. The lobbying effort continued into the new year. At their 1928 annual meeting held in Gulfport, the bar association members heard the good news. Just a week earlier, on April 26, the state's new governor, Theodore G. Bilbo (himself a member of their association since 1925) had signed a bill granting $1.6 million to the University of Mississippi for various improvements, including new buildings. And one of the major items listed in the bill was $150,000 to build a new home for the law school. Later, Dean Kimbrough told the members that, in fact, $140,000 of the $150,000 total would be sufficient to construct a new law building and that the additional $10,000 could be used to buy books for the law library, which would expand its holdings to far above the AALS's minimum requirement.[33]

At that same 1928 bar association meeting, the members also heard an interesting suggestion from their new secretary-treasurer, Louis M. Jiggitts. He proposed that Mississippi follow the example of Minnesota, where, the *Minnesota Law Review* was published monthly on a joint basis by both the state bar and the state university law school. Mississippi could not afford to do that, but it could begin publishing a quarterly "law review and journal" on the same basis. The first number of each volume would be published in the summer and would consist of the proceedings of the association's annual meeting held the previous spring. The bar association was already spending more than three hundred dollars a year to have the proceedings of its annual meeting published. That amount, combined with a little additional income from subscriptions and advertising, would suffice to pay for the new publication. A law student staff would do all of the actual editing and publication work under the supervision of a board of directors made up of Dean Kimbrough and the bar association's officers. Shortly before they adjourned on May 3, the membership voted to approve the journal plan.[34]

The first student editor of the *Mississippi Law Journal* was Dugas Shands of Cleveland. Its "Case Notes" editor was John C. Satterfield of Port Gibson, a future president of both the Mississippi State Bar (1955–56) and the American Bar Association (1961–62). At the end of September 1928, they proudly informed the campus newspaper, the *Mississippian*, that the first number of the *Journal* was ready to go to press. And, indeed, less than a week later, on October 3, the "July" issue was printed at the McCowat-Mercer printing firm in Jackson, Tennessee. Subtitled the "Journal of the State Bar Association," its contents consisted of the proceedings of the association's 1928 meeting. But volume I, number 2, bearing the date "October," contained Mississippi annotations, compiled by Chief Justice Sydney Smith of the state supreme court, to the "Restatement of Torts," recently issued by the American Law Institute. One of the *Journal's* most important functions, Shands had told the *Mississippian*, would be the publication of Mississippi annotations to the Institute's "Restatements" of American law.[35]

By the time the state bar association assembled for its 1929 annual meeting in Clarksdale all four numbers of volume I, totaling 468 pages, were in print, and at that meeting the members were told that 140 of them had subscribed to the *Journal*. So had all of the law students at the university and eighty-six American law libraries. The bar association had contributed $491.85 toward the cost of publishing volume I. Now, at Secretary Jiggitts's suggestion, on the understanding that every association member would get a free copy, a resolution was passed to contribute eight hundred dollars toward publishing volume II. The *Mississippi Law Journal*, it appeared, was there to stay.[36]

Indeed, at the time of the 1929 bar association meeting, things looked pretty good for the future of the University of Mississippi School of Law. At the meeting, heads were bowed in memory of her famous former dean, Thomas H. Somerville, who, after holding the position of "Dean Emeritus" for fifteen years, had died on June 11, 1928. Although suffering somewhat from ill health, he had continued practicing law in partnership with Robert J. Farley in their offices on the Courthouse Square in Oxford until just a few months before his death. And at the end of the meeting, the current dean, Kimbrough, who had initiated the practice of having a law school alumni luncheon as a regular item on the annual meeting schedule, succeeded to the presidency of the association for the coming year.[37]

Two years earlier, on November 23, 1927, the sixty-first chapter of the international legal fraternity Phi Delta Phi had been formally established in the law school. Named the Mayes Inn chapter in honor of the man who had served with distinction as both the law professor and as the sometime chancellor of the university half a century earlier, it replaced the Lamar Society as the honor society for law students. A chapter of the other major national honorary legal fraternity, Phi Alpha Delta, named the Lamar Inn chapter, was established two years later, in 1929.[38]

In the 1929–30 academic year, a record total of 105 students (including one woman—Lyda Gordon Shivers, who graduated "with distinction" in June 1930) were enrolled in the law program, with a law library of ten thousand volumes available to them. In 1929, a new paved bridge, named after L. Q. C. Lamar was built over the Hilgard railroad cut onto the campus from University Avenue. And that fall, work was begun on the "new building for the School of Law, to be known as *"Lamar Hall,"* a "beautiful structure" that was going to "provide ample accommodations in the way of classrooms, library, offices, etc."[39]

But more troubled times lay ahead. In October 1929, the nation saw the beginning of the major economic crisis that would come to be called the "Great Depression," and last for over a decade. The members of the large graduating law class of June 1930 could not have enjoyed reading an article by Oxford's Phil Stone that had been published in the February 1930 issue of the *Mississippi Law Journal.* Titled "The Greatest Good of the Greatest Number," it pointed out that, at that time, America in general, and Mississippi in particular, was suffering from a glut of lawyers: "The cold facts are that we have too many lawyers . . . in Mississippi. . . . I realize that this is not a popular thing to say, but the great majority of our lawyers know it to be a fact. According to the latest information I have been able to obtain, there are now over fourteen hundred licensed lawyers in Mississippi. Anyone knows that we don't need that many lawyers in Mississippi. The effect of this is that only a few lawyers are really making a decent living from their profession alone."[40]

Plans to hold the twenty-fifth annual meeting of the state bar association on the university campus at Oxford in the new law building during the first week in May 1930 had to be abandoned. Back in the fall of 1929, it had been confidently forecast that the building would be finished and ready to move into in April 1930, but it was not, and the new campus cafeteria that was supposed to have been ready for use by then also was not yet in operation. So the association's incumbent president, Dean Kimbrough and his executive committee had to make a very reluctant, last-minute decision to have the meeting that year in Biloxi instead.[41]

By then, however, most of the problems facing Kimbrough and his faculty were political ones. In January 1928, a new governor had taken office in Mississippi: Theodore G. Bilbo, a populist in the James K. Vardaman tradition. During the 1927 gubernatorial campaign, law school assistant professor Robert J. Farley had circulated petitions urging people not to vote for him. When Bilbo demanded that Chancellor Hume reprimand Farley for doing so, the chancellor refused, saying that the professor's political activities were none of his business. Bilbo had also campaigned to have the university (and perhaps the A&M College in Starkville also) moved to Jackson. There the new "Greater University of Mississippi" would be both centrally located—and, therefore, easier to access from everywhere in the state—and more easily able to assist and cooperate with the various departments of state government. Chancellor Hume had vigorously opposed that idea. Also in 1929, the puritanically inclined chancellor, in spite of strong opposition from the governor and many board members, had expelled two student editors of the *Ole Miss* yearbook, Fergus Lloyd and Howard Thames, for including in that year's number several "indecent and indelicate references to university women."[42]

By the spring of 1930, Chancellor Hume had readmitted the two erring editors to the university. And Governor Bilbo had also come to realize that his dream of a super-university in Jackson was never going to be accepted by a majority of the legislature. By then, however, he had been able to appoint a sympathetic majority of supporters to the university's board of trustees. At board meetings held in Jackson in June and July of that year, Hume was dismissed as chancellor and replaced by his predecessor, Joseph Neeley Powers, who had been put out of office as part of another political coup in 1924. In the law school, Dean Kimbrough was demoted to professor and replaced as dean by his sometime predecessor—both as a law school graduate and as a president of the state bar association—Judge Stone Deavours of Laurel. Also, because Bilbo complained that they had become improperly involved in the 1927 gubernatorial campaign, both Professors Hemingway and Farley were fired. Professor Roberds, on learning what had happened to his friends and colleagues, resigned.[43]

An article published in a national magazine alleged that the governor wanted the board to appoint one of his political lieutenants, George R. Smith, a Pass Christian lawyer who had never earned any kind of degree, as Hemingway's successor. If so, that did not happen. Actually, as things turned out, the law faculty for the 1930–31 school year were a not undistinguished group of legal scholars. Dean Stone Deavours, after all, had earned his LL.B. with special distinction under Dean Edward Mayes and Professor Simrall in 1892. Professors Hemingway and Roberds were replaced by Richard Franklin Payne, who had earned an LL.B. at Yale University, and Joseph J. Smith, who had earned an LL.B. at Harvard University. Part-time assistant professor Farley had been replaced by Oxford attorney and former circuit judge J. W. T. Falkner Jr. (a son of Colonel J. W. T. Falkner and uncle of author William Faulkner). Shortly before the 1930 summer vacation was over, they all moved across the Grove into the new Lamar Hall, leaving the old law building to be "remodeled for use by the Department of Geology."[44]

But more serious trouble was brewing. In that fall of 1930 a three-man sub-committee of the executive committee of the AALS, led by their secretary-treasurer Albert J. Harno, visited the campus to investigate the Bilbo impact on the law school. And, at the association's annual meeting, held December 29–31, 1930, in Chicago, they made a report that was far from favorable: Altogether, "approximately thirty-one" University of Mississippi "faculty members and employees" had been dismissed by the governor and his cronies on the board of trustees "without notice and without reference to their experience or qualifications." In conclusion, they noted that the university "has been and is so subjected to and affected by political influences and arbitrary actions by persons in authority over [it] as to render impossible the maintenance in its Law School of the sound educational policy contemplated by membership in the Association." They, therefore, offered a motion recommending "that the University of Mississippi be excluded from membership in the Association."[45]

The University of Mississippi's new law professor, Richard Payne, who was at the meeting, offered an amendment to that motion to make it read that "the dropping from membership shall not become effective until Sept. 1, 1931, and the Executive Committee is hereby vested with authority to set aside this order if in the judgment of the Committee conditions are such at the said University at that time to make such action on their part desirable." And new dean Stone Deavours "spoke at length" in support of the proposed amendment, ending with a plea to the Association to "let us alone." Then, a delegate from the Harvard Law School offered an amendment to Payne's amendment stating that "this action shall not take effect with respect to students now in the school until the first of September, 1931. A delegate from Ohio State University, however, spoke against the amendment. "Judge [not 'Dean'] Deavours," he noted, had pleaded: "We are all doing good work; let us alone." To applause, he suggested that "Deavours ought to make his appeal to be let alone, to the politicians of the state of Mississippi." The amendment was defeated and then the vote on the original motion was called for and approved unanimously. The University of Mississippi law school was no longer AALS associated.[46]

CHAPTER 4

The Early Decades in Farley Hall
(1930–1962)

In spite of the fact that the already semi-repentant board of trustees, meeting in Oxford on November 27, 1930, had rescinded their declared policy of the previous July, that faculty members at the university served at their will rather than at the will of the chancellor, the AALS's suspension of the law school remained in force for the next two years. The state's other institutions of higher learning, except Delta State University, were also under a general suspension by the Southern Association of Colleges and Schools (SACS), which had been decided upon at its 1930 meeting held two weeks before that of the AALS. As long as Bilbo remained governor, the firings he had favored remained in force and so did the suspensions. In January 1932, however, a new governor Martin S. Connor took office. A new state legislature went to work and soon passed Senate Bill 59, which abolished the university's old board of trustees and created instead a new board chaired by the governor and consisting of twelve, non-reappointable members serving staggered four-year terms.[1]

The new board members soon discovered that the main requirement for re-recognition was going to be the rehiring of Chancellor Hume and other administrators and professors fired at Bilbo's behest. In the summer of 1932 that was done, and in December 1932 both SACS and the AALS restored the recognition they had suspended two years earlier. Meanwhile, for the fall semester of 1932, T. C. Kimbrough was once again dean of the law school, and William Hemingway was back as a professor of law (and serving again on the university's athletic committee, along with Dean Kimbrough, who had remained on it over the past two years). The two other law professors were John Fox, a Mississippi College graduate who had earned his LL.B. at Yale University in 1922, and Robert J. Farley (after whom the building they then occupied is now named). After being dismissed from his part-time assistant professorship two years earlier, Farley had attended Yale University and earned a J.S.D. degree there in the spring of 1932. Nearly fifty years later, in an interview with Mississippi historian David Sansing, he would recall that, thanks to his Yale professor, he had been offered a position at the University of Wyoming law school (where the professor's brother was the dean) at a salary of $2,500. He had intended to accept it, but then Dean Kimbrough offered him the position back at the University of Mississippi also at $2,500. "And the difference was I had enough money to get back here and I didn't have enough to get to Wyoming! That was one of my main reasons for coming back here, although I wanted to come back." The man appointed that fall to fill Farley's old position of assistant professor of law, now apparently a full time one, was Landon C. Andrews, an alumnus of the program who had earned his LL.B. in 1905 and had since then practiced in Oxford, especially in the federal court. He was also a member of the state legislature.[2]

As the effects of the Depression began to lessen, the university's law program once again began to expand. Its total enrollment for 1932–33 was ninety-four, of whom fifty-one were in their first year, eighteen were in their second year, twenty-four were seniors, and one was a "special student." Twenty LL.B.s were awarded in the June 1933 commencement, and six more in August of that year. Only one of the university's other professional schools, the school of commerce and business education (established in 1917), which had 139 students that year, had a larger enrollment. The school of medicine had forty-five students, the school of engineering had thirty-one, and the school of pharmacy had fifteen.[3]

A brass plaque on the front steps of the building now known as "Farley Hall" states that the second Lamar Hall was "Erected A.D. 1929–30" under the supervision of a board of "Commissioners" that was chaired by Governor Bilbo and included Bidwell Adams, Sennett Connor, J. W. T. Falkner (the novelist's uncle, who had replaced Farley as the part-time assistant professor, 1930–32), J. H. Currie, O. J. Turner and B. G. Hazard, all of whom were prominent members of the state bar. W. C. Trotter had served as secretary to the commissioners. The Frank P. Gates Company had provided the "Architects and Engineers" who planned the building, and "Sanquist and Snow" had served as the "General Contractors" who built it.

"The building," the 1932–33 university *Bulletin* informed students and would-be students, was "one of the most modern in the country." "Located in a prominent place on the campus" and "complete in every respect," it had "offices for all instructors where students [might] consult with them about their problems."

"Ample classroom facilities" were available "together with a large assembly room where the entire law student body on occasions [could] assemble." A court room, "identical in every respect" to the courtrooms in courthouses all around the state, was available for the students to "try moot cases."

Its ground floor was "equipped with a club room, lounging room, locker room, and work rooms where the industrious students could "do their work."[4] And there was also on that floor "a large and commodious Law Journal room," which served as the "office of the Editor and Business Manager of the Mississippi Law Journal." The first editor to occupy that "large and commodious" office space was Hugh N. Clayton from Ripley, who, having served as business manager for volume II (1929–30) of the *Mississippi Law Journal,* in his senior year was the editor of volume III (1930–31).[5]

The law library in the new building contained some 10,000 "well selected law books" in 1931, and by 1933, it had "over 12,000," including "the reports of nearly every state down to the beginning of the National Reporter System, the entire National Reporter system, the U.S. Supreme Court Reports, several copies of the Mississippi Reports, the statutes of many states, numerous series of selected cases, the leading treatises and encyclopedias, and complete sets of several of the leading legal periodicals. Furthermore, there were "constant yearly additions to the library."[6]

Back in November 1931, the then board members had authorized Dean Deavours to "employ a Law Librarian and Stenographer," at a salary of $850 per year. For the 1934–35 academic year, Helen Patricia Maltby, LL.B., was serving as the "Secretary to Dean and Librarian," A year later, she was listed only as the "Librarian," and Rhoda Catherine Bass, B.A., was serving as the "Registrar of Law School and Secretary to the Dean." For 1936–37, both women held the same titles they had the year before; but, in 1937–38, "Mrs. Helen Maltby Lumpkin," "Law Librarian and Instructor," was instructing the first year students in "Legal Bibliography Lab." In 1938–39, though Mrs. Lumpkin was no longer on the staff, Rhoda Catherine Bass, B.A., LL.B., was teaching not only the "Legal Bibliography Lab" course to first-year students but also "Damages" to second- and third-year students.[7]

Meanwhile, in the fall of 1935, the University of Mississippi inaugurated a new chancellor, Alfred Benjamin Butts, who had previously served as vice-president of Mississippi State College at Starkville. He held both a B.S. degree and an M.S. degree from that same institution but had also earned a Ph.D. in political science at Columbia University in 1920 and a law degree at Yale in 1930. As chancellor, he was, ex-officio, a member of the law faculty, but he also held the title "professor of law" and did actually teach an administrative law course. He also contributed articles to several law journals. During the summers, he would leave the university and Oxford for several weeks to teach law at some other institution such as Ohio State University, UCLA, Duke, the University of Virginia, the University of Hawaii, or Yale University.[8]

While still a law student himself at Yale, Chancellor Butts probably had crossed paths with Myres S. McDougal, from Burton, Mississippi, who, after earning a B.A. and an M.A. at the University of Mississippi and a B.A. and a B.C.L. at Oxford University in England, had earned a J.S.D. degree at Yale in 1931. In March 1930, the Bilbo-appointed board of trustees had offered him a professorship of law at the University of Mississippi for the following year, but he went to Yale instead. From 1931 to 1934, he was an assistant professor of law at the University of Illinois and then returned to Yale as an associate professor. Evidently, however, the University of Mississippi still held a place in his heart. On May 8, 1935, the law faculty, in a meeting in which they reviewed several student petitions with regard to "incompletes," ruled that, if Myres McDougal would submit copies of his transcripts from both Oxford and Yale and also enroll in their law school for the upcoming eight-week summer session, they would grant him a University of Mississippi LL.B. He did so, and then returned to Yale where twenty-three years later, in 1958, he would be appointed the Sterling Professor of Law.[9]

By 1935, with the worst of the Great Depression over, the law student body had increased considerably in size. The enrollment for the 1934–35 school year consisted of sixty-six first-year students, twenty-three second-year students and thirty-five seniors.[10] A larger faculty obviously was needed. Fortunately, by then James Jefferson Lenoir, a native of McComb, Mississippi (who had earned a B.A. in political science at the university in 1927 and an M.A. in 1929), after getting a Ph.D. at the University of Illinois in 1934 had come back to the campus in 1934 as an assistant professor of political science. On May 21, 1935, the law faculty made the same deal with him that they had made two weeks earlier with Myres McDougal. And, after attending the summer session, he too was awarded an LL.B. in that year's August commencement. For the next two years, he served as an assistant professor of law, teaching constitutional law, but then he went on leave. Though he never did teach again in the University of Mississippi law program, he did eventually climax his career as a professor of law at the University of Georgia. Also John W. Wade, a native of Little Rock, Arkansas, who, after earning a B.A. in 1932 and an LL.B. in 1934 at the University of Mississippi, had gone on to get an LL.M. at Harvard in 1935, came back to Mississippi as an assistant professor of law in 1936. In 1938, he was promoted to associate professor.[11]

Robert J. Farley, on the other hand, having being offered "a tremendous advance in salary" (from $2,500 to $3,500), could not resist the temptation and left in 1935 to join the Tulane University law faculty in New Orleans.[12] He was replaced, in 1936–37, by Wex Smathers Malone, B.A., LL.M., J.D., who had served as an assistant professor under Dean Deavours in 1931–32. In 1937–38, Landon C. Andrews was promoted to full professor and Charles Tindall from Indianola, an alumnus who had earned his LL.B. in 1935, took up the assistant professor position. When Professor Hemingway died from a heart attack, on November 5, 1937 (just as the construction of "Hemingway Stadium" was getting under way), his place as a professor was filled by William G. Roberds, who had resigned from the faculty seven years earlier in protest at the ousting, by Governor Bilbo's board of trustees, of Professors Hemingway and Farley. In 1939, Professor Malone resigned his professorship and was replaced by Charles W. Taintor II, A.B., S.J.D., who until 1942 taught conflict of laws, oil and gas, and domestic relations.[13]

Into the early 1940s, enrollment in the law school continued at the same level, with just a few more than a hundred students enrolled every year, including two or three women. Approximately three out of every four members of each entering first-year class stayed on into the third year, and about two-thirds of those ultimately earned an LL.B. degree, in three or four cases with distinction. One or two of each year's graduates then went into practice somewhere out of state, but most of them stayed on in Mississippi.[14]

Beginning in 1934 and every year after that, a separate "School of Law" *Bulletin* was published by the university each spring. Until 1950, the front cover of every issue of proudly proclaimed that the school was a "Member of the Association of American Law Schools" and "Approved by the American Bar Association." Each issue contained a "Register" for the current academic year consisting of lists of the names of the university's board of trustees, of the law faculty, and of the students in each class. It also contained an "Announcement" of the entrance requirements, fees, curriculum, and class schedule for the coming academic year. Until 1943, inside the cover of each issue was a black and white photograph of "The Law Building," which, beginning in 1941, was also identified as "Lamar Hall."[15]

The university's general *Bulletin* each year continued to have a description of the law school's program in its "Professional Departments" section. The 1934–35 issue for the first time included lists of professional fraternities and student social organizations. Under the "Professional Fraternities" heading, Phi Delta Phi is listed for the law school. The list of "Student Organizations" includes the "Law Club," which is how the Blackstone Club was generally being referred to by then.[16]

The 1934–35 law school *Bulletin* informed prospective law students that, for 1935–36, the fees per semester would include a matriculation fee of $12.50, a tuition fee of $35.00, a library fee of $3.75, a physical training and athletics fee of $7.50, a hospital fee ("except for those living at home") of $3.25, plus a $1.00 subscription fee for the *Mississippian*. Out-of-state students were required to pay an additional fee per semester of $25.00. The fee for "late registration" was $1.00 per day up to a $5.00 limit, and the fee for changing courses, after the first week, was $1.00 for each change. "Living Expenses" would include $15.00 to $30.00 per semester for a dormitory room. Meals in the "men's dining hall" cost "about $16.00 per month"; meals "in boarding houses," $18.00 to $30.00 per month." One could expect to pay somewhere between $7.00 and $15.00 per semester for laundry bills, and about $30.00 to $40.00 per session for law books.[17]

The 1935–36 curriculum was organized as follows:

FIRST YEAR
Contracts
Torts
Property I
Procedure–Civil
Criminal Law and Procedure
Real Property
Agency
Legal Bibliography

SECOND YEAR
Equity
Bills and Notes
Insurance
Credit Transactions
Titles
Public Utilities
Mississippi Pleading Code and Cases
Evidence
Legal Bibliography

THIRD YEAR
Constitutional Law
Conflict of Laws
Private Corporations
Municipal Corporations
Trusts
Ethics
Wills and Probate
Damages
Chancery Practice
Mississippi Persons
Federal Procedure

Some of the courses would be given for two hours, or three hours "each semester"; others for one, two, three or four hours in either the first or the second semester. A footnote explained that, because "the Law School conceives it to be its duty to serve the people of Mississippi, . . . leading cases from the Mississippi Supreme Court [would] frequently be substituted" for the cases presented in the textbooks assigned for the various courses.[18]

Copies of each issue of the *Law Journal* were furnished to all students enrolled in the law school free of charge. The student editors of the *Journal* were "selected on the basis of their Law School records and aptitude for research." Second- and third-year students who were not on the editorial board but who desired to write notes for it could "do so under the direction of the Editor . . . and members of the Faculty."[19]

At a meeting of the law faculty on May 8, 1935, the decision was made to have in future years a law school summer program that would coincide with and be a part of the general summer school program offered by the rest of the university. It would have two terms—previous law summer sessions had only offered one—and would be taught by four law professors whose salaries would be part of the general summer school budget. So, in the summer of 1936, the law school's first term began on June 3 and ran for eight weeks ending on August 1. The second term ran for six weeks, from August 4 to September 15. Operating under the supervision of Dean Kimbrough, the instructors were Professors Andrews, Fox, Hemingway, and Malone. The courses offered were agency, three hours; criminal law, two hours; sales, two hours; personal property, two hours; legal bibliography, one hour; Mississippi pleading, two hours; federal procedure, two hours; bills, notes and checks, three hours; private corporations, three hours; wills, three hours; trusts, three hours; and judicial administration and ethics, one hour.[20]

Tuition for the first term, payable in advance, was fifty dollars, and for the second term, twenty-five dollars. The cost of room, board, and books for the first term would be approximately eighty dollars, and for the full summer session, one hundred twenty-five dollars. A student could earn up to eight credit hours the first term and up to six hours in the shorter second term. Altogether, a student could, by taking advantage of the full summer session, earn the equivalent of a full semester's credit hours. That meant, in fact, that a student could earn all of the credit hours needed to qualify for the LL.B. degree in just twenty-four months by enrolling full time for just two regular school years and two full summer sessions.[21]

The "practice court" was still a very important part of the curriculum. Used in conjunction with the second- and third-year "courses having to do with practice, procedure and evidence," and with the first-year students still serving as jurors and the professor sitting as the judge, the pleading was "required to be done with the same thoroughness and accuracy as done by the lawyer in the courts of the state." Regarded as "a necessary part of the student's work," it entered into and became a part of his final grade.[22]

Other important decisions made by the law faculty in 1935 included one that established a centralized record of all student absences from class to be kept by the currently serving "Secretary to the Dean" who, as noted above, now also held the title of Registrar of Law School." Students who had been out sick were now to be allowed, within reason, to make up for missed class time.

Students who transferred in from another institution would not be given credit for any work done at a law school that was not a member of the AALS. Law students who were members of the state legislature would be required to remain in school over the Christmas holidays and would take their final exams for the first semester on January 2, 3, and 4, which would enable them then to be in Jackson on January 7 for the legislature's opening ceremonies.[23]

Three years earlier, in April 1932, the legislature had enacted legislation that transformed the by-then twenty-six-year-old state bar association from a voluntary membership group into the "Mississippi State Bar," membership in which and the paying of annual dues to which was then required of all lawyers practicing in the state. The new state bar, of course, still retained close ties to the American Bar Association, and the ABA at its 1934 annual meeting in Milwaukee created a "junior section" made up of ABA members aged thirty-five or younger with its own separate by-laws and slate of officers. Over the next couple of years, several state bar groups (including the Tennessee State Bar, with the dean of the Vanderbilt University law school playing a leading role), organized their own junior sections. So it is not too surprising that on the opening night of the Mississippi State Bar's 1936 annual meeting, held September 3–4 in Greenville, Dean Kimbrough summoned former *Law Journal* editor and future judge Hugh N. Clayton up to his top floor room in the Greenville Hotel to talk about putting together a Mississippi bar junior section.[24]

In an interview forty-one years later, Judge Clayton recalled how his "close friend" Dean Kimbrough had told him: "Hugh, I want you to get several of these young fellas" and start putting together a plan for a junior section. And so, later that same evening, Clayton sat down in a corner of the Greenville Hotel lobby with a few of his contemporaries, including W. Calvin Wells Jr. and John Satterfield, who were both ABA members, and typed with two fingers on an old typewriter borrowed from the hotel a draft constitution and by-laws for a junior bar section of the Mississippi State Bar. At their business meeting the next day, the bar approved both of them as written. Then its thirty-five-year-old and younger members proceeded to elect Clayton president of the new section, to which all of them automatically belonged. Thereafter, it became customary for the section to meet and do business each year the day before the full state bar meeting began. And each graduating class from the law school every year thereafter immediately became part of an organized group of their near-contemporaries.[25]

Meanwhile, in 1936, the law school faculty made some more important policy changes. In February they ruled that students must have at least a C average to graduate and that accumulating nine or more hours of Fs would lead to automatic expulsion from the program. Just before Christmas they decided that a total of three absences from a particular class would automatically take a student's name off of that class roll and that three "tardies" would equal one absence. Early in the new year of 1937, they ruled that F's in 60 percent of a student's credit hours in one semester meant that he or she was out of the program for good. Later that same year, they also voted to add a taxation course to the curriculum to lower the number of hours needed to graduate from 88 to 78 (56 required and 22 elective) and to adopt a policy with regard to "Student Activities" that stated: "It is highly desirable, and practically imperative, that students in the School of Law devote their full time to the work of this School and engage in no extracurricular activities. Students who desire to engage in such activities must secure permission of the Dean."[26] The faculty also ruled around this same time that no law student could take work in any other department of the university without the express permission of the dean, and "in no event will he be permitted to take more than three semester hours of such work."[27]

By the mid-1930s, an honor system adopted by the law school students with regard to "all work and written examinations" had become a tradition of which the school's graduates were "justly proud." Currently enrolled students regarded it as being "something sacred," and no student could remain enrolled who was not willing to abide by it.[28] Meanwhile, by 1936, not only Phi Delta Phi but also two other honor societies had chapters in the law school. One of them, Phi Alpha Delta, was, like Phi Delta Phi, one of "the leading law fraternities of the nation" for men. The other, Phi Delta Delta, was "an international legal fraternity for women."[29]

By 1937, Phi Delta Phi was offering an award to the law senior class member each year who, "in 'the opinion of the law faculty, . . . best exemplified the attributes indicative of a successful lawyer, of character, scholarship, personality and general ability." By 1938–39, the faculty had resolved that there must be no discrimination between the sexes in selecting the winner each year, that the recipient must have been enrolled in the law school for at least two years, and that he or she must be a senior who was going to graduate in the coming spring or summer. Each recipient of the award was to be given a specially designed gold key as a token of his or her achievement, and the recipient's name would be inscribed on "a large bronze plaque" placed in the law building.[30]

By the 1940–41 school year, although World War II by then was raging furiously in Europe, the law school was operating much the same as it had over the previous few years. Almost all of the same faculty members were teaching: Chancellor Butts and Dean Kimbrough, Professors Malone, Roberds, Taintor, and Wade, and Assistant Professor Andrews. The only change was that in 1938 law librarian and instructor Catherine Bass had left and been replaced by Rebekah Elizabeth Dean, a graduate of the New York State Library School, who served as the law librarian but did not have "instructor" rank. On December 31, 1940, Professor Roberds left to accept a position on the state supreme court and was replaced on February 1, 1941, by Professor Lester Glenn Fant Jr. (holder of a B.A. degree from Vanderbilt University and an LL.B. from Harvard). Regular law students enrolled numbered 109, plus two "special students" (who had to be over twenty-three years of age and were not candidates for a law degree). Only two of the law students were females, but one of them, Evelyn Gandy, would become lieutenant governor of Mississippi (1976–80).[31]

In May 1941 the law faculty adopted a new policy whereby they, just as the students did, would have to check out any books they wanted from the library rather than simply walking off with them. In September 1941 they voted that liberal arts undergraduates should be allowed to take up to twenty-six hours of law course credits that could be counted toward meeting the requirements for their B.A. degrees. A month later, worried about the fact that a considerable number of their own students were "deficient in written English," they adopted a policy (recommended by a committee chaired by Professor Wade and also including Chancellor Butts and Professor Fox) that henceforth all law students would be required to demonstrate their competency in English in the form of either a *Law Journal* contribution, a legal research paper, or an appellate brief.[32] Meanwhile, on February 15, 1940, the first "Law Day" had been held on campus, and lawyers from all around the state had participated in a continuing legal education event called a "Law Institute." A second Law Institute (for which the intended topic was administrative law) was scheduled for December 12, 1941 (the Friday after Pearl Harbor), but it, apparently, was canceled.[33]

At a meeting held on December 12, 1941, the law faculty voted that their many students who already had been called up for service in the military (or, in some cases, the F.B.I.) could take their semester final exams (previously scheduled for

January 19–30, 1942) early. The total student enrollment at the beginning of the 1941–42 academic year had been eighty seven. One year later (1942–43) only ten seniors were enrolled, together with seven second-year students and seventeen first-year students. Three of the students were women—including Evelyn Gandy, then a senior, who served as the *Law Journal* editor—and four of them were from out-of-state.[34] Also, by then, three members of the regular law faculty, Professors Fox, Wade, and Fant were "on leave of absence in military service." Chancellor Butts, from January 1942 to January 1944, was in Washington working in the Judge Advocate General's office. Professor Taintor had left to take a position at the University of Pittsburgh. So the teaching in the law school was being done by Dean Kimbrough with the assistance of Professor Clifford H. Dixon, J.D., Assistant Professor Andrews, and Assistant Professor William N. Ethridge, a 1937 graduate of the law school who had gone on to earn an LL.M. at the University of Southern California in 1939, plus a few local lawyers.[35]

With the approval of both the AALS and the ABA, the law school was also, by then, offering an "Accelerated War Time Program." Any regularly enrolled student who "attended classes for one half of a semester or more" and then entered any one of the armed services, either as a volunteer or because he was drafted, provided his class work up to the time of his leaving was "of passing quality," was given full credit for those classes. The student would normally have had to take an examination on the work done in each class, unless the faculty agreed that it was impossible for him or her to do so.[36]

The 1944–45 enrollment was down to only twenty-two students. But in the first year immediately after the war, 1945–46, it was back up to more than one hundred. Twenty-eight seniors, twenty-one second-year students, and fifty-one first year students were enrolled, plus two "specials" and five alumni who were taking "Refresher" courses.[37] Also the faculty list was very similar to what it had been four years earlier. Chancellor Butts, by then, had been back on campus for a year and a half. Professors Fox, Wade, and Fant were back from serving in the military, and State Senator Landon C. Andrews was still serving as an assistant professor. One newcomer, at the professorial level was Associate Professor Forest Hodge O'Neal, who had earned both a B.A. and an LL.B. at Louisiana State University and then had spent the war years working as an associate in a law firm in New York City. Another newcomer was Corinne Bass, who held both a B.A. degree from Sophie Newcomb College in New Orleans and a B.S. degree in Library Science from Columbia University. She was both the law librarian and an instructor in law. After the last holder of both those titles, Rhoda Catherine Bass, had left in 1938, the law librarianship position had been held by Rebekah Elizabeth Dean, A.B., a graduate of the New York State Library School, until 1943. And, for the next two years after that, Grace B. Brown had served in the three positions of acting law librarian, law school registrar, and secretary to the dean, but she was now back again to serving in only the last two of those three capacities.[38]

By the spring of 1946, the dean with whom Ms. Brown was working, as both registrar and his secretary, was Robert J. Farley, the man after whom the building they worked in (then called "Lamar Hall") today is named. For, on the night of December 31, 1945, Dean Tommy Kimbrough had died in his sleep at his home on the campus. A few days later, Chancellor Butts and John Fox had phoned Professor Farley in new Orleans and invited him—he recalled in an interview many years later—to come back to Oxford "and see if [he] didn't want to be dean." So he did, and, as he recalled, very much "to the surprise of all my friends at Tulane, because I took a lesser salary as dean here than I was getting there, I did." Assuming the office on February 1, 1946, Farley held it for the next eighteen years.[39]

For a while, however, it seemed that he might not hold it for very long. Just a week earlier, on January 25, 1946, the board of trustees of the state's institutions of higher learning decided for a variety of reasons that it was time for the University of Mississippi to have new leadership at the top and voted to remove Butts as chancellor at the end of that academic year. And, for a while during that spring, Robert Farley was generally considered to be one of the leading candidates to replace him. The board, however, decided that they did not want to appoint anyone to the position who had considerable connections with any political factions within the state so, when Benjamin Butts left the campus that summer to return to Washington to serve as director of the war department's educational program, he was replaced as chancellor by J. D. Williams, a Kentuckian who had earned a D.Ed. from Columbia University in 1940 and since 1942 had been serving as the president of Marshall College in Huntington, West Virginia.[40]

Meanwhile, three students received LL.B. degrees on January 31, 1946, and seven more (including a future dean of the law school, Joel William Bunkley Jr. of Yazoo City) received them on May 27, 1946. On January 18, 1946, the law faculty voted to allow Thomas R. Ethridge (the future United States Attorney for the northern district for whom Oxford's new federal building is named) cred-it for three courses he had been taking in the 1941 fall semester. Because he had voluntarily enlisted in the United States Marine Corps on December 28 of that year, he had never taken the final examinations for them. Both in accordance with what had been their wartime practice and "in view of his service record," his peti-tion was granted. Just two days later, they approved a petition from future north-ern district judge William G. Burgin Jr. that, although he had twelve absences from his bills and notes class that semester, because ten of those absences had been due to his having to be off-campus either in his capacity as the university athlet-ic department's "Program Director and Director of Athletic Publicity" or in his capacity as "President of the Associated Student Body" and two were due to ill-ness—although the standing policy was that "any student absent from more than 20% of the total number of class meetings in any one course is not eligible to take the final examination therein"—he might still be allowed to take it.[41]

For the 1946–47 academic year, student enrollment was up to the unprec-edented total of 247. Forty-nine seniors, seventy-four second-year students, one hundred and twenty first-year students plus three "special" students and one "refresher" were attending. The only woman enrolled was in the first year. The eleven out-of-state students included six from Tennessee; one from Arkansas; one from Paducah, Kentucky; one from McPherson, Kansas; and two from as far away as Pennsylvania. The faculty, not surprisingly, was slightly expanded in size also. Although John W. Wade was "on leave of absence" as a visiting professor of law at the University of Texas and just a year later would become a permanent member of the Vanderbilt University law faculty, and Lester Glenn Fant Jr., who was now listed only as an assistant professor, pre-sumably was only teaching part time, there were three new associate profes-sors: Joel W. Bunkley (holder of a B.A. from the College of William and Mary as well as his LL.B.), Ford W. Hall (holder of a B.A. from East Texas Teachers College and an LL.B. from Tulane), and J. Hector Currie (a University of Mississippi alumnus and former Rhodes scholar, with an LL.B. from Yale). At one of their last formal meetings at the end of that school year, on May 19, 1947, the faculty kindly voted to permit four first-year students—two of whom were Noah S. Sweat Jr. and William Winter—to delay the taking of their final examinations because of medical problems.[42]

The 1946–47 law school *Bulletin* repeated the statement, made in every edi-tion of the *Bulletin* since the first one in the series published twelve years earlier, that "Lamar Hall, a commodious and well-equipped building, occupied exclusively by the School of Law," was more than adequate to meet every one of the school's needs. Its ground floor, it was noted, now contained "a club room, lounging room, locker room, and workrooms for students." But where was the *Law Journal*'s editorial office? At a meeting of the law faculty held a little more than a year earlier, on February 4, 1946, their attention had been called—now that more than a hundred students were again enrolled and many more expected in the next year—to "the crowded conditions existing in the law building and especially in the law journal board offices." And "in view of the crowded shelf room and office space" existing in it, "they deemed it "imperative that the small brick building immediately North of and behind the Law Building be allocated to the Law School for Law School purposes." The review recommended that the chancellor should "be requested to take such steps as necessary to obtain such allocation."[43]

The "small brick building" referred to had been built almost a century earlier, for Chancellor Barnard, just across the road from his residence (now known as "Barnard Hall"), to house a "magnetic laboratory." Because of the outbreak of the Civil War, however, that laboratory was never installed, and Chancellor Barnard, soon afterward, left the campus. After the battle of Shiloh on April 6 and 7, 1862 (while the "Chapel" was being used as a hospital for the wounded on both sides), the empty structure was used as a morgue to house the corpses of soldiers who had died from their wounds. So it came to be known as the "Dead House," and the name stuck. But that did not discourage Delta Kappa Epsilon fraternity from using it as their fraternity house into the early twentieth century. Then, in 1910, after a porch and additional windows had been added to it, it became a faculty residence. For a while, it was the home of physics professor W. L. Kennon, after whom the university observatory on All American Drive is named. The last faculty member to live in it was R. M. Guess, dean of students in the 1930s and 1940s. In 1946, it was turned over to the law school. And the 1947 law school *Bulletin* was able to report that "an office for the editorial staff of the *Mississippi Law Journal* is maintained in a small separate building just north of Lamar Hall."[44]

At the beginning of the 1948–49 school year, some 336 students were enrolled, twenty-eight of whom (including one woman—Jean Wilson, from Meridian) were scheduled to graduate in January 1949, and seventeen (all of them men) in May 1949. Of the 285 first- and second-year students, four were women and seventeen were from out of state (including four from New Orleans; three from Memphis; two from Jackson, Tennessee; and one from as far away as Gilchrist, Oregon). There were also three "special students" enrolled and three "irregular" students. Not surprising, the faculty had also increased in size. Although F. Hodge O'Neal had been away since 1947, serving as acting dean of the law school at Mercer University in Macon, Georgia (and would be appointed to hold that position permanently in 1949), and Ford W. Hall was no longer teaching, there were now four new names on the law faculty list. Professor Roscoe Cross, after earning an A.B. and an A.M. at the University of Kentucky, had earned a B.C.L. as a Rhodes Scholar at Oxford University's Pembroke College in 1929 and had then spent most of the next nineteen years (apart from three years in military service, rising to the rank of colonel) practicing law in Boston. William N. Ethridge Jr., after serving four years as an associate in the Wells, Wells, Newman and Thomas law office in Jackson, was back as a full professor and serving as the faculty adviser to the *Law Journal.* Two new associate professors were Walter Dunham Jr. (with a B.A. from the University of Texas and an LL.B. from Columbia) and William Lee McLane (a Tulane graduate, who also had an LL.B. from Columbus plus some experience practicing law in New York City). Also, Grace Brown continued to serve both as law school registrar and secretary to Dean Farley, and Sarah Katherine Cox was now serving as the "Secretary in the School of Law."[45]

Over the next four years, the faculty made it their practice to meet on the first Thursday of each month for lunch in the university cafeteria in Johnson Commons (presumably in one of the private dining rooms located in the basement).[46] Early in 1949, they were very much concerned with planning for the annual Southern Law Review Conference scheduled to be held on campus March 25–26 of that year. Local judge John M. Hutchinson had agreed to be the principal speaker, the Oxford Bar Association had agreed to sponsor a fish-fry for the conferees, and the law faculty themselves each pledged to contribute five dollars of their own money to help cover the hospitality expenses. They were also very happy to have their distinguished alumnus, Myres McDougal, the Sterling Professor of Law at Yale University, scheduled to appear as a guest lecturer April 5–8.[47]

In-house academic matters also had to be considered. On March 7, 1949, the faculty voted to shorten class periods during the regular school year from sixty minutes to fifty minutes but to retain sixty minute classes in summer school.

They also discussed the possibility of introducing a graduate degree (LL.M.) program. That fall, they were concerned with encouraging both faculty and student participation in the fourth annual Law Institute being put on in Jackson, December 2–3, by the junior bar section of the state bar. And in the spring of 1950, they were planning celebration of "Law Day" on the third Wednesday in March. No law classes, it was decided, were to be held after 10:00 A.M. on that Wednesday morning, or before 10:00 A.M. on the Thursday morning. Another topic discussed at both the March and April 1950 meetings was the problem of the growing number of law students who were members of the state legislature, a factor that impacted greatly on their class attendance records.[48]

In their January 1951 meeting, the faculty approved the placing of a glass-front, lockable bulletin board in the hallway on the "main floor" for notices and pictures. In their March meeting that year, besides again approving the cancellation of classes for Law Day, they also decided to begin, in the next school year, ten-minute rather than five-minute intervals between classes. And, in a special meeting held a couple of months later, they voted that, henceforth, "special commencements" should be scheduled each year, in both February and August, for the benefit of the law school's January and summer school graduating seniors.[49]

Meanwhile, nearly half the world away, the Korean conflict was raging, and it looked as though it was not going to end anytime soon. So, early in the new year of 1951, it was decided to offer, in the upcoming spring semester, not only an elective course for second- and third-year law students on "Military Law" but also an "elementary" military law course open to ROTC and other non-law students. Furthermore, at their April 1951 meeting, a decision was made that must have reminded many members of the faculty of how things had been back during World War II: Any student enrolled that semester who had to leave any time after April 1 to meet their military service obligations could take their final exams right away, or at some later date, and still receive full credit for the courses in which they had been enrolled.[50]

A year later, in the spring of 1952, a much more cheerful topic was taking up much of their meeting time. They were busy planning for a special new course that was going to be offered, through the university's extension studies office on campus that year, August 11–22, for members of the state bar. Its topic was going to be tax law. For a fee of only fifty dollars, lawyers from around the state would be given a thorough grounding in the latest tax law developments, receive free textbooks and other study materials, and also get to compete with one another on swimming teams or in golf matches.[51] A similar course was offered in 1953, and the extension courses soon became an established institution. Meanwhile, at a meeting held on September 26, 1952, the faculty voted to celebrate September 1954 through June 1955 as the "Centennial Year of the Law School."[52]

By 1954, the postwar glut of students had passed out into the working world, and the law school's enrollment was back to a number similar to the prewar level. For the 1953–54 school year, twenty-six seniors were enrolled. All of them were male; two were from out of state, one of them from Dunkirk, New York, and the other from Louisville, Kentucky. The number of first- and second-year students totaled 104. Among them were future dean Parham H. Williams Jr.; Omar D. Craig, later a leading Oxford lawyer; and William Faulkner's sister-in-law Dorothy Z. Oldham. Eight of them were women, thirteen were from out-of-state, and two were from Puerto Rico. One "special student" was also enrolled.[53]

The faculty, however, were only one fewer in number than the thirteen who had been teaching five years earlier. Two professors from that time were no longer on campus, however; Roscoe C. Cross had resigned in 1952 and returned to his boyhood hometown of Mayfield, Kentucky, to practice law, and William N. Ethridge had taken a leave of absence in 1950 to return to Jackson to serve as a commissioner for the state supreme court, and he had resigned in 1952 when he was elected to serve as an associate justice of that court. But Dean Robert Farley was still heading up the faculty, and Professor John H. Fox Jr. was still serving. Joel William Bunkley and James Hector Currie, associate professors five years earlier, were now full professors. One of two new associate professors was Arthur B. Custy (from Laurel, Mississippi). Having earned both a B.A. and an LL.B. at the university by 1949, Custy had been hired as an acting associate professor in 1950 and, after taking some additional course work at the Yale law school, had been made a regular associate professor in 1952. The other new associate professor, Ernest McLain Jones, had earned a B.A. from Southwestern at Memphis (now Rhodes College) and an LL.B. from the University of Virginia before practicing law for a while in Washington, D.C. Assistant professors Landon C. Andrews, Lester Glenn Fant Jr., and Charles B. Roberts were still serving in that capacity on a part-time basis while practicing law in and around Oxford. The staff had been joined in 1953–54 by Jackson D. Doty, a Tupelo native, who by 1949 had earned both a B.B.A. and an LL.B. from the university and now was practicing law in Pontotoc.[54]

Serving as a visiting professor in the 1953, 1954, and 1955 summer sessions was a gentleman from Carlsbad, Czechoslovakia. His name was Jan Paul Charmatz. In 1933, at the age of twenty-three, he had earned a doctorate in civil and canon law (J.U.D.) at the University of Prague and had taught there until shortly after the German takeover of Czechoslovakia in June 1939, when he left to go underground for political reasons. When the American armed forces liberated his country in the spring of 1945, he succeeded in talking his way into membership in the United States Army and from 1945 to 1948 had served in the office of the U.S. Counsel for the Prosecution of Major War Criminals, playing a major role in the prosecutions of both Albert Speer and Herman Goering. After teaching for a couple of years first in Cuba and then in Puerto Rico, he was awarded a Sterling Fellowship at the Yale Law School and earned a master of laws degree there in 1952. Then, from 1953 to 1955 he taught civil law at the Louisiana State University during the regular school year and, in the summers, both took courses and taught at the University of Mississippi law school. Awarded his LL.B. in August 1955, for the next two years, he served as a full professor on the Mississippi law faculty before going on to Tulane and, ultimately, ending up on the law faculty at Southern Methodist University in Dallas.[55]

Beginning in 1954, a bachelor's degree or the equivalent became a requirement for admission to the law school. However, by taking an approved number of law school courses as an undergraduate minor, a University of Mississippi student could, upon completion of just two years of additional law school course work, earn both a bachelor's degree and an LL.B. in just six years. In addition to the general semester fee of $81.50 (plus a non-resident fee of one hundred dollars for out-of-state students), law students still had to pay each semester a tuition fee of fifty dollars, plus a *Law Journal* fee of two dollars and a student government fee of two dollars. The summer session fee then was eleven dollars per semester credit hour taken. The student honor system with regard to the conduct of "all daily written work and examinations" was by then a well-established institution, and the law library contained "more than 30,000 well-selected books."[56]

In addition to the Phi Delta Phi Award given to the graduating senior each year considered by the faculty to be the most outstanding member of his or her class—won in 1954 by W. Emmett Marston—there was now also a Phi Alpha Delta Award given each year to the winners of the senior moot court competition. As was the case with the Phi Delta Phi Award, the winners' names were "engraved on a bronze plaque in the entrance of the law building." And the law faculty and the editorial board of the *Law Journal* were still handing out the Law Journal Awards—consisting of law books chosen by the winners themselves—to both the writer of the best case note and the best case comment appearing each year in the *Journal*. Also awarded then was the yearly Deposit Guaranty Bank and Trust Company Prize of one hundred dollars for "the student who, in the opinion of the faculty," had submitted "the best essay on some current matter of interest primarily in the field of estates, trusts or taxation." The Bureau of National Affairs offered a one-year subscription to the *United States Law Week* to the student who, in the faculty's opinion, had made "the most satisfactory scholastic progress during his senior year," and the American Society of Authors, Publishers and Composers awarded annually two Nathan Burkan Memorial prizes—a first prize of $150 and a second prize of $50—to the two students who, in the opinion of the dean, had written the best papers "on some phase of copyright law."[57]

In the spring of 1954, with the Centennial Year coming up that fall, the twenty-seventh Annual Law Day was celebrated on March 18. The program included an address by State Bar President Jerome Hafter, a noon banquet, an informal get-together at Spring Lake Lodge in the afternoon, and a student body dance at the law school that evening. An even more formal event was held on March 27, when United States Supreme Court Justice Felix Frankfurter was the featured speaker at an evening banquet held in connection with the 8th Annual Southern Law Review Conference. Other guests, besides the editors of law reviews from law schools all over the southeast, were the members of the Mississippi Supreme Court, the state's federal district judges, the state attorney general, the officers of the state bar, and the judges of the United States Court of Appeals.[58]

At the 1954 annual meeting of the state bar, held June 17–19 on the gulf coast at the Edgewater Gulf Hotel, Dean Farley was elected to serve as the state bar's president for the next twelve months At that same meeting, a future dean of the law school, Poplarville attorney Josh Morse, was elected president of the state bar's junior bar section for the coming year. A few weeks later, another future dean, Professor Joel W. Bunkley Jr., was reported as having presented to Chancellor J. D. Williams the flag that had flown on the USS *California* at Pearl Harbor on December 7, 1941. The flag was a gift to the university from the professor's father, Admiral Joel W. Bunkley Sr. of Yazoo City, who had commanded the flagship *California* at the time of the surprise Japanese raid on the Hawaiian naval base.[59]

The first major event of the 1954–55 "Centennial Year" was the Ninth Annual Law Institute sponsored by both the law school and the Jackson junior bar, held December 3–4, in Jackson at the Robert E. Lee Hotel. The institute opened on Friday morning with a seminar on estate planning offered by a panel made up of law professors John H. Fox Jr., Lester G. Fant, and Jack D. Doty, together with Noel Mills, trust officer of the Deposit Guaranty Bank. It closed on Saturday evening with a social hour followed by the Annual Institute Banquet. Dean Farley presided as master of ceremonies at the banquet, which concluded with "a very humorous talk" by the Honorable J. Ed Livingston, Chief Justice of the Alabama Supreme Court. Altogether, the December number of the *Mississippi Lawyer* reported, in a front page headline in big black capital letters, the institute was a "HUGE SUCCESS."[60]

Just two weeks later on December 17, at a meeting of state judges, municipal officials, and law enforcement officers held in the state bar office in Jackson, it was quickly decided that a traffic conference at a statewide level needed to be held in the very near future. Later, the decision was made to hold it at the university's law school, February 28–March 1, 1955. And again it was reported in the March issue of the *Mississippi Lawyer,* the verdict was that the traffic conference, which had addressed issues concerning "rules of evidence, civil and criminal responsibility in traffic collision cases, laws of arrest, search and seizure" had been "highly successful."[61]

The formal celebration of the law school centennial was held on the annual Law Day, March 14, 1955. The morning speaker was the newly elected mayor of Cincinnati, Ohio, Charles P. Taft. A son of United States President William Howard Taft (1909–13), this Taft had earned both a B.A. (1918) and an LL.B. (1921) at Yale University and had been a leading member of the Cincinnati bar for many years. The luncheon speaker, Congressman Clifford Davis, a native of Hazlehurst, Mississippi, had earned an LL.B. in the law school in 1918. After a distinguished career in Memphis city government, culminating in his serving, from 1938 to 1940, as both the commissioner for public safety and the vice mayor, he had been elected to represent the Tenth Tennessee district in the house of representatives in Washington, D.C. The evening speaker, Thurman W. Arnold, was, as were both Dean Farley and Mayor Taft, Yale University–connected. A native of Laramie, Wyoming, he had earned an A.B. at Princeton University in 1911, an LL.B. at Harvard in 1914, an M.A. from Yale in 1931, and an honorary LL.D. from the University of Wyoming in 1943. After three years as dean of the West Virginia

University college of law from 1927 to 1930, he had served on the Yale law faculty from 1930 to 1938. He then went to Washington, where he had served as an assistant attorney general of the United States in charge of antitrust enforcement from 1938 to 1943 and as a judge of the United States Court of Appeals for the D.C. Circuit from 1943 to 1945. For the past decade, he had been working as a member of the prestigious D.C. law firm Arnold, Fortas and Porter.[62]

Besides the outside speakers, another group of honorees invited to the centennial celebration were the twelve surviving graduates of the law school who had received their degrees in the nineteenth century. They were Alton Holt Stone (1891) of Greenville, William H. Watkins (1895) of Jackson, Charles Lowry Garnett (1896) of Columbus, Charles Frances Engle (1896) of Natchez, Wiliam Morris Hammer (1898) of Greenwood, Gordon Garland Lyell (1898) of Jackson, William Madison Whittington (1899) of Greenwood, Hazelwood Farish (1899) of Greenville, Walter W. Lockard (1900) of Oxford, James R. McDowell (1900) of Memphis, Gabe Herman McMorrough (1900) of Lexington, and W. Calvin Wells (1899) of Jackson.[63]

Many of the Centennial celebrants must have been very pleased to learn that the law school's Phi Alpha Delta chapter had been selected as that fraternity's "most outstanding chapter" that year in District Five. The district included law schools in the states of Mississippi, Louisiana, Tennessee, and Alabama. And later that spring chapter delegates from Vanderbilt, Tulane, and Cumberland universities as well as from the universities of Alabama and Tennessee came to campus for the Phi Alpha Delta Annual Conclave. Highlights of their get-together were an address by Florida Supreme Court Justice Elwyn Thomas and a dinner and dance at Sardis Lake Lodge.[64]

Altogether twenty law students graduated in that semester of celebration (eight on January 28, and twelve in May 1955). All of them were Mississippians, and all but one of them (June M. Dantin from Columbia) were men. The women law students were certainly holding their own, however. Two of them had been appointed to serve on the 1955–56 Moot Court Board: Mary Elizabeth Bickerstaff of Gulfport as its chair and Lenore Loving of West Point as its secretary. And that October, in the Federal Building on the Square in Oxford, Miss Euple Dozier, originally from Fulton, was sworn in as Mississippi's first-ever female Assistant United States Attorney.[65]

There was yet another reason for optimism by the end of 1955. Six years earlier, Dean Farley had noted in a *Law Journal* article on the history of the law

school, published in connection with the then on-going celebration of the centennial of the university, that the Lamar Hall law library, which by then contained only a few "more than 22,000 volumes," had "outgrown its physical
facilities." In a similar article, published in the March 1954 number of the *Law
Journal,* celebrating the upcoming centennial of the school of law, however, the
dean was happy to report that, with the library now having to house "more than
30,000" volumes, plans were "on foot to add to the law building so as to provide badly needed additional space, particularly for the library." With enough
added room, it would be possible "to systematically strengthen the library."
And, with a "substantially improved library," it would be possible to initiate
two projects that were already ongoing in several other states: first, a study of
needed improvements in the state's laws, which would have to be "undertak-
en cooperatively by the Bar and the law school, and, second, some method of
organized assistance in drafting desirable new legislation." With both of those
projects up and going, the law school would begin its second century "with a
vision of enlarged service to its students, the members of the Bar, and all the
people of the state."[66]

Adding the three-story extension onto the back of Lamar Hall in 1958 meant
pulling down the Dead House. But, once it was completed in 1959, there was
plenty of room in the enlarged law building to bring the *Law Journal* offices back into it, and for the "more than 30,000 well-selected law books" in the
considerably larger library. The school of law now possessed, its 1959 *Bulletin*
proudly proclaimed, "one of the most modern law buildings in the country."[67]

Inside that modern law building, however, some serious trouble was brewing. In the decade after the end of World War II, some black military veterans had developed ambitions with regard to gaining admission to the various
professional schools in their home states. Certain worried white politicians in
Mississippi were beginning to think that perhaps the only solution to the desegregation threat might be to close down all such schools in the state. Instead,
however, the state board of trustees, in August 1950, thought they had solved
the problem by instructing each of the state's institutions of higher learning to
"accept or reject any applicants according to the best interests of everyone."[68]

Just three years later, in the fall of 1953, Charles Dubra, a black minister from
Gulfport, applied for admission to the law school. He emphasized in his application that he did not want to cause any trouble. He would just attend the
necessary classes and otherwise spend his time in Oxford's black community.

Since he already had a masters degree from prestigious Boston University, Dean Farley considered him an "ideal" candidate for a breach of the color barrier and told Chancellor Williams so. The chancellor, therefore, took the dean with him to Jackson to meet with the board of trustees and try to sell them on the idea. One or two of the board members were agreeable to it, but the majority were appalled at the idea and firmly voted "no." The rationale they used, that Dubra's undergraduate degree was from an unaccredited school, Claflin College in Orangeburg, South Carolina, was not one that would have applied to a white holder of a Boston University graduate degree, but it worked in this case. And Dubra decided not to challenge it.[69]

A year later, in 1954, future civil rights martyr Medgar Evers, a graduate of fully accredited Alcorn A&M College, applied for admission to the law school. His case, like Dubra's, and in spite of the 1950 policy declaration, was also referred to the board of trustees in Jackson. Fairly confident that he would not be able to get them, the board members reminded him of a rule, then in force, that he must have two letters of recommendation from alumni of the university resident in his "home county" to qualify for admission. Rather to their surprise, he did find two Ole Miss graduates in his native Newton County who were willing to write such letters. Not good enough though, said the board. The letters had to be from alumni resident in Holmes County, where he was then living. And, while he was looking for a pair there who might be willing to write on his behalf, they raised the number of letters required to five. Just about that time, however, Evers was offered the position of NAACP state field secretary, and he decided to forget about going to law school and to do that instead.[70]

Meanwhile, just a few weeks earlier, on May 17, 1954, in Washington, D.C., the United States Supreme Court, presided over by Chief Justice Earl Warren, had handed down their unanimous decision in the landmark case of *Brown v. Board of Education* that racial segregation was unconstitutional at every level in public education. And a year later, in its *Brown II* decision, handed down on May 31, 1955, the Court said that desegregation must be carried out "with all deliberate speed. Those two decisions, straddling the law school's centennial celebrations time-wise as they did, soon began to have a very heavy impact. The law school's constitutional law expert, Associate Professor William Patrick Murphy, had replaced Walter Dunham in that capacity in 1953. And he soon made it clear that he had no doubt that the Court's order would have to be obeyed, even in Mississippi. Having grown up in Memphis and Jacksonville,

Florida, however, and with ancestral roots in Mississippi, he knew that getting it obeyed would not be easy.[71]

In a letter to the editor of the *Jackson Clarion Ledger* published June 30, 1954, Murphy noted that the decision did "create for the Southern states manifold problems of new school construction, school transportation, allocation of teachers and teaching space, health and sanitation, among others." He proposed, therefore, that the United States Congress should give some immediate consideration to how it might help the states out with such problems. In a letter dated June 24, 1954, mailed to Mississippi's junior United States Senator, John Stennis, he had made exactly the same suggestion. And Stennis, in a letter dated June 29, had thanked him for his letter and noted that its proposals had "a great deal of substance" and were "worthy of further study and consideration." In a second, longer letter dated July 9, 1954, however, the senator—after again thanking Murphy for his letter, which was "the best memorandum or writing" he had seen on the subject of desegregation and "as accurate, clear, and as sound as can be—nevertheless had to report that the chances for federal legislation of the sort he had suggested were "very, very remote." A constitutional amendment aimed at undoing *Brown* and upholding "separate but equal" would never get off the ground. As for addressing any problems at the grassroots level created by *Brown,* the southern conservative wing of the majority Democratic part did not want to do anything with regard to solving them; and its northern wing, while feeling that the south should do whatever was needed to solve them, thought also that the south should pay for those solutions themselves.[72]

The very next week, a story in the July 15 edition of the *Summit Sun*, a weekly paper published in Summit, the county seat of southern Mississippi's Pike County, under the headline "SOMETHING ROTTEN AT OLE MISS," opened with a copy of the letter from Murphy published in the *Jackson Clarion Ledger* on June 30, in which he made essentially the same suggestions he had made to Senator Stennis. Following it was a copy of a letter in response to it from Jackson resident W. J. Simmons. Professor Murphy's letter, he suggested, appeared to be an "elaboration of the position taken by Dean Farley of the Ole Miss Law School who, in a recent public speech had said that the State of Mississippi could not 'outsmart' the United States Supreme Court" and that they "had better accept racial integration if they knew what was good for them. It is my firm opinion," he concluded, "these two professors should be summarily fired from the faculty at the University." A final comment from the *Sun*'s editor was that

"Mississippians certainly need to feel concern when the Dean and his assistant suggest that this road to tyranny is the road for the South."[73]

The fact that Dean Farley had invited Supreme Court Justice Felix Frankfurter to be the principal speaker at the 1954 Law Day just a few weeks before the *Brown* decision had been handed down also was seen by many around the state as firm evidence that he was part of a plot to destroy the South's lifestyle. So great was the heat that the dean found it convenient to take a leave of absence, beginning on September 15, 1956, to return to teach for a semester at Tulane University in New Orleans. And, though he returned to Oxford and the campus in January 1957, some other university faculty members, suspected of similar hostility to the Southern way of life, around the same time decided that the safest and best solution would be to leave for good. *Time Magazine* included in the "Education" section of its July 29, 1957, issue a brief report titled "Exodus from Ole Miss." Based on a series of articles published a week earlier in the *Greenville Delta Democrat Times*, it told how that year 31 out of 136 professors had resigned from the University of Mississippi, in a few cases because salaries elsewhere were generally higher but in most cases because of the bullying pressure being put on faculty members by the state legislature and by the segregation-championing white "Citizens Council" on any of them who were not outspoken champions of maintaining the racial status quo.[74]

Meanwhile, word got out that Professor Murphy in 1955 had joined the American Civil Liberties Union (whose publications, naturally, were of great interest to a constitutional law scholar), and that aroused a great deal of suspicion with regard to him in some circles around the state. Then, in a letter published in August 1957 in the *Memphis Commercial Appeal*, he reminded readers that "Judicial review has been a basic part of our constitutional system throughout our history," and it meant that "the Supreme court is the final interpreter of the Constitution and can invalidate national and state laws which it finds to be in conflict with the Constitution." And, while it was true that "constitutional history discloses periodic denunciations of the court's exercise of power and drastic proposals to restrict it, when emotions have subsided responsible men have concluded that on net balance, we are better off with the Supreme court as it is . . . with its powers unimpaired." Just a few months later, in a review published in the December 1957 issue of the *Mississippi Law Journal* of a book titled *The Sovereign States* by James Jackson Kilpatrick, editor of the Richmond, Virginia, *News Leader*, which passionately championed the doctrine of state sovereignty, he remarked scathingly: "It is an almost infallible rule that, whenever a newspaperman expounds on a legal subject, what he says will be unreliable." And as for Kilpatrick's thesis, "that the government provided for by the Constitution, 'was intended to be . . . a federation of sovereign states jointly controlling their mutual agent, the federal government," it was "untenable because it was untrue."[75]

In the autumn of 1958, two alumni of the law school practicing law in Lexington, Mississippi, State Representative Wilburn Hooker and H. Edwin White, a former state representative, denounced Dean Farley to the state press for having been, over the past four years, "an ardent admirer of the Supreme Court's 'judicial legislative decisions' of which the integration cases are the foremost example." On September 18, they made an oral complaint to the board of trustees, which, at the board's invitation, was backed up by a thirty-page, written list of complaints handed in on November 18. In it Hooker, White, and two other alumni of the university accused Farley, Murphy, and several non–law school members of its faculty of "conspiring to accomplish apostasy, subversion and the violation of Mississippi law and tradition." Those charges were referred to a "Special Committee." Nine months later, after having studied the committee's report, the board, at a meeting on August 27, 1959, announced, first, that they wanted to express "unanimously and unreservedly . . . their confidence in Chancellor J. D. Williams and his administration of the University of Mississippi" and, second, that their committee's investigations revealed that "the allegations that chancellor Williams and others at the university developed or engaged in a plan or scheme of operation to subvert the constitution, laws and customs of Mississippi or that there is a communist cell at the university are without foundation in fact."[76]

So things were calmer for a little while. But the pro-segregation White Citizens Council chapters kept up their attacks statewide. And, in the 1960 session of the state legislature, members of both houses attacked Farley and even more so Murphy, the outsider, as enemies of the state. Though Farley, of course, had long ago qualified for tenure, Murphy had not done so yet, and the calls for his immediate ouster were numerous. A state senate resolution passed in May, in fact, called upon the board of trustees "to forthwith terminate the contract of employment of Dr. William P. Murphy, professor of law."[77]

A substantial majority of the law student body, however, wanted to keep him on the faculty. In that same month of May 1960, 121 of the 182 law students enrolled that year (66 percent) signed a petition calling on the legislature "to

abandon the attack now being made on the honorable William P. Murphy."
"Mr. Murphy," it said, has never advocated integration in any of his classes to
the best of the knowledge of the undersigned." And they wished "to take this
opportunity to publicly voice [their] complete faith, trust, and absolute confidence in the teaching ability and integrity" of Professor Murphy. On May 28,
1960, student body vice-president Pat H. Scanlon of Jackson, as the presiding
officer, signed a student-body resolution calling for the delivery of the petition
to Dean Farley, who was authorized to publish it if, "in his discretion, the need
arose" and stating furthermore that, if it was published, a list of those who had
signed it should be attached to it.[78]

Apparently it never was published. And Murphy found it expedient to accept
an invitation to spend the 1960–61 academic year teaching as a visiting faculty member at the University of Kentucky Law School. In the spring of 1961,
he received the J.S.D. degree from Yale University he had been working on
for some time. And, for the 1961–62 academic year, he was again on academic
leave, teaching as a visiting faculty member in the law school at the University
of Missouri.[79] Meanwhile, the board of trustees, which now included five new
Ross Barnett appointees, kept insisting that he must never come back onto the
University of Mississippi payroll. Finally, a compromise was reached whereby
he was allowed to return to the law school for the 1962 summer session. He was
not, however, allowed to do any teaching, and the salary that supported him,
his wife, and three children through that summer was paid not out of university
funds but from funds raised by some of his very grateful former students.[80]

Years later, Murphy told an interviewer that perhaps he should have strug-
gled to hold on to his position but that might very well have resulted in his
being fired and the law school losing its accreditation. Also, he and his wife
had reached a point where they did not feel able to put up with any more job-
related conflict and financial uncertainty. So, that fall of 1962, he went back
to the University of Missouri Law School as a regular member of their faculty.
Eventually, he became a member of the law faculty of the University of North
Carolina. Meanwhile, just a few weeks after the Murphys left Oxford, amidst
scenes of bloodshed and violence, James Meredith integrated the University of
Mississippi campus.[81]

CHAPTER 5

From Law School to Law Center
(1963–1975)

Dean Farley's departure from the law school occurred not very long after that of Professor Murphy. On December 7, 1963, he was due to celebrate his sixty-fifth birthday. At that time, the university policy was that any administrator, on reaching the age of sixty-five, must resign his administrative position, though if his department or school wished for him to do so, he might continue teaching for a few years longer. But, in the spring of 1963, Chancellor J. D. Williams cautioned Farley that, although the members of the board of trustees were divided as to whether he should be retired right away on his birthday, at the end of the first semester of the 1963–64 academic year, or at the end of that year, in June 1964, a substantial majority of them were in agreement that go he must. And, although the chancellor said he would do his best to get them to change their minds about it, Farley saved him the trouble by resigning on June 6, 1963, to accept a position he had been offered at the University of Florida Law School.[1]

During the early months of 1963, the speculation was that the law school's next dean would be Professor John H. Fox. The board of trustees' choice to fill the position, however, was Joshua Marion Morse. A Poplarville native, Morse had earned an LL.B. at the law school in 1948 and then returned to his Pearl River County hometown to start up a practice. Poplarville in earlier decades had also been the hometown of Governor Theodore G. Bilbo, who, following his retirement from politics, shared office space with Dean Morse's father. And "Josh" Morse, while practicing there in the 1950s, had developed a fairly close professional relationship with Hattiesburg attorney M. M. Roberts, who was now Governor Barnett's principal ally on the board of trustees. Mainly because of Roberts's backing, Morse had been appointed to an associate professorship on the law school faculty in the autumn of 1962. And now, just a year later, he was chosen by the board to serve as Farley's successor in the deanship. Furthermore, presumably to further enhance his academic prestige and standing, he was given a leave of absence for the 1963–64 academic year so that he could engage in some postgraduate law work at Yale University as a Sterling Fellow. That, ultimately, turned out to have been a very big mistake on the board's part.[2]

During that year, meanwhile, Professor Fox did serve as the "acting dean." And, on November 11, 1963, "Dean Emeritus" Farley was honored in a ceremony held in the law school. After some opening remarks by the minister of Oxford's First Presbyterian Church, speeches praising Farley's record of service were made on behalf of the bench and bar by Judge Claude F. Clayton of the United States District Court for the Northern District and on behalf of the teaching profession by Dean W. Ray Forrester of the Cornell University Law School, a former member of the University of Mississippi law faculty. Then law school professor Sylvester J. Hemleben, on behalf of himself and his colleagues, presented a portrait of Farley to be hung in the law building. The master of ceremonies for these proceedings was then law student body president Mr. W. Scott Welch.[3]

Through the next ten years, Robert J. Farley continued to be listed in the law school *Bulletin* as both "Dean Emeritus" and "Professor of Law Emeritus."[4] Meanwhile, many changes were taking place. The second African American student admitted to the university was a law student named Cleve McDowell. A twenty-one-year-old graduate of Jackson State University, McDowell met all of the admission requirements and was approved by the law faculty for admission in the 1963 summer session. Though the board of trustees ordered that he not be admitted, to no one's surprise, that order was soon overruled by the U.S. District court for the Southern District, and McDowell came to campus on June 5.[5]

During that 1963 summer, McDowell roomed with James Meredith in Baxter Hall. But on August 18, Meredith graduated. When McDowell returned to campus in September, all of the federal troops and marshals that had been protecting Meredith over the past year had departed. When he asked both the local sheriff and university officials for permission to carry a firearm for his protection, they told him no, for that was very much contrary to university policy. He continued, however, to carry a small handgun, concealed in his coat pocket, both on campus and on weekend visits to his hometown of Drew, located in Sunflower County in the heart of the Mississippi Delta. On September 23, returning to campus after a visit with the United States attorney in Oxford to ask for better protection, and a little late for class, as he ran up the steep front steps of Lamar Hall he dropped his sunglasses. When he bent over to pick them up, the gun fell out of his pocket in full view of two totally unsympathetic student witnesses.[6]

When he came out of the class a little while later, the Lafayette County sheriff was waiting to arrest him for unlawful possession of a firearm. Before the semester was over, the student judicial council had recommended, and the chancellor had ordered, his expulsion from the university. An appeal to the board of trustees, not surprisingly, was turned down "unanimously" on November 11, 1964. And much to the relief of the law faculty, the "Racial Committee" of the AALS, meeting in Chicago just a couple of weeks later, over Thanksgiving, were sympathetic. The university, they concluded, was "not following a policy of discrimination with regard to Cleve McDowell" and was within its rights in the handling of that situation." Therefore, they recommended no further action with regard to his case. McDowell himself, Dean Farley recalled years later, did not claim that, at least as far as the law school was concerned, he had been unfairly treated.[7]

In fact, after spending a few years working for the NAACP in Mississippi, McDowell would resume his legal studies at Texas Southern University, earn a J.D. degree, qualify for admission to the Mississippi bar in 1971, and begin practicing law in his hometown of Drew. Meanwhile, by the autumn of 1964, two more African American students had enrolled in the university, and, by 1966, fourteen African Americans were enrolled. Included in their number were Patricia Anderson and Reuben V. Anderson, who was destined to become in 1967 the law school's first black graduate.[8]

Some other major developments were occurring in the law school by the mid-1960s. In the fall of 1962, the faculty had voted to make the "Law School Entrance Examination" a prerequisite for admission. Indeed, the 1963 Law School *Bulletin* stated that "All applicants for admission in September, 1963, and thereafter" would be "required to take the Law School Admission Test administered by the Educational Testing Service" of Princeton, New Jersey. Beginning with the 1965 summer session, a system of identifying students taking final examinations by an anonymous number known only to the law school registrar was implemented.[9]

By 1963–64, the law student body numbered 284, including three women and thirty-three non-Mississippians. The full time faculty, now nine in number, included Professors Joel Bunkley, Roscoe Cross (who had rejoined the faculty and begun again advising the university's would-be Rhodes scholars, in 1961), Art Custy, Acting Dean Fox, and George W. " Casey" Stengel, plus two "visiting professors" (replacing Dean Farley, now at Florida, and Dean Morse, on leave of absence). There also were two associate professors, Parham H. Williams and Sylvester J. Hemleben (both of whom were newcomers), two assistant professors, Charles B. Roberts and Edward P. Connell, and law librarian and instructor Corinne Bass. Also, in accordance with what was now a long-established custom, two local Oxford lawyers, Thomas Henry "Hal" Freeland and Gerald Alexander "Gerry" Gafford, were teaching part time as "acting assistant professors.[10]

At the state bar's 1964 annual meeting (held that year, for the last time, at the Edgewater Gulf Hotel, in Gulfport), at the customary law school alumni luncheon, the constitution of the newly organized Law Alumni Chapter of the University of Mississippi Alumni Association was formally voted on and adopted. The new organization's purpose, its constitution stated, would be "to promote effective legal education at the University of Mississippi School of Law, to perpetuate the traditions of the University of Mississippi and of its School of Law, to promote the best understanding between the University of Mississippi, the School of Law and its alumni to the end that the work of said School of Law may be of the highest caliber, to cooperate with the University of Mississippi Alumni Association in all matters affecting the welfare of the University of Mississippi, and to cooperate with all other agencies of the School of Law, the state government, or private interest which might affect the welfare of the School of Law."[11]

By the next year, 1964–65, with Dean Morse now in charge, things were changing. Ms. Bass was promoted to assistant professor and would hold that position until her retirement in 1967. Although Parham Williams was on a leave of absence (taking his turn engaging in advanced study at Yale on a Sterling Fellowship), five more new associate professors were on the faculty. Luther L. McDougal III (a nephew of Myres S. McDougal), who, after graduating from the law school in 1962, had been practicing law in Tupelo) had been chosen along with four 1964 Yale LL.M.s whom Dean Morse had recruited while at Yale himself during the previous year: Michael P. Katz (a South African who had earned an LL.B. in 1961 at the University of Cape Town), William E Holder (an Australian), "Bill" (James M.) Brown (a University of Illinois B.A. with a J.D.

from the University of Florida), and Kenneth Vinson (holder of a 1959 LL.B. from the University of Texas Law School).[12] Instead of two or three Oxford lawyers coming in to lecture occasionally as "acting assistant professors," a slate of twenty-nine "visiting lecturers," made up of experienced members of the Mississippi bar (including both M. M. Roberts and Ross Barnett) and also of the bars of neighboring states came in to give single talks on a wide variety of jurisprudential topics to a student body that was now too large to be listed individually, by name and hometown, in the law school *Bulletin*. Also, in September 1965 the board of trustees approved an expenditure of $12, 630 "for renovation to the Law School Building."[13]

Sadly, however, by the 1965 spring semester, John Fox's attendance at law faculty meetings was being adversely affected by worsening health problems and, early in the fall, the highly regarded professor died. On October 8, 1965, a memorial resolution in his honor, presented by the law alumni chapter chairman, Mr. William Winter, was approved at the homecoming general meeting of the university alumni association.[14] A few months later, a very happy event that occurred in the form of a dinner party that took place on January 11, 1966, in the Paul B. Johnson Commons, at which the law school's class of 1935 alumnus, Myres S. McDougal, who was now the Sterling Professor of Law at Yale University and generally recognized as "the outstanding authority on International Law," became the first recipient of an L. Q. C. Lamar Fellowship, an honor that was, henceforth, going to be awarded to outstanding "graduates of the Ole Miss Law School who have distinguished themselves in professional life." State Bar President Orma R. Smith came over from his home in Corinth to preside over the proceedings as master of ceremonies. Dean Morse presented Professor McDougal with his certificate of appointment as a fellow, and United States Supreme Court Justice Byron R. White was the "Principal Speaker" at the proceedings.[15]

The law school's thirty January 1966 graduates were its first to be awarded "Juris Doctor" (J.D.) degrees instead of the customary LL.B.s. The change of degrees had been authorized by the board of trustees eighteen months earlier, in June 1964. Making the change, in fact, put the law school in tune with a growing national trend that had been pioneered by the Harvard Law School. Many of the law school's alumni, however, felt cheated. They still only had bachelor degrees while their junior colleagues now were "doctors." Encouraged by the board of trustees to do so, the law faculty finally, in November 1967, voted to award the J.D. degree retroactively. By the spring of 1968, in return for a small fee, alumni could exchange their LL.B. diplomas for new ones according them J.D. status.[16]

By then, another kind of doctoral degree also was offered by the law school, thanks to a new member of the law school faculty, Professor Steven Gorove. A refugee from Communist Hungary, Professor Gorove had earned a J.D. degree at the University of Budapest in 1939 and by 1955 also had earned an LL.M., a J.S.D., and a Ph.D. from Yale. During the following decade, he had taught at New York Law School, the University of Akron, and the University of Denver before being hired not only as a professor but also as the "Chairman of the Graduate Program" at the University of Mississippi Law School in January 1965. Thanks to his efforts, by the fall of 1966, the school was offering three graduate degrees: "Master of Laws (LL.M.)," "Master of Comparative Law (M.Comp. L.)," and "Doctor of Laws (J.S.D.)."[17]

The M.Comp.L. degree was "designed essentially for graduates of foreign law schools" who did not intend to practice or teach in the United States. Candidates for all three graduate degrees—unless given an exemption by the program chairman—were required to take "six hours of graduate course work" in other divisions of the university's graduate school. The first graduate degree to be granted was earned by Mark Krauss, upon whom an LL.M. was conferred at the June 1966 commencement.[18]

In fact, in spite of all the storms of controversy over racial integration raging around it, the University of Mississippi law school in the mid-1960s was continuing to grow and prosper. One aspect of everyday life that improved was the food service in the Alumni House. Built in 1951 and located just one short block east of the law building, it was much more convenient for law faculty and students than either the Union "Grill" located in Weir Hall or the university cafeteria in Johnson Commons. So it had been very good news when, in the spring of 1961, the alumni association budgeted ten thousand dollars to pay for an extension of the Alumni House "Snack Bar." And it was even more exciting when, in the summer of 1968, they voted to spend $42,400 "for the expansion of food service in the Alumni House."[19]

The alumni chapter, meanwhile, also was contributing very generously to the expansion and development of the law library. In 1965, they had donated $1,150 for "law library books." In 1966 they donated $7,000; in 1967, $2,350; in 1968, $4,500; and, in 1969, $2,500. And various, very large commercial firms were also contributing to the law library in the mid-1960s. The list of in-state contributors in 1965 included the Mississippi Power Company (Gulfport), Mississippi Power and Light (Jackson), the International Paper Company (Natchez), and Ingalls Shipbuilding Corporation (Pascagoula). Out-of-state contributors that same year were Humble Oil (Houston, Texas), the Gulf, Mobile and Ohio Railway Company (Mobile, Alabama), the Southern Railway System (Washington, D.C.), and the United States Fidelity and Guaranty Company (Baltimore, Maryland) as well as the Gulf Oil Company and the Cities Service Company. Meanwhile, the *Law Journal* was greatly helped by a decision by the board of trustees, in 1967, to raise the fee that law students had to pay for it from $2.00 to $2.50.[20]

In December 1965, Mrs. Margaret B. Wynne of Greenville signed an agreement in the Washington County Chancery Court, donating to the university more than two thousand shares in the Union Compress and Warehouse Company of Memphis to create the William T. Wynn Memorial Trust Fund. Intended to commemorate the memory of her recently deceased husband, a 1911 graduate of the law school and a highly successful Greenville lawyer who had practiced his profession as far afield as Memphis, New Orleans, and New York and also had served on the university's alumni association board of directors in the 1950s, the fund was to continue to pay for her support as long as she lived. But at her death, it was to go to the law school to create scholarships for deserving, needy students, to buy books, journals and other materials for the law library, and to help supplement law faculty salaries.[21]

Just a few months earlier, in July 1965, the Rockefeller Center in New York City had given the law school a grant of forty thousand dollars to fund a proposal drawn up by two of the new Yale men on the faculty, Professors Holder and Vinson. It was to be used to underwrite, in cooperation with the state bar, a new course on "professional responsibility" that would better prepare the law school's graduating seniors to handle the kinds of ethical problems that were inevitably involved in practicing law. The classes would focus on various aspects of the ABA's code of ethics, with particular emphasis on the legal profession's responsibility for devoting a reasonable percentage of their working hours to pro bono work on behalf of members of the indigent classes.[22] Under the overall direction of Judge William N. Ethridge, who was now the Chief Justice of the Mississippi Supreme Court, during the 1965 fall semester, a total of thirty-seven members of the state's bench and bar (including former governor Ross Barnett and future governor William Winter) took part in the weekly seminars that the members of the senior class were required to attend.[23]

The law school's prestige was rising, and so was the size of its student body, which in the fall 1965 semester totaled 344, including four black students. In addition to the continuing activities of two academic honor fraternities, Phi Delta Phi and Phi Alpha Delta, the moot court competition team, made up of second-year law students Don Allen and Don Stacy, not only won the south-eastern regional championship, defeating teams from schools such as Duke, Virginia, and North Carolina, but also went on to come in third in the national championship. And a very active student body now had eight of their number, appointed by their president, serving on a "visiting speaker's bureau."[24]

Early in 1966, the speakers bureau invited United States Senator Robert F. Kennedy, who at the time of the Meredith crisis, two and a half years earlier, had been the United States attorney general, to come to the campus in mid-March as their guest speaker. Around the state, of course, the news of the invi-tation provoked the wrath of a substantial number of the white citizenry, but not enough to force the invitation to be retracted. An attempt early in March to get a resolution denouncing it approved by the legislature failed to get major-ity support and so did an attempt to get the board of trustees to order that the invitation be retracted. On March 18, the senator and his wife flew into the uni-versity airport and, escorted by a sizeable force of local law officers and nation-al guardsmen, eventually appeared on the speaker's platform in the Coliseum, where they received an enthusiastic standing ovation from an audience of more than five thousand students, faculty, staff, and visitors.[25]

That scene was shown on at least one network national newscast that eve-ning, together with comments that things seemed to be changing in Mississippi. Introducing Senator Kennedy, Ed Ellington, chairman of the speakers bureau, had remarked that his appearance proved that the University of Mississippi was a place where every kind of view or opinion could be freely expressed and that it was in no way was part of "a closed society." Then, in a "calm and concilia-tory" speech, Kennedy observed that race relations and civil rights were issues that were cause for concern not just in the South but throughout the nation. "You have no problem the nation does not have," he told the audience. "You share no hope that is not shared by students and young people across this coun-try. You carry no burden they too do not carry." In the question period his ver-batim accounts of his telephone negotiations with Governor Ross Barnett, back in 1962, with regard to James Meredith's early attempts to register on campus—about how many marshals should put their hands on their guns and when—provoked loud gales of laughter from the audience. And, before leaving, he circled the auditorium and shook hands with hundreds of them who came down to greet him personally and to thank him for coming.[26]

The university board of trustees, though they had not prohibited Kennedy from coming, had felt it necessary to appoint a "special committee" to look into just how, and why, his visit had been arranged and conducted. At their April 1966 meeting, having received a "written explanation" from Dean Morse as to the circumstances behind it, together with an "apology" for all the trouble it had caused, they decided to discharge that committee. Just seven months later, however, after hearing that state NAACP President Aaron Henry had been a guest lecturer in a civil rights class in the law school, they adopted a policy that, henceforth, any outside speaker, at any of the universities and colleges under their jurisdiction, must be approved in advance by them.[27]

By then, however, other important new developments were taking place in the law school. At the beginning of the 1965–66 academic year, Dean Morse had succeeded in getting from the Ford Foundation a development grant for his school "in excess of $667,000." A small portion of the grant was used to enhance further the academic caliber of its student body by creating a number of new scholarships "for deserving students of exceptional ability."[28] A large amount of it was used to create a new course on "Problems of Public Law." In the fall 1965 semester that course was taught, for two weeks each, by Dean Louis H. Pollak, and Professors Eugene Rostow, Alexander M. Bickel, Myres S. McDougal, and four other visiting members of the Yale University law faculty. In the spring 1966 semester it was taught, similarly, by former United States Solicitor General Archibald Cox and six other members of the Harvard Law faculty. For the 1966–67 academic year, the course was taught on a similar basis by members of the New York University Law School faculty in the fall and members of the Columbia University law faculty in the spring.[29]

Most of the Ford money, however was used to beef up, in both size and caliber, the law school's own faculty. For 1965–66, the faculty had twenty permanent members. For 1966–67 it had twenty-six. That number included Professor Arthur B. Custy (who, after earning a J.S.D. at Yale in 1965 was actually still on a leave of absence) but not Associate Professor Holder, who had left to go back to his native Australia. The newcomers to the list included three of the law school's own outstanding graduates: Associate Professor John Robin Bradley, a 1962 graduate of the law school, who in his senior year had served as the editor-in-chief of the *Law Journal* and also earned the Phi Delta Phi honor award; Assistant Professors Aaron S. Condon, a 1952 graduate, who now came back to the campus from a law practice in Kosciusko; and Robert C. Khayat, a June 1966 graduate (and future chancellor of the university), who during his senior year had served as the articles editor of the *Law Journal* and now was serving as the school's director of law extension. Another was Associate Professor Thomas A. Edmonds (a future dean of the law school), who had served as articles editor of the Duke University *Law Journal* before earning his LL.B. there in 1965.[30]

New Associate Professor Michael Horowitz was a 1962 Yale Law School graduate who had been working in a New York Law firm for the past three years. There were also five new associate professors who had just graduated that year from the Yale law school. They were Joseph A. Chubb, a New Yorker, who had earned both his bachelor's and his law degree at Yale; Walter E. Dellinger, who had done his undergraduate work at the University of North Carolina before going to law school at Yale; Frederick B. McLane, a Californian with a bachelor's degree from Stanford University who had served on the *Yale Law Journal* board of editors; George M. Strickler, who had a B.A. from Southern Methodist University; and Michael B. Trister, who had an A.B. from Princeton. Both Strickler and Trister had been employed as instructors by Yale during their senior year there.[31]

Given all that was going on, it is not too surprising, perhaps, that *Time* magazine, in the "Law" section of its September 23, 1966, issue under the heading "Law Schools" had run a report on the "New Mood at Ole Miss." "For a century," the report observed, the University of Mississippi Law School had "allowed its all-white student body to ignore the winds of U.S. constitutional change, while steeping itself almost entirely in local law, customs and politics." As a consequence, its graduates had "emerged with their Deep South views untouched" and then went on to run their state "with an isolated narrow-mindedness that has mired Mississippi in racial tragedy." But, now, the article reported, their new dean, Joshua Morse III, "once a country lawyer in Poplarville, Miss.," after a one-year mind-altering experience at the Yale University Law School, had come to realize that (in his own words) "many of the problems which plague the University of Mississippi and our state stem from a provincial outlook—our students are accustomed to examining every question in the light of its impact upon Mississippi culture rather than taking a broader view." But he was determined to change that, and his Yale-educated instructors were determined to assist him in doing so. "It's like the Peace Corps, except we're given much more responsibility," one of them told the *Time* reporter. The course for seniors taught by the guest faculty from the Ivy League, which the students were now referring to as the "jet-set course," was also helping. And, thanks to all of their efforts, "the Ole Miss law school," Yale's law school dean Louis H. Pollak had told *Time*, was "at the threshold of becoming a focus for the kind of thinking that can bring Mississippi into the 20th century."[32]

Some other successes achieved by the law school around the same time, however, were, no doubt, much more pleasing to most of Mississippi's citizens. A 1964 grant from the Department of Agriculture in Washington made possible the creation in the law school of a Legal Institute of Agricultural and Resource Development (LIARD). The institute's mission was to be the compilation "from secondary sources physical and economic information" on the state's "water resources" and to "conduct a critical study of the effect of water regulatory measures on irrigation and other water development measures in the state." And another grant, obtained from the Tennessee Valley Authority, was to be used to "conduct research and studies pertaining to land tenure policies and problems" in the north Mississippi area served by the TVA.[33]

Another new member of the law faculty in 1965 was Professor Joel Blass, who, after earning an A.B. and an LL.B. at Louisiana State University, since 1942 had been practicing law in New Orleans as well as in Gulfport and Wiggins, Mississippi. In 1966, he also was accorded the secondary title of "Research Director of the Legal Institute of Agricultural and Research Development." Yet another faculty newcomer in 1965 was Assistant Professor William Montgomery Champion, a Mississippi State B.S. and a 1961 alumnus of the law school, who also had earned an LL.M. at George Washington University in 1962; since then he had been practicing law in Jackson, the state capital. From the beginning, on campus he held the secondary title of "Research Assistant" to LIARD.[34]

Another Mississippi State alumnus, William G. Walker, who had earned an M.S. there, was hired in 1965 to work as the "Research Economist" for LIARD but was not accorded law faculty status. Two years later, in July 1967, however, the board of trustees did approve the appointment of Walter E. Chryst, B.S., M.A., and Ph.D., as both a "Professor of Law and also the "Director of Economic Research in the Legal Institute of Agricultural and Resources Development."

He thus became the only non-lawyer to-date in the history of the law school ever to serve on the law faculty. During the two years that he served (prior to his tragic, sudden death early in the autumn of 1969) he was paid an annual salary (one third of which came out of grant funds) of thirty thousand dollars, which was some 25 percent higher than what was being paid at that time to the law school dean.[35]

The law school faculty, by 1966–67, was meeting weekly rather than month-ly, though meetings were still being held at noon, over lunch, in the faculty din-ing room of the university cafeteria (Johnson Commons). In March 1966, they had voted to change the grading system from a letter-grade one to a numeri-cal one. Under the new system, which went into effect in 1967–68, the range of grades given ran up from 0.0 to 4.0., with any grade below 1.0 counting as an F and an average of at least 2.0 required to qualify for graduation. Some courses, such as individual reading courses, up to a limit of ten hours could be taken for a passing grade of Z, which meant that one got credit for the course but that it did not impact on ones' grade point average.[36]

In November 1966, the compilers of a "Role and Scope" study on Mississippi's institutions of higher learning commissioned by the board of trustees noted with regard to the law school's program of study that it was "planned to serve the people of Mississippi" and that, therefore, "leading cases from the Mississippi Supreme Court [were] frequently assigned to students in addition to the cases appearing in the case books" and "important Sections of the Mississippi stat-utes [were] studied in classes." Also "Special courses [were] given in Mississippi pleading and practice." All of these practices, it was said, enabled the law stu-dents "to acquire a working knowledge of the substantive and procedural law of the state." The six full semesters that were required to graduate also included "training in the principles of English and American law" sufficient to "constitute adequate preparation for the practice of law." The curriculum also included "an intensive study of decision making," "collateral reading chosen from the lead-ing texts and law journals, and mock trials." "From time to time," guest lectures were given "by leading judges, lawyers, and other legal scholars." And, finally, "to give students experience and training in conducting themselves in courts, actual practice, and in the handling of general office matters, a Moot Court Board, composed of students chosen on the basis of their scholastic records [was] appointed by the faculty." And the students were "required to conduct actual cases in [that] court." The fields of study covered were "commercial law, jurisprudence, property law, trials and advocacy, governmental regulations and personal relations."[37]

At their meeting on May 10, 1967, the law faculty got the good news that the chancellor would no longer require them, or their students, to attend the annual baccalaureate ceremony in the Coliseum at which the undergraduate and graduate school degrees were awarded but instead they could hold their own, in Fulton Chapel or elsewhere, a few days later.[38]

On July 26, 1967, the faculty voted to begin holding some classes on Saturdays, a practice that was not continued for very long. But, at the same time, they also voted to cease having a bell rung in the law building to mark the beginning and ending of classes, and that policy was one that has continued to this day. Another major concern of the law faculty in 1967 was whether either of the two law fraternity chapters, the Mayes Inn chapter of Phi Delta Phi or the Lamar chapter of Phi Alpha Delta, was showing any discrimination in their recruitment of new members. That concern was augmented by an application for recognition of a third fraternity, Delta Theta Phi, which required only a 2.0 grade point average to be considered for admission and which proposed to name its campus chapter in honor of Jefferson Davis. After some modification of its statement of membership requirements, it was finally recognized that fall. But a year later, in December 1968, the faculty voted to inform the national offices of all three legal fraternities on campus that, because the fraternities were "not primarily professional" but had become instead "primarily social," they would no longer formally sponsor them. Although in the spring of 1969 the faculty decided—though by only a one-vote majority—to continue awarding the annual Phi Delta Phi outstanding student award, they also judged it expedient to drop from the 1969 and subsequent issues of the law school *Bulletin* the customary section on "Legal Fraternities and Organizations." It was replaced by a section headed "Student Organizations," which listed only "the Lamar Society of International Law" (newly founded by Professor Steve Gorove) and "a Student Body Association with an active Speaker's Bureau."[39]

On April 4, 1968, the speakers bureau formally notified the faculty that the vice-president of the United States, Hubert H. Humphrey, had agreed to speak on campus just three weeks later. His presentation in the Coliseum caused almost as much excitement, and drew almost as big a crowd, as Robert Kennedy's had two years earlier. Also, because it was widely believed that the vice-president would use the occasion to announce his candidacy in that year's upcoming presidential election (though he actually did not), it received at least as much national press coverage as Kennedy's had, and even some notice overseas.[40]

By the summer of 1968, some major new developments were occurring in the law school. During the academic year just ended, 384 students had been enrolled. For the fall 1968 semester, 440 (including more black students than were enrolled in any other non–historically African American school in the United States) were pre-enrolled. Meanwhile, several faculty members were departing. Assistant Dean Arthur B. Custy was going to Salem, Oregon, to become dean of the law school at Willamette University. Other "Yalies" who left that year were Fred McLane, who returned home to practice law in California, and Walter Dellinger (a future acting solicitor general in the Clinton administration), who had just been appointed to serve as a law clerk to United States Supreme Court Justice Hugo Black. On the other hand, Professor William Champion was back on campus after a year of graduate study at the Harvard Law School. And six new faculty had been hired, together with four part-timers, including State Supreme Court Chief Justice William N. Ethridge. The law school, in spite of its greatly increased enrollment, had one of the lowest faculty-student ratio figures in the entire nation.[41]

In addition to fulfilling their teaching responsibilities, the law faculty was also publishing; graduate program chairman Steve Gorove, very appropriately, had the longest list of publications to his name. His article, "The Outer Space Treaty," published in the 1967 volume of the *Bulletin of the Atomic Scientist,* and his co-editorship of the *American Journal of Comparative Law* were both significant signs of things to come.[42]

LIARD was still the major source of research funds for the law school. But two other major outside money grants were soon about to cause the school a great deal of trouble. One was a grant from the National Defender Project, out of which second- and third-year students enrolled in the on-campus course in criminal procedure were paid to assist local attorneys who had been appointed by the judges of both the local state courts and of the United States District Court for the Northern District to represent indigent criminal defendants. Doing that gave the students, who were given a maximum of one week's leave to participate in it, "vital experience in the preparation and trial of actual cases involving the life or liberty of human beings." In the 1966–67 academic year, 192 of the law school's students participated in the program.[43]

Because many Mississippians had no doubt that any indigent defendant was certainly guilty, such a program could provoke a certain amount of political hostility. But far more potentially troublesome, for both the law school and the university, was the other major new grant, from the Office of Economic Opportunity in Washington, D.C., to set up a legal services office in the Oxford area. Second- and third-year law students were to be assigned to assist the office's staff attorneys "by interviewing clients and performing general research on cases received by the office." Initially, the clinic was supervised by Professor Aaron Condon and Mr. Earl Laird. By the autumn of 1967, Professor Michael Trister was the instructor in a new two-hour seminar course for the students involved in the system. Serving as a substitute for Moot Court II, it required the twenty students selected to participate in it to spend the first two weeks of the semester doing background reading on "such topics as the purpose and structure of the Legal Services program, office procedures, interviewing techniques, investigating problems, and record keeping." Also they would be introduced to the legal areas with which they were going to be dealing and the major reference sources for those areas. They would then start serving, for twenty hours a week, at $2 an hour, in one of the legal services offices, while still attending the weekly seminar, doing research, and writing up reports on relevant topics.[44]

The OEO grant was also used to place forty-four students in legal services offices around the country during the summer of 1967. An arrangement was worked out with the legal services office in Clarksdale whereby senior law students would work there for one week during their final year and gain some very useful practical experience.[45] But inevitably, all of this legal work, for free, on behalf of the destitute, the discriminated against, and the downtrodden, soon aroused animosity in certain circles around the state. As early as December 1966, *Jackson Clarion Ledger* columnist Tom Ethridge commented that some Mississippians already were convinced that Dean Morse's "liberal" innovations and projects had made the law school "a tool of the leftist Ford Foundation, the Negro Revolution and the politically minded U.S. Justice Department's efforts to 'change Mississippi.'" By the spring of 1968, the state board of trustees had a "law committee" in existence to address law school related concerns, and one of its alumni, prominent board member M. M. Roberts around that time commented mournfully: "I'm embarrassed by my law school."[46]

That same spring, the North Mississippi Rural Legal Services office in Oxford had become involved in a lawsuit to force the desegregation of the Holly Springs public school system, and that was widely seen as certainly going too far. At the state bar meeting down in Biloxi in June, Dean Morse was not invited to give his usual speech at the luncheon for law school alumni. Also by then, the university's new chancellor, Porter L. Fortune Jr., under heavy pressure from the board of trustees, had already informed members of the law faculty that they would have to choose whether they were going to stay with the OEO program (now being funded through a two-year institution for black women, Mary Holmes College, in West Point, Mississippi) or keep their law school positions. And, when Luther McDougal, Michael Trister, and George Strickler protested, they were immediately removed from the payroll for the upcoming summer session. By that fall, McDougal, concluding that protest was in vain, had given up his title of "executive director of the legal services program" and been promoted to a full professorship. But Strickler and Trister, claiming that their civil liberties had been violated, had taken their case into federal court. "The great experiment at the law school is almost dead," Trister told *Time Magazine*.[47]

In the fall of 1968, the board of trustees' law committee took on the responsibility of finding counsel for Chancellor Fortune and Dean Morse, who were the two defendants in the Strickler/Trister lawsuit but billed the university for the defense counsel's services.[48] Meanwhile, Dean Morse was not at all happy with the way things were developing. Like the "Yalie" professors he had hired, he was not given a pay raise for the 1968–69 academic year. There was talk of the AALS and the ABA again canceling their respective relationships with the law school. And, in the 1969 session of the state legislature, there was talk again of moving the law school to Jackson. In March 1969, the dean announced that he would be leaving at the end of that semester to take up the deanship of the law school at Florida State University in Tallahassee.[49]

On June 19, 1969, the board of trustees approved the appointment of Professor Joel Bunkley as the new dean of the law school.[50] His term of office, however, was to be a brief and troubled one. On September 3, 1968, federal Northern District Judge Orma R. Smith, with regard to the Strickler/Trister lawsuit, had found in favor of the university. But on October 9, 1969, the Fifth Circuit Court of Appeals, by a two-to-one decision, reversed Judge Smith and ordered the board and the university "to grant to [the] appellants injunctive and declaratory relief." A state university that allowed its faculty to accept outside and part-time employment, they ruled, could not single out the OEO legal services program and prohibit part-time employment with it.[51]

An appeal by the university to the Supreme Court in Washington, D.C., against that Fifth Circuit decision was "denied without prejudice" on January 19, 1970.

Right around that same time, the board of trustees modified their no-outside-employment rule to say that it was all right for a faculty member to engage in it provided he or she had the permission of the head of the institution. And both Strickler and Trister were invited to return for the upcoming spring semester, as part-time associate professors, with the understanding that the remainder of their working hours would be devoted to working with legal services. Strickler responded that he might return to the campus that fall but never did. Instead he began practicing a combination of both public and private law in New Orleans and eventually joined the Tulane law faculty in 1979. Trister was somewhat interested at first, but when he learned that as a part-timer he would not be a voting member of the faculty, his interest quickly evaporated. Instead, he stayed on in Oxford as the full-time director of the legal services program. Ken Vinson, meanwhile, having been, like Dean Morse, the victim of board pressure and denied a pay raise for 1969–70, took a leave of absence that year, and in the fall of 1970 joined the dean on the Florida State law faculty. Also that same fall, Luther McDougal left to join the law faculty at the University of Arizona. Although the long-term Yale connection would continue, the brief "Yalie" era in the history of the University of Mississippi's law school had come to an end.[52]

Another problem still had to be faced. Neither the AALS nor the ABA were very happy with how Morse and his young men from Yale had been treated. They also were troubled by how Morse's successor as dean, Joel Bunkley, had been selected. Soon after Morse's impending departure had already been announced, the law faculty, at their weekly meeting on April 9, 1969, had elected a decanal search committee whose members were to take the lead in finding his successor. And, although just one week later, John Robin Bradley, the search committee chair, noted for the record that the law faculty, by a 13 to 3 majority, were in favor of looking off-campus for their new dean, in fact, candidates both on- and off-campus were considered. One of the on-campus candidates was Professor Bunkley. And, although Bradley reported to Chancellor Fortune on May 22, that the faculty had classified Bunkley, by an 11 to 5 vote, as "unacceptable," he was the one who took up the office less than six weeks later.[53]

Meanwhile, back in December 1968, at the ABA annual meeting in Chicago, their committee on academic freedom and tenure had reported a complaint with regard to the restrictions imposed on Professors Strickler and Trister with regard to their off-campus activities. In response to that complaint, an investigative subcommittee of the academic freedom and tenure committee had visited the campus on May 11–13, 1969. After hearing the sub-committee's report later that year, the full committee had added to the list of complaints against the University of Mississippi's handling of its law school two additional charges: One was "its failure to recommend appropriate salary increases for Dean Joshua M. Morse III, and Professor Kenneth Vinson for the academic year 1968–69." The other was "its failure to permit meaningful faculty participation in the selection of a successor to Dean Morse following his resignation in June, 1969."[54]

At the AALS annual meeting in December 1969, after hearing their committee's report, the association went on record with the opinion that "in the absence of positive and effective action by the University of Mississippi to redress the clear impediment of academic freedom at [their] Law School as well as the harm to individuals involved, . . . the appropriate sanction is expulsion of the . . . Law School from the Association." To be fair, however, instead of taking immediate action they were prepared to allow "the appropriate officials of the University of Mississippi an opportunity to be heard at the earliest possible date by the Association's executive committee" to demonstrate to them that "acceptable conditions of academic freedom and tenure" had been put into place in their law school. If they failed to do so, however, then the executive committee, at the association's 1970 annual meeting, would recommend that they be expelled from membership in it.[55]

It was that threat that had motivated the board of trustees, in January 1970, to offer Trister and Strickler re-employment on a part-time basis and also to assure Kenneth Vinson that he could expect to be paid a fair and reasonable salary when he returned from his one-year leave of absence. They also at that same time went on record as stating that the school of law "has and will continue to have authority to conduct its affairs in a manner which is consistent with the Articles and Rules of the Association of American Law Schools."[56] And the law school faculty, meeting in the dean's office in Lamar Hall on January 19, 1970, by secret ballot, approved by a 10 to 4 majority a resolution stating that:

> Whereas, the . . . School of Law was faced with the possibility of the loss of its accreditation by the Association of American Law Schools, and Whereas, Dean J. W. Bunkley Jr. was instrumental in persuading the Board of Trustees . . . to agree to the recommendations of the faculty for retaining accreditation.

> Now, therefore, be it resolved by the faculty of the . . . School of Law
> that they commend [Dean Bunkley] for his actions and express their
> support and confidence in his remaining Dean of the . . . School of
> Law."[57]

In early April 1970, Chancellor Fortune received a letter from a friend who told him that at the annual meeting of the Conference of Western Law Schools, which had been held in San Diego at the end of March, the word was that the University of Mississippi was "looking good" now to the AALS. And, although a two-man AALS team visited and checked out the law school in October of that year, they were, in fact, only there for "the usual five years inspection," There was no further talk of reconsidering the school's AALS membership.[58]

Race relations in the law school, meanwhile, although strained at times, were improving. In 1967, Reuben V. Anderson, who had earned a B.A. degree at Tougaloo College in Jackson in 1964, earned his J.D. degree. Less than twenty years later, in 1985, he would become the first black jurist to be appointed to the Mississippi Supreme Court, and in 1997–98 he would serve as the first black president of the Mississippi bar. In 1970, Constance Iona Slaughter became the first black woman to earn a J.D. degree from the law school.[59]

Ms. Slaughter (now Ms. Constance Slaughter Harvey) had played a leading role in organizing in the law school a chapter of the Black American Law Students Association (BALSA). In the autumn of 1963, a handful of both black and white law students, who had spent the previous summer living in and assisting a number of black communities in the state, had organized the "Law Students Civil Rights Research Council." Just a few years later, the black members of the LSCRRC had organized a campus chapter of the national organization known as BALSA. The chapter was actively backed by the Magnolia Bar Association, an organization of black Mississippi lawyers organized in the late nineteenth century. During the two-year period following the assassination of Martin Luther King in April 1968, the black student body on the campus quickly became much more active in asserting their rights than they had been during the mid-1960s. And the black law students, being generally older, more oratorically practiced, and more conscious of legal and constitutional issues, provided them with a corps of very articulate leaders.[60]

Two of their most outstanding spokesmen were Eugene McLemore and John Donald. McLemore, a native of Walls, Mississippi, was a graduate of Mississippi

Valley State University, where he had been student body president in his senior year, and had done some graduate work in political science at Atlanta University before enrolling in the law school in 1969. Donald, from Jackson, was a younger brother of the university's third black enrollee, Cleveland Donald, and had done his undergraduate work on the Oxford campus also before enrolling in the law school. On February 26, 1970, they led a small delegation of black students that went before a special session of the university's faculty senate and presented to its members a list of some two dozen complaints and grievances they had with regard to their on-campus lives and careers.[61]

A majority of the senate members were not prepared to approve a motion by law professor John Robin Bradley calling for all misconduct charges pending against black students stemming from their protest demonstrations of the preceding few months—most notably the one on the evening of February 25, when they had marched up on the stage in Fulton Chapel, where the "Up With People" group were giving a song and dance performance, taken over, and turned it into a civil rights protest—be dropped. In the hours immediately following that incident, any black student seen out anywhere around the campus had been taken into custody and eventually bussed down to the state penitentiary at Parchman. The senate did, however, approve a motion recognizing that the black students on the campus did "have urgent legitimate grievances" and urging the university administration to "address itself to them immediately." In a follow-up meeting with McLemore, Donald and the other members of their Black Student Union delegation on the following night, the senators went so far as to urge the administration to drop all criminal charges pending against black student demonstrators. They also agreed to a motion calling for the immediate creation of five faculty committees to look into the various categories of grievances complained of by the black students. One of those committees, the one created to address academic grievances, was responsible for putting into place, by the next academic year, a Black Studies program in the college of liberal arts. And many other good results followed as well.[62]

By the early 1970s, the law school, like every aspect of higher education everywhere around the nation, was expanding and flourishing. The first post–World War II "baby boomers" were now arriving at college age, and the winding down of the Vietnam war meant that many veterans of the armed forces were returning home, eager to use their veterans' benefits to procure professional training.

Fall semester enrollment, already at the unprecedented level of 331 by 1969, increased to 399 in 1970 and rocketed up to 645 by 1971.[63]

More students meant that more faculty members were required. For the 1970–71 academic year, fourteen full-time and six part-time faculty were employed. One old, familiar face on the full-time faculty was Dean Emeritus Robert J. Farley, who returned as the first holder of the school's newly endowed Farley Chair of Law. Two 1970 newcomers on the full-time faculty were Associate Professors Guthrie T. Abbott, an alumnus who had graduated with honors in 1967, and Aaron Condon, an alumnus who had graduated with honors in 1952 and had occasionally taught part-time over the past two decades. Two new part-timers were William B. Shaw, an assistant professor in the school of education who specialized in school law and held not only a Ph.D. degree from Northwestern University but also a J.D. degree from the University of Chicago law school, and Adjunct Professor A. Eugene Lee, M.D., the assistant physician in the university's student health service who in his spare time had earned a J.D. degree in the law school.[64]

By the beginning of the 1971–72 academic year there were eighteen full-time faculty members in residence, ready to instruct the greatly increased student body. Professor Shaw was full-time. Professor George ("Casey") Stengel was back from a year's leave of absence which he had spent teaching at the University of Kentucky School of Law. Judge Noah S. ("Soggy") Sweat, an alumnus from the class of 1949, had gone on to earn an LL.M. from George Washington University in 1952 and then spent the 1952–53 academic year serving on the faculty of law at the University of Paris. He then had done some part-time teaching while serving, 1962–70, as circuit judge for the first judicial district; and, in 1970, he had become full-time with special responsibility for overseeing intern training programs under grants from the Law Enforcement Assistance Administration in Washington, D.C. Other newcomers included alumnus Don L. Fruge, who after earning his J.D. in 1970 had spent the intervening year at the New York University Law School, and Thomas R. ("Tommy") Ethridge, the World War II veteran, whose interrupted law school career had finally ended with his graduation in 1946. Since then he had also earned an M.A. degree from the university in 1951, served in the state senate from 1948 to 1954, held the office of United States attorney for the state's northern district from 1954 to 1961, and then gone into private practice in Oxford for nine years. The handful of part-timers, meanwhile, included, among others, Adjunct Professor "Gene" Lee, who was now a regular, and Adjunct Professor Edward P. Connell of Clarksdale, who for some years had been teaching his special field of estate planning and estate and gift taxation.[65]

The number of faculty available for 1971–72 was, however, diminished slightly just as the new school year was getting under way. In August 1971, Associate Dean Joel Blass, after six years of service, decided suddenly that he wished to return to private practice on the coast at Gulfport. And, just a few weeks later, on September 30, 1971, Dean Bunkley died suddenly from a heart attack.[66]

On October 3, the law faculty, meeting under the chairmanship of their new associate dean, Parham Williams, were told, first, that Mrs. Bunkley wished to thank them all for the support and assistance they had given her with her regard to her sad and sudden loss and, second, that Chancellor Fortune wanted to know what they wished to do with regard to filling their now vacant deanship. Following a lengthy discussion, a motion was made by Professor Ethridge and seconded by Professor Sweat that the new dean be chosen from among the existing faculty. Then, Professor Williams (who must have known already how things were going to go) excused himself and asked Professor Khayat to preside in his place, and the Ethridge motion was quickly approved by a voice vote. There was a general consensus, however, that the actual deanship vote should be by secret ballot. Such a ballot was quickly held, and the count "revealed that Professor Williams was the unanimous choice of the faculty for the decanal appointment."[67]

Less than three weeks later, on October 22, when Chancellor Porter L. Fortune recommended Professor Williams for the law school deanship to the board of trustees, who were meeting on campus prior to Homecoming, they quickly approved his appointment at an annual salary of $29,000. A native of Lexington in the Mississippi Delta and the son of lawyer parents, the new dean had earned a B.A. at the University of Mississippi at the age of twenty-two in 1953 and an LL.B. degree from its law school in 1954. His next few years had been spent back home in the Delta, practicing law and eventually serving as the district attorney for the fourth judicial district. He returned to the law school as an associate professor in 1963 and had been promoted to a full professor in 1965, before going to the Yale law school as a Sterling Fellow and earning an LL.M. there in 1966. In 1967–68, he had taken another leave of absence in order to serve as a fellow in law administration at the New York University law school, and he had been appointed to his first administra-

William Forbes Stearns (1854–1861)

Lucius Q. C. Lamar (1866–1870)

Edward Mayes (1877–1892)

Garvin D. Shands (1894–1905)

Thomas Somerville (1905–1913)

Leonard J. Farley (1913–1921)

Thomas C. Kimbrough
(1921–1930, 1932–1945)

Robert Farley (1946–1963)

Joshua M. Morse III (1963–1969)

Joel W. Bunkley Jr. (1969–1971)

Parham H. Williams Jr. (1971–1985)

Guthrie T. Abbott
(acting dean, 1985–1986)

Thomas Edmonds (1986–1988)

Larry S. Bush
(acting dean, 1988–1990)

David E. Shipley (1990–1993)

Carolyn Ellis Staton
(acting dean, 1993–1994)

Louis Westerfield (1994–1996)

William M. Champion
(acting dean, 1996–1997)

Samuel M. Davis (1997–present)

Ventress Hall. When it was the home of the School of Law, from 1911 to 1930,
it was called Lamar Hall.

Professor John Fox, much loved (and feared) professor who served from 1932 to 1964.

Class photo of Constance Slaughter Harvey. In 1970, she became the first African American female graduate of the School of Law.

LOOKS LIKE THE WINNER GOT IT WORST IN THE END

A scene from the aftermath of a Murder Bowl game, a full-contact football game that once was an annual contest between University of Mississippi law students and pharmacy students.

Farley Hall. It was known as Lamar Hall from 1930 to 1978, when it was home to the School of Law.

A scene from the law library in old Lamar Hall, now known as Farley Hall.

The current Lamar Hall, occupied in 1978 and present home of the School of Law.

Class composite of the 1902 graduating class.

Noah S. "Soggy" Sweat Jr., author of the famous "Whiskey Speech."

Class photo of Senator Thad Cochran, 1965 graduate of the School of Law and senior senator from Mississippi at the time of the School's sesquicentennial.

Class photo of Reuben V. Anderson, who in 1967 became the first African American graduate of the School of Law.

Class photo of Senator Trent Lott, 1967 graduate of the School of Law.

Class photo of Roger F. Wicker, 1975 graduate
of the School of Law and congressman representing the First District of Mississippi, where
the school is located.

Class photo of John Grisham, 1981 graduate of
the School of Law and noted writer.

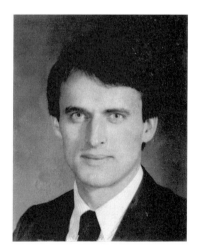

Some alumni may recognize Professor George Cochran's famous Karmann-Ghia.

Professor (now Chancellor) Robert C. Khayat teaching a class.

The late Professor George "Casey" Stengel (right) with his student (and later a beloved School of Law professor) Guthrie T. Abbott (middle).

Oil portrait of Lucius Q. C. Lamar, who served on the law faculty from 1866 to 1870. He also served in both houses of Congress, as secretary of the interior under President Grover Cleveland and as an associate justice of the United States Supreme Court. Lamar Hall, home of the University of Mississippi School of Law, is named for him.

tive post, as the law school' s assistant dean, in 1969. Now only forty years old, he was, as the *Oxford Eagle* noted, "one of the youngest deans of a major American law school."[68]

On November 18, 1971, just a few weeks after Williams took over as dean, a Vanderbilt law professor, Paul Sanders, arrived on campus to conduct the annual AALS accreditation inspection. In a letter written a few weeks later to the AALS president, Sanders reported that there had been "no reoccurrence" of the conditions that had led to talk of a withdrawal of accreditation just two years earlier. He had met with personally with Chancellor Fortune, who had assured him that the law school would be "fully protected against repressive interference." And the record supported "an expression of confidence in the disposition and ability of [the chancellor] to protect and promote academic freedom at the University of Mississippi."[69]

But there were some problems brewing that the new law dean had to confront quickly. One of them was a concern on the part of several board members that too many nonresidents of Mississippi were attending the state-subsidized law school and getting their legal training at the Mississippi taxpayers' expense. In October 1971, board member M. M. Roberts of Hattiesburg, told a colleague that he believed that the school was "being ruined" by an influx of outsiders. His understanding was that "approximately 55%" of the first year law class that year was from out of state.[70]

Replying to Roberts a couple of weeks later, Dean Williams explained that, in the aftermath of the Vietnam war, not only was there a great increase in applications for admission but also that many Mississippi natives were residing temporarily out of state. Also, although it was true that up until this time there had been no distinction made between admission standards for in-state and out-of-state applicants, the law faculty were now putting some in place. Meanwhile, of the 617-strong law school student body for that year, only 213 (34 percent) were from out-of-state. A little over a year later, on February 11, 1972, he reported to the chancellor with regard to admissions for the fall of that year, that, as of that date, fifty-one Mississippi residents and only thirteen nonresidents had been accepted. And, while only thirteen resident applicants had been rejected, 163 nonresidents had been told "no."[71]

Through the early 1970s, the number of women students in each law school class continued to be around twenty. There were slightly fewer black students and virtually no Asian, Latino, or Native Americans enrolled.[72]

The blacks, however, continuing the tradition established by their predecessors in the closing years of the previous decade, continued to be very politically active. In July 1970, they were rather upset when the first-ever, serious African American candidate for a place on the law faculty was not hired. But the school was then still under heavy scrutiny from the AALS because of the Strickler/Trister and Morse/Vinson cases, and it was to no one's interest to have it disaccredited. In the fall of 1970, the university did hire an African American professor serve in the sociology department. So the matter was finally dropped.[73]

A few months later, in February 1971, the LSCRRC took the lead in organizing a "Pre-Law Committee." The five student members of its racially mixed governing board were James Minor, Johnny Walls, Freida Gunn, Max Kilpatrick, and Julie Epps. And they were, in consultation with their faculty advisor, Robert Khayat, to work at organizing four-person teams of law students that would go out, in March and October of every year, on one- or two-day recruiting trips, to visit every public and private four-year institution of higher learning in the state, including all of the historically black institutions. They would take with them recruitment packets made up of admission forms, catalogs, and LSAT materials to distribute to interested undergraduates. Also, the 1971 edition of the law school's *Bulletin* for the first time announced that (in compliance with the Federal Civil Rights Act of 1964) it was "the policy of the University of Mississippi to make available its teaching, research and service programs and its facilities to every qualified person regardless of race, color, religion, sex or national origin."[74]

The African American student enrollment in the law school in the fall of 1971, however, was still only nineteen out of a total enrollment of 359 (5.26 percent). And there was still no African American on the law faculty. Early in April 1972, Firnist J. Alexander, president of the Magnolia Bar Association, and law school alumnus Reuben V. Anderson, who was now chairman of the Magnolia Bar's standing committee on black legal education, in a letter addressed to Chancellor Fortune, Dean Williams, and state bar president Lester F. Sumners, reported that they had been petitioned by the law school's black students "to inquire into their charges of systematic and institutional racially discriminatory practices by the Law School administration and faculty." Two weeks later, on April 19, Anderson and his Magnolia Bar committee members met on campus with Williams, Sumners, and members of the law faculty to discuss the charges that had been made. The only immediate consequence of their meeting, however, seems to have been a decision made by the faculty, in a meeting held the next day, to counter accusations that had been made of biased grading by adopting, beginning in the next academic year, a blind grading system whereby on student exams and papers the author was identified to the grading faculty member only by an assigned number, with the assignee's identity being only known by the law school registrar. Apparently that change did not help much. By the fall of 1973, the African American enrollment was down to sixteen out 649 (2.47 percent). In the fall of 1975, it was only a little bit better, with twenty-two African Americans out of a total enrollment of 584 (3.77 percent).[75]

Meanwhile, the fact had to be faced that Lamar Hall, even with its still less than twenty-year old rear addition, had been designed to accommodate a law school with around 250 students and ten faculty members and now had nearly two and a half times that number of students enrolled and nearly twice as many faculty occupying office space. All of them were using a law library that had been designed to hold around 30,000 volumes, now, in fact, held some 49,000, and was expected by the AALS to hold at least 60,000. It was becoming, in fact, obvious that a new law school was needed. But where was the money for it coming from, and where should it be built? Back in 1955, the university medical school had been moved to Jackson and renamed the "University Medical Center." Many people thought that the law school should be handled in the same way. Members of the Jackson bar were generally in favor of moving it there, and the idea was particularly favored by its junior bar members, intrigued by the thought of having the school's law library located just a few minutes away from the offices where they worked.

In the 1972 session of the state legislature, two bills were introduced with regard to the law school. A senate bill, authored by Senator Bobby G. Perry from Horn Lake and Senator George M. Yarborough from Red Banks, would appropriate 4.5 million dollars to pay for building a new law school on the Oxford campus. A house bill, introduced by Morris Cohen of Canton, directed the board of trustees to "establish a law school of the University of Mississippi at Jackson." The latter was strongly endorsed by the executive committee of the Jackson junior bar, whose members issued a statement in its support contending that "as long as the Law School is situated in a corner of the state distant from the vast majority of attorneys and businesses, it can't serve the people of Mississippi to the greatest possible degree." Specifically the Jackson junior bar argued that greater opportunities for legal training would be afforded to the law students by being in closer proximity to the state's principal administrative, legislative, and judicial bodies and that both they and their spouses would be economically much better off in the much larger Jackson community with its "greater employment opportunities," including a large number of "positions in law firms." Early in the session, the legislature had received a petition that had been signed by more than half the law students then enrolled on the Oxford campus requesting removal of the law school to Jackson for essentially those same reasons.[76]

Though neither bill passed that year, the controversy continued. At the 1972 state bar annual meeting in Biloxi, the junior bar meeting as a whole voted 64 to 46 against moving the university law school to Jackson. There was, of course, actually already a law school in Jackson. The private, unaccredited Jackson School of Law, founded in 1935, four decades later had a large number of alumni in Jackson and around the state, who, after attending its night classes on the Millsaps College campus over several years, had then gained admission to the bar by taking the bar examination. But it was still unaccredited. And, by 1972, the American Bar Association was in the process of adopting a new set of "Standards for Legal Education" that strongly favored the idea that a law school ought always to be attached to an accredited university. As early as 1968, Mississippi College, a private Baptist institution located in Jackson's southwestern suburb, Clinton, had shown some interest in buying the school. And Millsaps College itself also had considered doing so, for a while. At the state bar convention in Biloxi, in June 1973, members of the Jackson School of Law's single legal fraternity, Sigma Delta Kappa, took the lead in organizing an alumni association of the school's graduates. Just a few weeks later, the association's officers were meeting with Mississippi College officials to discuss the possible buy-out.[77]

The University of Mississippi, meanwhile, was fighting back both by emphasizing the importance of the ABA's university-connection standard and by arguing that the heavy emphasis on the large number of law office internships that would be available to law students in Jackson was tantamount to advocating a return to the old-fashioned system of lawyer training by apprenticeship rather than scholarship. At the same time, however, it was also, in fact, looking for ways to greatly expand the reach of its law school in Oxford down to Jackson. In the autumn of 1972, Dean Williams's plans for the law school included, in cooperation with the legal education committee of the state bar, the idea of a greatly expanded program of legal education housed on the grounds of the Universities Center on Jackson's Eastover Drive that would "provide an opportunity for the practitioner to upgrade his knowledge and skill in specific areas of the law." At their March 1973 meeting the board of trustees, by an 11 to 1 vote, approved a request by Chancellor Fortune to authorize also the establishment, there at the Universities Center, of a "fulltime, degree-granting branch" of the university law school. The idea was to admit its first freshman class in the autumn of 1973 and then to add a second-year class in 1974 and a third-year class in 1975. Doing so, Dean Williams had assured them, would "both relieve the over-crowded condition on the Oxford campus and . . . meet the growing needs for legal education in the Jackson area."[78]

The cost of doing all that, it soon came to be generally realized, however, was just going to be too great. To put in place a twenty-thousand-volume branch law library and to pay an associate dean, two faculty members, two librarians, and a secretary for just the first year the trustees were asking the legislature to approve an appropriation of $339,147.00, which they declined to do.[79] By the summer of 1973, therefore, it was very apparent that the future of the university of Mississippi law school, like its past, was going to happen in Oxford, Mississippi.

On the Oxford campus, meanwhile, law school business was being carried on as usual. The total student enrollment for 1972–73 was at a record level of 690, and the full-time faculty now numbered twenty-three. One of the faculty newcomers that year was Associate Professor Michael D. Featherstone, a graduate of Davidson College who had earned his J.D. degree from the University of South Carolina Law School in 1970 and an LL.M. from the University of Georgia Law School in 1971. Another was George C. Cochran, who had served as editor-in-chief of the law journal at the University of North Carolina Law School before earning his J.D. there in 1964. From 1964 to 1968, he had been in Washington, D.C., clerking for Supreme Court Chief Justice Earl Warren and then for Justice Stanley Reed before going to work in a private law firm. From 1969 to 1972, he had been at Duke University serving as the director of their center on law and poverty. Dr. Gene Lee, director of the student health service on campus, and Clarksdale attorney Edward P. Connell both were continuing to serve as part-time adjunct professors. And another new recruit to the faculty in the spring of 1973 was Assistant Professor Tom Mason, holder of a law degree from the University of Oklahoma, where he had served as editor of the

Oklahoma Law Review. Dean Emeritus Robert Farley had been going to return to campus to teach in the spring 1973 semester but instead had gone to teach at the Cornell University law school, which had made him an offer he could not refuse. He was going to be back for the fall semester, however, and the law alumni were going to pay his salary.[80]

During each semester, the law faculty met, usually every other Tuesday or Thursday afternoon, at 4:00 or 4:30, in the dean's office. And also, every once in a while, they held a weekend afternoon and evening get-together at professor Harry Case's cabin retreat, "Buzzard Roost," located out in the country between Highway 7 North and Sardis Lake, near Hurricane Landing. On January 27, 1972, besides approving the candidates for January graduation, they adopted a rule that no more than thirty transfer hours from another law school could be counted toward a degree. On February 2, 1972, they voted both that law journal candidates should be given one hour of credit for law journal work and that moot court board members should receive two hours credit for service on the moot court board. On April 17, 1972, they adopted a rule that prohibited smoking, eating, or drinking in class. Just three days after that, they unanimously endorsed future federal judge Rhesa Barksdale as the winner of the Phi Delta Phi outstanding student award.[1]

A continuing concern of the law faculty was the law school library. Both its condition and its size were cause for concern. In March 1971, they had voted to ban eating or drinking anywhere in the library. Over the next couple of months, they had adopted a policy that no law student could register for classes, graduate or have his transcript forwarded to him until the librarian certified that he had returned all books, journals, and other materials and also adopted a rule that henceforth the library was to be completely "non-circulating" as far as students were concerned.[82]

By that time the library itself had become grossly inadequate for meeting the needs of students and faculty. Designed two decades earlier to meet the needs of some 250 students and a dozen or so faculty, it was now much too small. Its seating capacity of 125 was two hundred below the AALS requirement for 650 students; the chairs and reading desks were old and decrepit. Insufficient office space meant that students were reading and studying amid the clatter of typewriters operated by staff members sitting at desks just a few feet away from them. Inadequate funding meant that not everything that should have been available on the shelves was, in fact, there. In the spring of 1970, law librarian

Bill Murray had warned the faculty that he was "desperately short of funds" needed to keep the library up to national accreditation standards.[83]

Chancellor Fortune, in a December 1971 letter to the board of trustees, had noted that whereas the law library's share of the general library funds allocated by them to the university currently totaled $77,000, what was needed annually to meet accreditation standards was $255,000. Noting that members of the legislature in their session earlier that year had requested that special consideration be given to meeting the law library's needs, he asked that the board, in future, fund the library both separately from the rest of the university's library budget and adequately. And, nearly two years later, by the spring of 1973, the law library's budget situation was considerably better. The legislature had come up with a special appropriation of $200,000 for acquisitions in 1972 and a further $100,000 in 1974. Also a number of major law firms around the state had made generous contributions to the acquisitions fund. The library's grossly inadequate size, however, and the worn-out state of its equipment and furniture were still major problems.[84]

In spite of all the inadequacies that had to be dealt with, an impressive amount of both teaching and scholarly work was being done, and being done well. The J.D. candidates were being required to complete ninety credit hours during six semesters, or the equivalent (three full summer sessions were the equivalent of two semesters), of residence. Because they still enjoyed the diploma privilege, it was a curriculum designed particularly to prepare them to practice very competently as members of the Mississippi bar. Required courses (with their number of credit hours) were:

FIRST YEAR
Contracts (6)
Property I (4)
Constitutional Law (4)
Legal Bibliography (2)
Jurisprudence (2)
Torts (4)
Legal Writing (2)
Property II (3)
Federal Courts (4)

SECOND OR THIRD YEAR
Commercial Law (6)
Introduction to Tax (6)
Circuit Court Practice (2)
Wills and Estates (4)
Business Units (3)
Chancery Court Practice (2)
Criminal Procedure (4)
Evidence (4)

THIRD YEAR
Legal Profession (2)
Moot Court I: Trial Court and Appellate Procedure (1)
Employer-Employee Relations (3)[85]

Of the twenty-two additional hours, most of which were taken in a student's third and final year, a few had to be earned in such required courses as Readings in Law 513 and 514. Others were earned in courses for which a student had to compete for admission, such as Moot Court II or the research, writing, or editing work for the *Law Journal.* A few of the nonrequired third-year courses, in fields such as business or legal history, were taught by business school or liberal arts faculty members, for "Z-grade" (hours only) credit.[86]

In the summer of 1972, Professors Sweat and Gorove launched a "Law Program Abroad" summer school, conducted at the University of Dijon in eastern France, in which interested members of the senior class could earn up to six hours of credit in an exotic and also highly educational setting. Meanwhile, the dozen or more graduate students (most of whom were foreign students enrolled in the Master of Comparative Law program), were writing, under the direction of Professors Gorove, Champion, Stengel, and Condon, and sometimes Dean Williams and others, theses on a wide range of subjects having to do with both American and international law.[87]

Professor Gorove, in 1965, while still a newcomer on the faculty, had inspired and assisted in the foundation of a new student organization called the Lamar Society of International Law. And on April 10, 1969, just three months prior to the first manned landing on the moon by Neil Armstrong and Ed Aldrin on July 20 of that year, the society in conjunction with the law school speakers bureau had sponsored an on-campus conference entitled "Man's Landing on the Moon—Legal Implications and Perspectives." At the conference, held in the law building, an audience made up both of students and members of the general public heard a panel, chaired by Professor Gorove and including the general counsel to the National Aeronautics and Space Administration, a special consultant to the U.S. Senate's committee on aeronautical and space sciences, and the counsel employed by the General Electric Company's test center in Bay St. Louis, Mississippi, address questions such as "What law is to govern man's activities on the moon? Can any nation exercise sovereignty, jurisdiction or control? Can John Doe, AT&T or the U.N. acquire land or other valuables on the moon?"[88]

At another conference, held at the law school three years later, April 7–8, 1972, sponsored by both the Lamar Society and the American Society of International Law, the topic addressed was "Earth Resources, Survey Satellites and International Law." The visiting panelists for it included, among others, the director of what was then the NASA Test Center in Bay St. Louis; a Plainview, New York attorney who was serving as the president of Peace Studies, Inc.; and, from Washington, D.C., both the scientific counselor on the staff of the Italian embassy and the senior specialist in international relations at the Library of Congress. A number of student members of the Lamar Society also served as panel members.[89]

Just one year later, in the spring of 1973, the proceedings of that conference were published in volume I, number 1, of a new publication called *The Journal of Space Law*, published by the Lamar Society. The new journal had an editorial advisory board chaired by Professor Gorove that included scholars from Philadelphia, Pennsylvania; Buenos Aires; Geneva; Neuen Kirschen, Austria; London; Paris; Belgrade; Washington, D.C.; and New Haven, Connecticut (Yale University's Sterling Professor, Myres S. McDougal). Its student editorial board, headed by editor-in-chief John H. Fitch Jr., also included Johnnie. M. Haley, Robert E. Williford, Jerry Mills, Mickey Mauldin, William M. Sigler, Luther S. Ott, and William L. Youngblood. As Dean Williams pointed out in the foreword to number 1: "By limiting its scope to problems arising out of man's activities in outer space" it was going to fill "a void in international law publications."[90]

By that spring of 1973, it had become obvious that the law school was not, either wholly or in part, going to be relocated to Jackson; it was going to stay on the university campus at Oxford. As of July 1, 1973, with board of trust-ees approval, the "University of Mississippi Law Center" was officially created. That transformation put the institution that had for a century been known as "the law school" in tune with what was now an important developing national trend. During the preceding decade, approximately half of the AALS-accredit-ed "schools"—including those at LSU, Vanderbilt, the University of Houston, the University of North Carolina, the University of Tennessee, the University of Georgia, Florida State University, and the University of South Carolina—had become "law centers." By 1980, it was predicted, "most of the major law schools" would have made the same transformation.[91]

In all but name, the center already existed in embryonic form. Besides the "law school," engaged in training and educating would-be members of the state bar, several other programs were then being used to strengthen and sup-port the law's operations in Mississippi. The Legal Institute of Agricultural and Resources Development, being directed by Professor James W. Zirkle, a gradu-ate of the University of Tennessee law school and a Yale LL.M., was employing a three-person staff and using its $150,000 research grant funding both to con-duct extensive research on behalf of several committees of the state legislature and several state agencies and also in conjunction with the Mississippi-Alabama Sea Grant Legal Program funded by the federal government in 1972. A Clinical Education Program, directed by Professor Sweat, was using $91,000 in grants from the Law Enforcement Alliance of America (LEAA) to run a "prosecu-tor training program" that placed senior law school students, for one semes-ter, in the offices of district, county, and municipal prosecutors, and also in public defender offices and youth courts throughout the state. Under another LEAA grant of approximately $166,000, Professor Sweat was also operating the Mississippi Judicial College, which provided comprehensive training programs for officers at all levels of the state's judicial system. And with the support of the state bar, the Continuing Legal Education Program, under Professor Khayat's direction, was offering CLE classes, varying from one day to six weeks in length, on such newly developing fields as land-use planning, marine law, and the uni-form commercial code for members of the bar both at the Universities Center in Jackson and at various regional centers around the state.[92]

There still remained, however, the major problem of the law building, orig-inally constructed in the late 1920s and enlarged twenty years later to accom-modate a student body of around two hundred fifty. Other universities in the south that had converted their law schools into law centers had also constructed immense new buildings to house them. The LSU law center occupied a massive new structure covering 133,795 square feet. The University of Houston law center was made up of a huge five-building complex. And the University of Alabama had been allotted $7,500,000 to build theirs. In the autumn of 1971, Chancellor Fortune had advised the board of trustees that at least three million dollars would be needed to construct a suitable law center building, of approximately 120,000 square feet, on the campus at Oxford. Law center funding had been on the agendas of both the 1972 and 1973 sessions of the state legislature, but the prevailing uncertainty as to just where that center was going to be located had discouraged any final decision with regard to funding it.[93]

But when the question of where the law center was to be situated was settled, planning a new building for it could go ahead. At a meeting on September 4, 1973, the law faculty approved a plan presented by architects Jernigan, Hawkins and Harrison of Jackson. The state legislature, in their 1974 session, appropriated $4.3 million to build it. A little less than a year later, on March 8, 1975, the formal groundbreaking ceremony took place at the chosen site, located a little to the east of the then law building and just across the street from the west side of the Alumni House.[94]

Meanwhile, some other important developments were taking place. Although, nationally, law school enrollment, which had doubled in the previous decade, was continuing to soar, the University of Mississippi law school's enrollment, by the fall of 1974, had been cut back to just 575, and the faculty were determined to keep it there, at least as long as the law center remained housed in its present quarters. Of the entering class of 231 students that fall only 7 percent were nonresidents of Mississippi. But some things had not yet changed very much; only 12 percent of the new students were women, and only 4 percent were black.[95]

Although the make-up of the student body was not yet changing, the make-up of the faculty, to some extent, was beginning to do so. One of the law school's own African American alumni, A. C. Wharton, who had earlier earned a bachelor's degree at Tennessee State University, joined the faculty as a part-time adjunct professor in that same fall of 1974. And new Assistant Professor Catherine Sullivan, a 1970 graduate of the University of Massachusetts who had earned a J.D. degree at Yale in 1974, became the first woman to teach full-time on the law faculty.[96]

Other good things were happening too. In 1973, a major Jackson law firm made a commitment to provide three thousand dollars every year to fund what were going to be called "the University of Mississippi School of Law Memorial Lectures." The first lecturer, in the spring of 1974, was Professor Philip Kurland of the Univeristy of Chicago School of Law. The second, in 1975, was Professor Charles Frankel of the Columbia University School of Law. Their lectures were published each year in special editions of the *Mississippi Law Journal*, which, thanks to the generous support it continued to receive from the state bar, then had the fourth largest circulation of any such publication in the United States.[97]

On February 5, 1975, the law faculty, in a meeting that the dean did not attend, passed a unanimous resolution expressing their appreciation and thanks "for his outstanding service and leadership." They thanked him "particularly for his untiring efforts":

> 1. As an extremely effective and congenial administrator;
> 2. In Implementing the University of Mississippi School of Law Memorial Lectures;
> 3. In being the impetus and guiding force in the planning and financing of a new Multi-million dollar law center for the University of Mississippi; and
> 4. In representing the School of Law, on and off campus, in a manner that gives reason to each member of its Faculty to be justly proud.

The resolution was attested and sealed by both Associate Dean of the Law School Robert C. Khayat and Mrs. Joan Murphy, Law School Registrar and Secretary to the Law Faculty.[98]

CHAPTER 6

THE RECENT PAST
(1975–1994)

T he law center's last three years in its first home, the building now
known as Farley Hall, were ones of continuing growth and development. In January 1976, volume 1, number 1 of the *Ole Miss Law Center
Newsletter* was published, and its front page contained an exciting news item.
William Wayne Drinkwater Jr., a graduate of the class of 1974, had just been
chosen to clerk for Chief Justice Earl Warren of the United States Supreme
Court. A Meridian, Mississippi, native, Drinkwater had served as articles editor for the *Law Journal* in his senior year and graduated first in his class, thus
winning the Dean Robert J. Farley award for the student with the highest grade
point average in his graduating class. In the 1940s alumnus Huey B. Howerton
had clerked for Associate Supreme Court Justice Hugo Black, and in the more
recent past, Rhesa H. Barksdale, the first winner of the Farley award in June
1972, had clerked in 1972–73 for Justice Byron White, and Raymond L. Brown
had clerked for Justice Tom Clark in 1962–63. But Drinkwater, who, since
graduating had been clerking for Mississippi's northern district federal judge
William Keady, was the first alumnus ever to clerk for the supreme court's chief
justice.[1]

By the time Catherine Sullivan joined the law faculty in 1974, there were
already a number of women lawyers serving in administrative positions on the
law center staff. Dixie Criddle was director of the Criminal Justice Research
Service, Ann Ball was director of the Mississippi Prosecutors Association, and
Frieda Gunn Collins was assistant director of the Sea Grant Legal System. For
the 1975–76 school year, Professor Catherine Sullivan had another female colleague. Professor Judith Ittig, of the University of Tennessee law faculty, was
serving as a visiting member of the law center faculty, taking the place of
Professor Khayat, who was on a two-year leave of absence gaining front-line

experience by working with an Oxford law firm. And, at the beginning of the spring 1976 semester, Karen Green, a member of the 1974 graduating class who had gone on to earn an LL.M. in tax law at the New York University law school, was also added to the faculty. In the summer of 1976, Professor Sullivan left to join the New York University law school faculty, but in the fall of 1977 Carolyn Ellis, who had earned a J.D. at the Yale law school in 1972 and since then had been practicing law in New York and New Jersey, was recruited as a new assistant professor. Although that same year Professor Green went back to the NYU law school for one year as a visiting professor, by the autumn of 1978 there were again two women, Ellis and Green, working on the law center faculty.[2]

The law school's student body was now becoming much more co-educational than it had ever been (except briefly during World War II). By the spring of 1974, Karen Green and Judy Johnson were on the editorial staff of the *Law Journal.* A social organization called "Women in Law" had been organized, and the two law student fraternities, Phi Delta Phi and Phi Alpha Delta, were enrolling women. In the fall of 1974, a "Women in Law" day was held in the law center on the first Friday in November "to encourage undergraduate women to attend law school," and another one was held on the same day in 1975. "More than fifty" of the 525 students enrolled for the 1974–75 school year were women. Although the total number of women graduates in the May and August 1975 classes was only five, the 1978 spring and summer total was thirteen. Just three years later, in 1981, that total would be twenty-seven.[3]

The African American enrollment, meanwhile, remained at about the same level that it had been down into the early 1980s, and A. C. Wharton Jr. continued to serve only half-time as an adjunct professor. In the summer of 1975, however, a black "visiting distinguished professor" of law was brought in to teach in the summer session. He was Doctor Larry Gibson, a member of the law faculty at the University of Virginia who was a graduate of Howard University and had earned an LL.M. at Columbia. Professor James Chandler, a graduate of the University of California at Berkeley and the holder of a J.D. from the University of California at Davis, became the third black faculty member to teach in the University of Mississippi law school when he was hired as visiting distinguished professor in 1976. The fourth, Dr. James D. Minor, an alumnus as was Wharton, had received his J.D. in 1972. Since 1974, he had been serving as director of the state's criminal justice research service.

As of June 1, 1978, he became both an assistant professor of law and an assistant to the dean with the responsibility for directing the school's minority affairs program.[4]

Back in 1969, the law school had applied to the Council on Legal Educational Opportunities for funding to conduct a southern regional CLEO institute in the summer of that year, but without success. In the summer of 1976, they applied again and this time were successful. Headed by Professor Tom Mason, the institute ran for six weeks beginning in June. Funded by the federal government, it gave minority students with good undergraduate records the opportunity to come to the law school for the summer session and enroll in special, noncredit law classes and be graded and evaluated by members of the law faculty. Students who performed well were then awarded scholarships that would enable them to attend the law school of their choice in a five-state area of the south. Thirty-two students attended the 1976 institute, which was "highly successful," and a number of the student participants came back to enroll in the law school in the fall. The 1977 entering class of 189 students included eleven African Americans.[5]

One very unpleasant incident occurred in the last few years of the law school's sojourn in what is now Farley Hall. One weekend night in October 1975 two notable portraits, one of L. Q. C Lamar and one of Dean Robert Farley, that hung in the building's main floor hallway were stolen. Probably done in connection with one of the "scavenger hunts" that were then a very common part of some fraternities' pre-initiation, pledge-harassment tests, the crime resulted in the two missing portraits being discovered, a few days later, outside the back door of one of the apartment buildings in married student housing. The 5.75 x 6.5 foot Lamar portrait had suffered severe damage and had to be turned over to a professional restorer, and the cost its restoration was paid out of a special fund established by the law school alumni.[6]

But very good things were going on then also. In 1974, the Jackson law firm of Butler, Snow, O'Mara, Stevens and Cannada established an endowment to fund a lecture series at the law school in memory of their firm's founding partners. The first of the lectures was presented in the spring of that year by Professor Philip Kurland of the University of Chicago. For the next couple of years, they were made part of the annual "Law Weekend" held on campus every spring. But because of competition that same weekend from such events as the annual "Red and Blue" spring football game, beginning in 1977, the lectures were scheduled separately a little later each spring.[7]

In 1975, Percy A. Matthews of Hazlehurst, willed money to the law school to endow another lecture series in honor of his surviving wife, Judge Burnita Shelton Matthews. A native of Burnell, Mississippi, Judge Matthews had earned an LL.B. at the National University Law School in 1919 and an LL.M. there in 1920. While qualifying as a member of the Mississippi, D.C., and United States Supreme Court bars and practicing law in D.C., she had become very active in the national women's rights movement. She was appointed to the bench of the United States District Court of D.C. by President Truman in 1949, becoming the first ever female federal district judge. The first Matthews lecture was given on March 4, 1976, by Professor James P. White of the Indiana University School of Law, Indianapolis, the consultant on legal education to the American Bar Association and an "author of numerous legal publications."[8]

Another Washington, D.C., legal luminary honored that same spring was United States Senator James O. Eastland. An alumnus of the university, though not of the law school, Eastland had first practiced law in Forest, Mississippi, from 1927 to 1934, and then settled in Sunflower County. Elected to the senate in 1942, he had been serving as the chair of its judiciary committee since 1956 and as its president pro tem since 1972. On March 8, 1976, at a testimonial dinner held in Jackson to "honor the veteran senator," at which the principal speaker was United States Supreme Court Chief Justice Warren Burger, the launching of a new fund drive among alumni and friends of the university was announced. Its aim would be to raise a two-million-dollar fund that would be used to establish a number of "Eastland Scholarships" to assist needy students who wished to enroll in the law center. By July 1977, more than half a million dollars had already been raised, and four of the scholarships were already being offered to deserving candidates.[9]

Soon after that, the law center was finally able to move into its newly constructed home building located just west of the Alumni House and right across from the north side of the Grove. Back in December 1974, the state's higher education board of trustees had voted to name the new building "the James Oliver Eastland Hall," but just six months later, on June 3, 1975, at the state bar's annual meeting in Biloxi, the law school alumni chapter passed a resolution stating that their school's new home should "continue to carry the name L. Q. C. Lamar" and that the trustees should be promptly so informed. In fact, it took a while to get the trustees to change their minds, but in their March 1977 meeting they finally agreed that their earlier decision had been somewhat "premature."

They then ruled instead that the law center's new home should be named "the Lamar Law Center" but that the law library that it housed would be officially known as "the Eastland Law Library." When Senator Eastland retired from the senate just a year later, in 1978, he made a gift of all of his historically valuable papers and other memorabilia to the archives section of that library.[10]

Through the mid-1970s, things remained cramped and crowded in the law school building. In December 1975, Chancellor Fortune told concerned alumnus Judge Hugh N. Clayton that not only might the old athletic dormitory (now Miller Hall) be designated as a dormitory exclusively for law students who wished to live on campus but also the old chancellor's residence (now Barnard Hall) could be used to provide additional office space for the law faculty. Neither of those things, in fact, happened, but in that same fall of 1975 the law school student body president, Jim T. Thomas, persuaded Alumni Secretary Bill Griffin to agree—on a trial basis at first—to allow fifty spaces in the Alumni House parking lot to be used by law student parking sticker holders every day, except on days when large meetings were being held, when a least one day's advance notice would be given to the law school. And that arrangement remains in effect, essentially, to this day.[11]

The new law building, meanwhile, was slowly materializing. Like the one other major new building constructed on the campus in the 1970s, the Student Union, it represented a major departure from the red brick and columns of the Greek revival style in which most of the buildings on campus, echoing the example of the Lyceum, had been built. It was constructed instead in the then very fashionable *bauhaus* style, which had originated half a century earlier in Germany and which featured walls made up of large blocks of cement or granite topped by flat roofs very susceptible to leaking (which is presumably why most of mankind throughout history have avoided using them). Nevertheless, at a law faculty meeting on September 14, 1976, it was noted with great pleasure (and, on a motion by Professor John Robin Bradley, recorded in the minutes of the meeting) that the huge crane employed in the construction of the new building was being dismantled that very day.[12]

The 1978 *Law School Catalog* (published in the summer of 1977) had on its cover a picture of the steps leading up to the second-floor main entrance to the new building, shown with several students standing on them. Inside, on its first page, was a photograph of Dean Williams (with a confident grin on his face and his right hand in his right trouser pocket) walking out from the building's south-side entrance accompanied by two white males, one black male, and a white female student. On page 4 was a statement that the new Lamar Hall would be "occupied during the Fall 1977 Semester." On May 6, 1977, however, the law faculty was informed that probably it would take at least two more months to complete all of the basic construction work on the building and that January 1978 was the best estimate for the move-in date. As things turned out, however, and as the 1980 *Catalog* noted, the new hall, in fact, "opened for the Summer 1978 semester."[13]

The members of the board of trustees were not totally pleased, apparently, with how the new building looked from the outside. On May 18, 1978, they laid down a rule that, henceforth, all of the institutions of higher learning in the state could only build new buildings on their campuses that were "compatible" architecturally with the already existing buildings. To help enforce that rule in the future, a colored picture showing exactly what the exterior of a new building would look like must be submitted to the board before construction was begun.[14]

At the same time, however, the board members were generously approving of various liberal expenditures for interior furnishings, office equipment, and a Dictaphone system for the new law center building. An "electronic information system, two fully-equipped moot court rooms, fully up-to-date classroom seating arrangements and sliding, compactable bookshelves for the library" were all authorized.[15] They were also generous in paying for the renovation of the "Old Law Building," which in February 1979 was formally renamed "Farley Hall" in memory of both Dean Leonard J. Farley (1913–21) and Dean Robert J. Farley (1946–63), the only father and son team ever to have both served as the deans of any major law school in the United States. In September 1979, they formally approved the building's takeover by the university's journalism department.[16]

Over the course of the 1978–79 academic year, the law center's faculty, students and alumni happily celebrated their move into their new home. In October, an open house was held that enabled the entire university community to see and admire the marvelous new example of modern academic architecture, including its rising tiers of seats in the new acoustically excellent classrooms, its ultra-modern moot court rooms and library, and its very contemporary pair of "conversation pits" in the middle of the main hall on the first floor. A highlight of the occasion was an art show organized by the university's director of museums, Ms. Valerie Braybrook. Appropriately labeled "The Eye of the Law," it featured exhibits of famous original paintings from the Smithsonian, the Metropolitan Museum of Art, the Chicago Art Institute, and many other galleries around the nation. The show remained on exhibit through December 1978.[17]

The formal dedication of the new law center complex took place on March 22, 1980. The principal speaker at the dedication ceremony was Justice Byron R. ("Whizzer") White of the United States Supreme Court. Other speakers were Governor William F. Winter, Chief Judge J. P. Coleman of the United States fifth circuit court of appeals, former Senator James Eastland, and Chancellor Fortune. The crowd of more than fifteen hundred included representatives from many other law schools and universities. Other guests of note were Mrs. Margaret Hearn, a great-granddaughter of the law school's first professor, William Forbes Stearns; Mr. Longstreet Heiskell, a grandson of L. Q. C. Lamar; and Mr. Thomas C. Kimbrough, a grandson of the late Dean Kimbrough. In a small side-ceremony that same day, presided over by United States Senator Thad Cochran, the "Clayton Law Journal Suite" on the main floor was "Dedicated In Honor Of The Only Father And Son Who Each Served As Editor-In-Chief Of The Mississippi Law Journal," Judge Hugh N. Clayton (1907–94), the editor in 1931, and Hugh C. "Buzzy" Clayton (1945–72), the editor in 1970.[18]

The law faculty, meanwhile, even as they were getting ready for and then actually moving into their new home, had to worry very seriously about something else. The 120-year-old "diploma privilege," whereby all of their graduates were automatically entitled to immediate admission into membership in both the state and federal bars, was being severely challenged. By then, the American Bar Association had been on record as opposed to such a privilege for more than fifty years, and Mississippi was one of only five states that still offered it for its state university law school graduates. The Mississippi College School of Law, by now, was functioning as a fully fledged, three-year law school, but its graduates, as well as the graduates of out-of-state law schools, had to take the state bar examination to gain admission to the bar. Furthermore, the average passing rate for that exam was very low, only 24 percent. The reason for that, one critic had suggested, was that the exam was "compiled by Ole Miss professors and graded by Ole Miss graduates."[19]

In the spring of 1976, a committee of the young lawyers section of the state bar that had been created to consider whether the diploma privilege should be also extended to Mississippi College's law graduates ended up recommending that the privilege should be abolished altogether. The YLS board took no action with regard to the matter that year, however, and, in both 1976 and 1977, a bill to abolish the privilege was passed by the state senate but died in committee in the house. On Tuesday, May 31, 1977, YLS members arriving in Biloxi to get ready for the opening of the state bar annual meeting were confronted by a front page story in the *Gulfport Herald* headlined: "Ole Miss Professor charged with lying." The story detailed a report that had appeared three weeks earlier in the Mississippi College law school newsletter, the *Legal Eye*, recounting that University of Mississippi Law School Dean Parham Williams had told the house committee on colleges and universities that the YLS board were not in favor of abolishing the privilege when, in fact, on March 26 they had voted to do so.[20]

The next day, however, another front page story in the *Herald* quoted YLS President Mike Bush as saying that, because a motion to abolish the privilege made in the December 1976 YLS board meeting had not even been seconded, Dean Williams's report, made to the house committee in February 1977, was a perfectly reasonable one. The YLS board had been ready to vote to abolish the privilege a month later, on March 26, Bush explained further, because, by then, not only had their committee on bar admissions presented them with a very convincing report in favor of their doing so but the legislature had passed a bill that made the bar examination grading process a much fairer one.[21]

On the day after that second *Herald* story was published, the YLS section, in their general business meeting, by a standing vote of 83 to 77, approved a motion from their board that stated that the section of the state code "which provides that graduates of the University of Mississippi School of Law are eligible to practice law in the Courts of this State without the necessity of passing the Bar exam should be repealed." Two days later, that same recommendation was approved by the state bar as a whole. A year later, at the end of the 1978 annual meeting, the bar commissioners met and passed a resolution avowing that, for the coming year, the state bar's "primary" goal should be to make the state's supreme court "the ultimate authority on admissions and discipline of lawyers and to remove the executive and legislature from any control over the same." In their 1979 session, both houses of the legislature approved a measure that was practically the same, word for word, as the YLS motion approved two years earlier. All candidates for admission to the bar, it said, must hold both a bachelor's degree from an accredited college or university and also a degree from a school of law that was fully, or at least provisionally, accredited by the ABA. The preceptor program, whereby one could study law under the supervision of a bar member and then qualify for bar admission by taking the bar exam, was abolished immediately, and the diploma privilege for graduates of the university law school was to expire as of the end of November 1984. Governor Cliff Finch talked about possibly vetoing the measure, but an intensive barrage of letters from its YLS supporters finally got him to sign it on April 16, 1979.[22]

A concession in the new law that allowed university law school graduates to continue to enjoy the diploma privilege for another five and a half years—so that all of those students who were already enrolled in its program or were very soon expecting to enroll in it, could still benefit from it—was matched by another one that protected Mississippi College's law graduates from the ABA accreditation requirement until November 1984. In fact, however, the national body at its 1980 annual meeting in Honolulu, Hawaii, accorded provisional accreditation to the new school, which in January 1981 moved into a new home on Griffith Street in downtown Jackson. So, by the early 1980s Mississippi had two law schools competing with one another on a fairly balanced basis.[23]

One very important advantage that the university law school still enjoyed over its Mississippi College competitor, however, was the existence of a large corps of loyal alumni, both in state and out of state, most of whom were very active in the law alumni chapter of the university's alumni association and entertained very warm feelings of loyalty to and regard for the institution and the faculty that had provided them with their professional skills. A particularly important development in that anniversary year was the alumni association's creation of a new entity called the "Lamar Order" the purpose of which was to both solicit and manage "large gifts . . . for the School of Law in order to encourage its recognition as one of the outstanding legal education centers of the United States." Membership in the order was to be open not only to law school alumni but also to other individuals and to families and organizations that were "friends" of the law school and dedicated to its "well-being." And it could be earned either by making a gift to it of five thousand dollars, payable at the rate of five hundred dollars over ten years or in a shorter period if desired; or by arranging for a minimum future gift of at least ten thousand dollars by means of a bequest, trust arrangement, or life insurance policy.[24]

During its very first year, under the presidency of Stokes V. Robertson Sr. of Jackson, the order recruited fifty-two charter members who began making the payments that soon were being used to "insure excellence" in the law school's various programs.[25]

During the same year that saw the birth of the Lamar Order, two other examples of alumni loyalty to and regard for their law school were manifested. The trustees of the Wynn memorial trust fund created the law school's first endowed chair, the Wynn Professorship in Law, and James McClure Jr. of Sardis, Mississippi, and his sister, Mrs. Tupper McClure Lampton of Columbus funded the establishment of the James McClure Memorial Lectures in Law in honor of their father.[26]

James McClure Sr., a native of Fayette, Mississippi, had begun his higher education at Millsaps before coming to the university, where he was elected to membership in both the ODK undergraduate leadership fraternity and Phi Delta Phi and earned both a B.S. and an LL.B. degree in 1917. After service in the army in World War I from 1917 to 1919, he was admitted to the bar in 1919 and began practicing law in Charleston, Mississippi. Soon afterward, however, he became associated with a law firm in Sardis and continued to practice law there until shortly before his death in 1976. By then he was the senior partner in the law firm of McClure, Mclure and May. He had also had a very distinguished civic career, serving as a member of boards of trustees of institutions of higher learning and as chairman of the Mississippi oil and gas board. Always a very loyal alumnus of his university, he had also served as president of its alumni association and as a member of its committee on intercollegiate athletics.[27]

The first McClure memorial lecture was given in 1979 by Mississippi Supreme Court Chief Justice Neville Patterson, whose topic was "The Mississippi Judicial System: Some Observations on Its Past, Present and Future." Over the next fifteen years, the list of lecturers would include some of the nation's most outstanding legal scholars and also United States Supreme Court Justices Harry Blackmun, Sandra Day O'Connor, Antonin Scalia, and Clarence Thomas.[28]

For its 125th anniversary year, 1979–80, the law school had thirty faculty members, of whom four were "adjuncts," serving only on a part-time basis, and one was "visiting." Their number included sixteen professors, six associate professors, and seven assistant professors. Three women members were Assistant Professors Carolyn Ellis, a Yale J.D., and Karen Green and Mary Anne Connell, both alumni. Two "Distinguished Visiting Professors" invited to teach in the 1979 summer session were Professor William O. Morris, of the University of Virginia law school, and a class of 1966 alumnus of the law school who was destined to be its dean at the time of its sesquicentennial, Professor Samuel M. Davis of the University of Georgia law school. The "Visiting Distinguished Professor" for the summer of 1980 was another future dean, Professor Louis Westerfield, an African American member of the law faculty at Loyola University in New Orleans.[29]

In that anniversary year, 572 students enrolled for the fall semester, and 497 for the spring semester. The entering class of students in the 1979 summer and fall totaled 190, of whom 180 were Mississippi residents. Twenty-seven percent (51) were female, and 5 percent (19) were African American. The "resident" majority had to pay a tuition fee of $353.50 each semester, and nonresidents, $753.50. In addition they all had to pay, each semester, a school of law "professional fee" of $100 and a "law student body fee" of $8, which went to support the *Law Journal*, the speakers bureau, and the student body association. The per-semester residence hall rate for a room for two with air-conditioning and a telephone was $282.50 for men and $294 for women. For needy students there was, of course, "financial aid" from various public sources. Also by that time the law school had some twenty scholarship or loan funds available to deserving students from its various endowment funds.[30]

New students, on arrival, were given an orientation pamphlet that began with a greeting and a few introductory remarks from Dean Williams. Probably, he suggested, most of them believed that they had come to law school "to learn 'the law.'" But the faculty would have to disappoint them in that regard. For they "could not begin to teach you all the rules and principles of law" in just three years. Instead, they were "going to try to give them an understanding of what law is" is by teaching them "a number of rules and principles, and then showing you how they interact with other rules and principles in real life situations." Also, they would be studying "how law has developed through history" and all of the "forces, legal and extra-legal, that shape the law." By the time they were finished, they should have achieved "the ability to recognize problems or issues" and to "clearly express their thoughts about them." Also they should know "how to find the law and what to do with it when it is found." Finally, they were expected "to develop a sense of professionalism and a commitment to your profession."[31]

The pamphlet also contained a greeting from the student body president for the beginning academic year and information on the various student body organizations, the honor code, and such things as "hornbooks," "gilberts," and "skinnys."[32]

Most of the students, of course, were candidates for the J.D. degree; however a handful of them were enrolled in the "graduate program," still chaired by Doctor Stephen Gorove, working for either a Doctor of the Science of Law degree or one of the Masters degrees. In addition to the LL.M. and M.Comp. L., beginning in 1973 the law center also offered a Master of Marine Law and Science degree (M.M.L.&S.) through the sea grant legal program administered by the center's Mississippi Law Research Institute on the Gulf Coast at Ocean Springs.[33]

Law school publications, in addition to the *Mississippi Law Journal* and the *Space Law Journal,* included the *Graduate Record* and the *Law Center Newsletter.* The *Record,* containing biographical data and photographs of graduating seniors, was mailed each year by the law school's placement office, to approximately four thousand potential employers, including the members of the state bar, state and national government agencies, banks, and business corporations. The quarterly *Newsletter* was distributed to the law school's approximately thirty-five hundred alumni and some two hundred other law schools around the nation.[34]

The student-operated Phi Alpha Delta Legal Research Exchange was by that time providing a unique service to lawyers around the state. Twenty-four hours of research service in the law library, carried out by students with excellent academic credentials, was available to them on request. In the National Student Trial Advocacy Competition, sponsored by the Association of Trial Lawyers of America, the law school's team, consisting of Merle Bouchard and Samuel Keyes and coached by Professor Tom Mason, swept the 1979–80 southern regional tournament. And third-year law student Rogers Druhet won the 1980 John W. Davis Award for being "the outstanding Black male law student in the United States.[35]

Senator Eastland's papers had been placed in a permanent repository on the first floor of the annex to Farley Hall. And, in the law school's Eastland law library, a room adjoining the main reading room and open to visitors, was furnished with the desk and other furniture, along with numerous autographed photographs and other notable memorabilia that had been in the senator's office in the Dirksen Senate Office Building in Washington, D.C. The law library staff was now fully trained in the use of the new computerized shared cataloging system known as SOLINET and were busy teaching the law students, who assembled in small instruction groups, how to use the newly installed computerized legal research system known as LEXIS. Meanwhile, the faculty had their own "faculty library" up in room 544, which provided them with easy access to the federal reports and other basic research materials.[36]

In addition to the law school, the law center, now in its seventh year, though its organizational structure was slightly changed, still had three other operating branches. Its Criminal Justice Institute, directed by Professor N. S. Sweat Jr., used nearly half a million dollars in grants from the Law Enforcement Assistance Administration in Washington and a small amount of support from the state legislature to operate a "criminal law intern program" as well as the Mississippi Prosecutors College and the Mississippi Judicial College.[37]

The intern program, each year had placed some three dozen student interns in prosecutors' offices around the state, where, as authorized by a state statute and under the supervision of a prosecuting attorney, they conducted the prosecution of criminal cases. Recognized by the LEAA as a "model program," it had been much imitated by other law schools around the nation. The prosecutors college, in addition to providing training for the state's prosecutorial officials, produced every year a number of useful publications and statistical studies. Operated out of an office in Jackson, it relied primarily on the law center's faculty and their library in Oxford, to do a lot of much needed research. Meanwhile, the judicial college was busy compiling such useful publications as a manual of model jury instructions, a chancery clerk's handbook, a circuit judge's desk book, and an appeals procedure desk book.[38]

The Mississippi Law Research Institute carried out a number of both basic and specific research projects that were requested by members of the state legislature, various state government agencies, the state bar, and the state judiciary. During that year, they researched and drafted proposed legislation dealing with a personal property exemption in the state's bankruptcy laws, a new uniform fraudulent conveyance act, and a new uniform marketable record title act for the state. They also drafted and published a handbook of forms for criminal affidavits to be used by inferior court judges and clerks and began work on the development of a model code of municipal ordinances for the state's towns and cities. Its sea grant legal program, under the auspices of the Mississippi-Alabama Sea Grant Consortium, did research work with regard to the development of appropriate legal controls for the management of the coastal zone.[39] The now three-year old Institute of Continuing Legal Education meanwhile continued to offer, in collaboration with the state bar, a broad-ranging program of seminars and workshops for members of the bar.[40]

Five years later, in the 1984–85 academic year, there were twenty-seven full time faculty members in the law school, including three women, and also

Professor Louis Westerfield, an African American who had come to campus in 1980 as that year's "visiting distinguished professor," had returned as a visiting professor in 1983–84, and then became a full time regular member of the faculty. Professor Robert Khayat, after serving for seven years as the law school's associate dean, was now working in the Lyceum as the vice chancellor for university affairs, and the new associate dean was Professor Thomas R. Mason.[41]

The student enrollment, now that veterans of the war in Vietnam were no longer applying in large numbers to take advantage of their G.I. bill benefits by going to law school, was down nearly 20 percent. Only 144 new students enrolled for the fall 1984 semester, and the total enrollment was down to 483, of whom only seventy-six were from out of state. Twenty-nine percent of the total enrollment was made up of women, but only 4 percent were African Americans. There was also one female Asian student in the senior class. For the spring 1985 semester, the total student enrollment was 441, of whom 121 were senior class members.[42]

By 1984–85, though occasionally a graduate student from another program might enroll in a law school course, there were no longer any law school graduate students. The 1983 law school *Catalog*, under the heading "Admission to the Graduate Program," briefly noted that the program was "currently being revised" and that no applications for admission to it would be accepted that year. The *Catalogs* for the next few years contained the same statement, but the 1989 one finally made no mention of a graduate program. The LL.M., the M.Comp.L., the M.M.L.& S., and the J.S.D. degree programs no longer existed.[43]

Beginning in 1982, however, a new degree program was being offered for ordinary law students, the Juris Doctor/Master of Business Administration (J.D./M.B.A.) degree. Administered jointly by both the law school faculty and the faculty of the school of business administration, the new degree required 114 hours of course work done over three years (as compared to the ninety hours required for a J.D.) In addition, students wishing to enroll in it were required to take, prior to enrollment (if they had not already done so), the undergraduate courses in business that the business administration faculty required for admission to their graduate program.[44]

Apparently because a fairly good knowledge of the French language was necessary if one was going to take part in it, the summer study abroad program at the University of Dijon in the mid-1970s had been abandoned after a couple of years. But, in the summer of 1983, a new program was initiated in England, at

Cambridge University's Downing College, and, not just because there was no language problem involved with it, it very quickly became a great success.

The idea for a summer program in England originated with Dean Williams, who recruited a new young member of the law faculty to organize it. Professor Larry Bush, by 1974, had earned both a B.A. degree and a J.D. degree at the University of Florida, and then, except for the year 1978–79, during which he had taken off in order to go over to England and earn an LL.B. degree at Fitzwilliam College at Cambridge University, had spent the next seven years working as a lawyer for the Tennessee Valley Authority. Recruited into the law school faculty in 1981 as an associate professor, he was soon asked by Dean Williams to assist in developing a summer program in England, which he did with great enthusiasm. For obvious reasons, in looking for possible sites he focused on Cambridge and eventually arrived at a very satisfactory agreement with Professor John Hopkins of Downing College.[45]

The first group of students went over to Cambridge with professor Bush in 1982, and by 1984 the format for the summer sessions there was established pretty much as it would remain over the next two decades. The program was required to be self-supporting from the seven-hundred-dollar fees charged for enrollment in it and could not draw on law school funds except for a small amount to be used up front for advertising, which had to be reimbursed later. An additional £670 was charged each student by Downing College for room and board. The teaching was done by law school professors Bush, Mason, and Bell and also by four members of the Cambridge University law faculty. Only classes from the law school's elective curriculum were offered, none from the required curriculum. The classes began on the second Monday in July and ended on the second Tuesday in August, with final exams on the following Wednesday and Thursday. Each week, classes were only given Monday through Thursday. One Friday was taken up through the early afternoon with a bus trip to London to visit first the royal courts of justice in the Strand and the historic "Inn of Court" known as the Middle Temple. Otherwise, the students had Fridays through Sundays free, either for studying or for travel to other points of interest around the British Isles.[46]

In the second year that the program was offered, 1983, under the auspices of the institute of continuing legal education members of the state bar were invited to enroll in the session, for three weeks, as auditing graduate students. Though there was a great deal of interest shown in that idea, in the end, only seven bar members actually enrolled. So in 1984, that segment of the program was reduced to just two weeks, with special CLE classes being offered for the participants in it. From then on it became a regular, and very popular, part of the law school's "Cambridge Summer Program."[47]

Another interesting development in the early 1980s was the beginning of the publication, about halfway through each semester, of an independently published student news sheet called *The Solicitor*. Financed by advertisements from such major Oxford businesses as Neilson's Department Store, the Warehouse Restaurant, and Rainbow Cleaners, it had a lot of good news to report: There was available, at 1610 Van Buren Avenue just off the Square, a not-for-profit, law school student-body managed store selling used law textbooks. In the last week of February 1984, at the Annual Southern Regional Black Law Student Association Convention, a team representing the law school's BALSA chapter that had been coached by Professor Lou Westerfield, consisting of third-year students Mary Brown and Wanda Turner and second year students Bill Catledge and Veronica Anderson, had placed third in the moot court competition and so would compete in the national competition in St. Louis. Furthermore, Brown and Turner had won the trophy for the best petitioner's brief, and Turner had won the trophy for best oral advocate. In November 1984, it was reported that his law faculty colleagues had recommended Professor Westerfield for tenure, which meant that he would be the first African American faculty member to receive that honor. And the law student soccer team was having an undefeated season.[48]

Another important development in the autumn of 1984 was the transferring of the university's court reporting program into the law center. Founded in 1976, the program for its first eight years had been offered in the business school's department of business education and office administration. By 1984, the program had already graduated forty students, conferring upon them a bachelor of science degree with a major in court reporting (the only such degree offered anywhere in the United States). During its first year in the law center, eleven more completed the requirements for graduation, and its director, Mrs. Janice K. Bounds, was granted faculty tenure.[49]

That autumn too, for the first time, a panel of judges from the United States fifth circuit court of appeals, including class of June 1962 graduate E. Grady Jolly, visited the law school. In addition to conducting a docket of oral arguments in the moot court room, they participated in a number of other activities with both faculty and students and had such a good time that they tentatively agreed to visit again, at least every three years.[50]

Meanwhile, back in the spring of 1984, Chancellor Porter L. Fortune, troubled by ill-health, had announced that he would be retiring from office at the end of the academic year. Of the on-campus candidates that were suggested as his possible successor, Dean Parham Williams of the law center was generally considered the front-runner.[51] Ultimately, however, the board of trustees chose as the new chancellor a youthful Texan named R. Gerald Turner, who had been serving as a vice-president at the University of Oklahoma. Perhaps that had made things a little awkward for Dean Williams in 1984–85, but he had been dean of the law school and director of the law center for a decade and a half, and perhaps he just felt it was time for a change.

Back in 1924, both of Dean Williams's parents had been enrolled in the Cumberland School of Law in Lebanon, Tennessee, where they both graduated and soon qualified for admittance to the Mississippi bar. Now the Cumberland School was located in Birmingham, Alabama, as a division of Samford University and was building quite a reputation. In 1984, one of their national mock trial teams had won the national championship, and the American college of trial lawyers had awarded the school their Emil Gumpert award for excellence in the teaching of trial advocacy. But much more needed to be done to improve the academic record of the school and its faculty, their present dean suggested in a final report submitted shortly before his retirement in the spring of 1985.[52]

Meanwhile, one Saturday, early in December 1984, Samford University's President, Thomas E. Corts, accompanied their basketball team over to the University of Mississippi for a scheduled match in the Tad Smith Coliseum. Samford lost the match, but Corts did succeed, while in Oxford, in meeting with Parham Williams and in persuading him to apply to fill the soon-to-be-vacant Cumberland Law School deanship. And Williams was the candidate eventually picked to fill the position.[53]

During the 1984–85 academic year, the law faculty usually met in Room 508 of the Lamar Center building on the first Wednesday of each month. At an extraordinary meeting held there on March 20, 1985, however, Dean Williams, just back from a visit to Washington, D.C., reported first that funding for the proposed Jamie Whitten chair of law was proceeding favorably and that the creation of the chair should possible in just one more year. And then he announced to his amazed colleagues that he was going to be resigning from the deanship "immediately" in order to fill the same position at the Cumberland School. At another meeting held just one week later, however, it was explained that, in fact, he planned to resign from the deanship as of June 30 that year.[54]

On July 1, 1985, Professor Guthrie T. Abbott began serving as acting dean of the law school and, because finding a replacement for Parham Williams was not easy, held the office until the end of December 1986. There were plenty of candidates for the position; by the end of the fall 1985 semester, thirty-five persons had applied to fill it. But the members of the search committee, chaired by Professor Bill Champion and made up of five members of the law faculty, one other university faculty member, and two members of the state bar, in consultation with Chancellor Turner, were not able to agree on any one of them who was willing to accept the terms offered. In the spring 1986 semester therefore, a new search committee was appointed and went to work.[55]

The new dean that they eventually did hire was not unknown around the campus. Thomas A. Edmonds, after earning a B.A. degree at Mississippi College in 1962 and a LL.B. in 1965 at the Duke University law school, where, as a student, he had served on the editorial staff of their law journal, had practiced law for a year in Orlando, Florida, before returning to Mississippi, in 1966, to join Dean Josh Morse's law faculty. During the politically stormy 1968–69 academic year, however, he had retreated back to Duke as a visiting faculty member there. In 1970, he had followed Dean Morse to Florida State University, where he was promoted to a full professorship in 1974. For the 1975–76 academic year he had been a visiting faculty member at the McGeorge Law School at the University of the Pacific in Sacramento, California. And, in 1977, he had accepted the deanship of the T. C. Williams Law School at the University of Richmond, in Virginia.[56]

Edmond's term as dean at the University of Mississippi's law school, however, was destined to be brief. He was not able to hand over his responsibilities to a successor and leave Richmond until January 1987. Then, after just twenty-four months in his new position, he relinquished it, in January 1989, to accept the prestigious office of executive director of the state bar in Virginia.[57]

Meanwhile, however, during the five years that followed Dean Williams's sudden and unexpected departure, much that was good continued to happen in the law center. In July 1985, the ABA voted to continue its full accreditation of the of the law school, keeping it still the only one in the state that was both ABA-accredited and AALS-associated. In the dean's office, when Joan K. Murphey, after fifteen years of hard work and cheerfully dedicated service as both the administrative assistant to the dean and the law school registrar, retired in 1985, her duties were divided up. Constance E. Parham became the new registrar and a number of different persons were appointed as "assistant to the dean" with regard to a number of different programs. In 1986–87, Joyce M. Whittington was the first winner of the newly instituted "outstanding law school staff member award" for her contributions over the previous six years as the conference and publicity coordinator for the Mississippi Judicial College. Two years later, she would become the law school's new director of placement and scholarships.[58]

Among the faculty, acting Dean Abbott, in April 1986, was the winner of the university-wide "Teacher of the Year" Award. And at the end of that academic year Professor Lou Westerfield left to take up the deanship of the North Carolina Central University Law School in Durham. Alumnus Reuben Anderson, who in January 1985 had made history by being appointed the first-ever black member of the Mississippi Supreme Court, was one of six black Mississippians honored by the university with an Award of Distinction as part of its celebration of Black History Month in February 1986. Also in 1986, law school graduate Bobby Harges of Grenada, winner of that year's Phi Delta Phi Outstanding Student Award, at a banquet at the Sheraton Center in May of that year received the NAACP's John Warren Davis Award given each year to the nation's most outstanding black male law student.[59]

By 1986–87, three issues of the *Law Center News* were being published annually, in the fall, winter, and spring, and they had much good news to report. The first alumni "phon-a-thon," conducted in the spring of 1986, had brought in six thousand dollars, and the Lamar Order endowment by then had reached a total of $275,000. Oxford attorneys Jack Dunbar and his wife Wylene (a sometime philosophy professor in the university), in 1986, endowed a second annual lecture series to focus on the theme of "law and philosophy." And that same year, the Jackson law firm of Young, Scanlon and Sessums endowed a Legal Writing Award for law students. Meanwhile the drive begun in 1985 to raise money for funding a chair of law in honor of Congressman Jamie L. Whitten, the 1931 law school alumnus who had been representing north Mississippi in the House of Representatives in Washington, D.C., for more than forty years, was making steady progress.[60]

The law school's summer program in England, run by Professor Larry Bush at Downing College, Cambridge, received full accreditation from the American

Bar Association in 1986. Dean Edmonds, while serving as dean at the University of Richmond, had started up a similar program at another college in Cambridge, and he gave full support to and had some exciting new ideas for the Downing program, which was attracting more applicants (including some from Canada) each year than it had room for.[61]

Just two years later, in the spring of 1988, applications for admission to the Cambridge program were pouring in from all over North America. Harvard Law Professor Archibald Cox, who had served as solicitor general of the United States from 1961 to 1965 and as a Watergate special prosecutor in 1973, returned to the campus where he had been a visiting distinguished professor in 1968 to speak on behalf of the Common Cause movement for which he was now the national chairman. Law school alumnus Leonard B. Melvin Jr. of Laurel made an initial gift of twenty thousand dollars to create an endowment fund that would underwrite and upgrade a professorship on the law faculty. Things were certainly looking good.[62]

But, in the middle of the night of April 2 (Easter Eve), 1988, a terrible fire broke out in the central area of the fifth floor of the law center building. Its point of origin was the small kitchenette adjoining the faculty lounge (Room 508), which was reduced to a small heap of blackened rubble. The lounge itself was ruined. The faculty library next door, in Room 544, was damaged slightly, and most of the faculty offices and other rooms on the fifth floor suffered serious smoke and water damage. "Repair work [is] expected to continue for at least six months," Dean Edmonds reported to Chancellor Turner a few weeks later.[63]

In fact, the fall 1988 *Law Center News* reported that the job of putting everything back right would "soon be completed." The faculty and staff would be "moving back to their offices and everything should soon return to normal." "It will be wonderful," Dean Edmonds was reported as saying, "to have our offices and seminar rooms on the fifth floor back in service." Certainly, it would "make it much easier to conduct our program in an effective and efficient manner."

Things generally were going well again for the law school in the autumn of 1988. The McClure lecturer that semester was Sandra Day O'Connor, the first woman member of the United States Supreme Court. A new member of the faculty was Assistant Professor Katherine M. Gorove, daughter of Professor Emeritus Stephen Gorove, thus creating the first, to-date, father/daughter team on the law school faculty. In a message to "alumni and friends" published in the fall 1988 issue of the *Law Center News*, Dean Edmonds reported that state support for the law school was now better than it had ever been; the law alumni chapter was doing a great job of fund raising and the Lamar Order endowment was now very close to three hundred thousand dollars.[64]

It is not surprising, therefore, that the same issue of the *News* also carried a report that the southeastern chapter of the American Association of Law Schools, at their recent annual meeting in Louisville, Kentucky, had chosen Dean Edmonds as their president-elect. That meant that at their next meeting, scheduled to be held in Biloxi, he would have automatically become their next president. But, because of his resignation and return to Virginia in January 1989 to serve for the next decade and a half as the executive director of the Virginia state bar, that did not happen. Meanwhile, Associate Dean Larry Bush had become the acting dean of the law school and, with the assistance of the new associate dean, Tom Mason, would be responsible for managing it and the law center for the next year and a half.[65]

A major highlight of the spring 1989 semester, and the first major event of Larry Bush's career as acting dean, was a national symposium on "The Civil Rights Movement and the Law," held on campus March 31–April 2, sponsored jointly by both the law center and the university's Center for the Study of Southern Culture. Some university officials had been a little reluctant to schedule such a symposium, fearing that it might stir up some adverse publicity— particularly after Richard Barrett, a noted racist agitator, threatened to come to campus and demonstrate against it. But it went ahead as planned and was a great success.[66]

Including as its participants Judge Charles Clark, a law school alumnus who was chief judge of the federal fifth circuit court of appeals; Judge Elbert P. Tuttle, senior judge of the federal eleventh circuit court of appeals and a former chief judge of the fifth circuit; Judge Minor Wisdom, senior judge of the federal fifth circuit court; and Constance Baker Motley, James Meredith's counsel in his court suit to gain admittance to the university twenty-seven years earlier and now senior judge on the federal district court for the southern district of New York, "the symposium attracted a national audience who were given the rare opportunity to hear landmark cases discussed by those who were there when the cases passed through the courts, thus providing unique perspectives and insights." It was also broadcast nationally on the C-SPAN cable satellite television network.[67]

That summer of 1989, Aaron Condon retired from the law faculty after twenty-three years of service. Robert Khayat, who for the past four years had been based in the Lyceum, serving as the vice chancellor for university affairs and raising nearly sixty-two million dollars for the "Campaign for Ole Miss," moved to Mission, Kansas, where he began serving as the executive director of the National Collegiate Athletic Association Foundation. However, in the fall of 1989 four new members were added to the permanent faculty. The newcomers were Associate Professor Bryn R. Vaaler (J.D., University of Minnesota), and Assistant Professors William A. Edmundson (J.D., Duke University), Timothy L. Hall (J.D., University of Houston), and Gary Myerson (J.D., Duke University). The faculty now totaled twenty-two full-time professors, four adjunct professors, and one visiting professor.[68]

More faculty were needed because the student enrollment, after being in the four hundreds through most of the 1980s, was now (in tune with a national trend that was perhaps partly due to the fact that several high-audience TV shows were now featuring lawyers as hero figures) increasing notably. The law school had received 921 applications for admission in the 1989 entering class, of whom 442 had been accepted and 226 had enrolled. The entering class was made up of 149 residents and 77 nonresidents: 161 males and 65 females; 209 whites, 15 blacks, and 2 members of other ethnic minorities. The total enrollment for the fall 1989 semester was 563, for the spring 1990 semester 515, and for the 1990 summer session 216. During the year, a total of 179 J.D. degrees were awarded. Student organizations active in the law school were the Law Student Body Association, the Black Law Students Association, the Lamar Society of International Law, the Law Wives, the Christian Legal Fellowship, the Honor Council, and Phi Alpha Delta, Phi Delta Phi, and Delta Theta Pi fraternities.[69]

The fees charged to a full-time in-state student for each semester of 1989–90 included a tuition fee of $810, a student activity fee of $183.50, a "professional" fee of $150, and a law student body fee of $11. An out-of-state student had to pay an additional nonresident fee of $591. The residence hall rent for a shared room (with one other occupant) was $632, or single rooms were available (for law students or graduate students) in Guess Hall (the east wing for women, the north wing for men). Happily though, some sixty endowed scholarships, each bringing in a sum of around two hundred thousand dollars now existed to help law students who either had a good academic record and/or were from a particular geographical area of the state.[70]

The Department of Court Reporting turned out fourteen more graduates in 1989–90, and during the year Department Chair Janice K. Bounds served on the National Shorthand Reporters Association's standards revision task force.[71]

In the Eastland law library, this was the year that the old-fashioned card catalog system was replaced by an electronic online cataloging system, and each volume on every shelf was painstakingly provided with a barcode strip which would make both shelf-reading and the checking in and out of books much easier in the future. The librarians were also very happy to see the work needed to complete the second floor portion of the library brought close to completion. When it was ready, the library would meet the student-seating standards required by the ABA and also have much more room for housing its collection. The funding available for acquisitions, however once again was some two hundred thousand dollars short of what was needed. The online legal research services were costing more every year, and because it seemed very likely that journal subscriptions might soon have to be canceled, faculty were being asked to give some consideration as to which titles should go first.[72]

The law center's court education program, funded annually by the state legislature, and directed by Krista R. Johns, was now running both the continuing legal education program and also the Mississippi judicial college. Now in its twentieth year of operation, the college in the 1989–90 academic year conducted thirty-three training programs for state court personnel, including in-depth training for new trial judges, new justice court judges, and new mayor/judges. Its publications included a *Handbook of Legal Terminology*, a manual called *The Uniform Rules of Circuit and County Court Practice*, and the *Guide to Mississippi Youth Court* as well as others.[73]

The center's Mississippi Law Research Institute, which had evolved out of the LIARD program established back in October 1964, had been given its final organizational structure by a state statute in 1983 and was generously provided for out of state funds. Under its director William Hooper, it also accomplished a great deal that year. One of its staff attorneys, Richard L. Carlisle, had researched and drafted a unified theft law (aimed at replacing the numerous current ones that dealt with many different kinds of thievery) for consideration by the state legislature in its 1991 session. Albert L. Sage III had updated the institute's 1978 report on *An Analysis of the Law of Separation of Powers Applicable to the Government of Higher Education*. And the Sea Grant Legal Program, under the direction of Richard J. McLaughlin, had published studies concerning seafood inspection and quality insurance and the impact of the petroleum industry on gulf coast tidelands as well as publishing a *Guide to Laws and Regulations Governing Hard Mineral Mining on the Continental Shelf.*[74]

One major highlight of the fall 1989 semester was the unveiling of a bronze plaque that was to be placed on the south wall just inside the main second-floor entrance to the law center, honoring Congressman Jamie Whitten and celebrating the one-million-dollar endowment of the new Whitten Chair of Law and Government. The ceremony took place on "public officials day," observed every year on a Saturday in October. Present for it, besides Chancellor Turner, Acting Dean Bush, various local dignitaries, and, of course, Congressman Whitten himself, was law school alumnus (LL.B., 1949) and former governor (1980–84) William Winter, who as the first holder of the chair taught a class on "Law and Public Policy."[75]

During that same fall semester, a search committee chaired by Professor Guthrie T. Abbot was busy conducting a nationwide search for a new dean for the law school. On December 6, 1989, they began reviewing the numerous applications that had come in for the position. Early in the new year, the position was offered to, and, on February 6, accepted by David E. Shipley.[76]

Shipley had earned a B.A. in 1972, at Oberlin College in Ohio, and a J.D., in 1975, at the University of Chicago Law School, where he had served as executive editor of the law journal. After being admitted to the bar in Rhode Island that same year, he had worked for two years in a law office in Providence before joining the University of South Carolina law faculty as an assistant professor in 1977. His areas of academic specialization were copyright, intellectual property, civil procedure, administrative law, legal and equitable remedies, and domestic relations. After being promoted to associate professor at South Carolina in 1981, he had been on leave as a visiting associate professor of law at William and Mary for the 1983–84 academic year. And, after being promoted to a full professorship in 1985, he had been away again, in 1986–87, as a visiting professor at Ohio State University. Then, back at South Carolina, he had served as the associate dean there for 1989–90 and been proclaimed the school's "Professor of the Year."[77]

So the new dean who took over control of the law center on July 1, 1990, had been around and had also had some administrative experience. Two other new members of the faculty who began teaching that year were Bobby M. Harges and Donna Adler. Harges, the 1986 alumnus who had won the award that year for the nation's most outstanding black male law student, had practiced law in

New Orleans for three years, "to build on what I had learned in the classroom." Recruited as a faculty member in 1989, he had taken a leave of absence that first year in order to complete work on an LL.M. at the Harvard Law School. Now he was back on campus, teaching torts, and would stay on the faculty for three years before returning to New Orleans to join the Loyola University law faculty. Adler, a total newcomer, was a graduate of both Harvard University and the Boston College Law School who, while working on an LL.M. at the University of Florida Law School, had been recruited to fill a temporary vacancy on the faculty there. In spite of her very different background, she said she found living on Oxford, Mississippi, "very easy" and, for relaxation, she liked to read the local history.[78]

On December 13, 1990, the new dean and both the old and the new members of the law faculty met and adopted a formal statement with regard to their Mission, which said:

> The primary mission of the school of law is to provide high quality legal education that prepares graduates for the practice of law in the United States, for entry into governmental and public service, or for any other endeavor in which legal education is necessary or helpful background.
>
> The Law School believes that lawyering skills, legal ethics, and professionalism must be emphasized throughout the curriculum. Because this is a state-assisted school, some courses use Mississippi precedent as a basis for exploring the subject matter. Recognizing that the teaching mission cannot be fulfilled without an intellectually strong program, the School of Law adheres to a continuous commitment to scholarly research and writing. In addition, the school undertakes to provide, as appropriate, services to the Bar, to the judiciary, to state, federal, and international agencies, to academic organizations, and to the public.[79]

In 1991, three members of the law school faculty came very close to setting a national record for a law school of any size by being awarded Fulbright scholarships for the next academic year. Associate Professor Larry S. Bush was awarded one that would enable him to spend the 1991–92 academic year in the Romanian province of Transylvania, where they were just beginning to throw off the burdensome restrictions of communism, teaching labor law at the University of Cluj-Napoca. Assistant Professor Katherine Gorove was going to be lecturing that same year on international trade at the university in Budapest, where a similar transformation was taking place (and where her father had been a student several decades earlier). And adjunct Professor Richard McLaughlin, director of the Sea Grant program in the Law Research Institute, was going to spend six months at Nihon University in Tokyo, Japan, discussing with experts there possible types of private industry and government cooperation in carrying out oceanic research programs.[80]

The most prestigious faculty position now was, of course, the Whitten chair, held for one semester each year by a distinguished visiting member of the state bar who lectured on his particular field of expertise. During the fall 1990 semester, the chair was held by Jackson attorney Joe Daniel, the class of 1940 law school alumnus who was now the senior partner in the prestigious law firm of Daniel, Coker, Horton and Bell. Teaching a course in trial practice, he gave the students "instruction and practical experience information related to the skills and techniques of modern courtroom litigation." During the spring 1992 semester, the chair was held by former law school faculty member and sometime associate dean Joel Blass, Named a fellow in the American College of Trial Lawyers in 1965, winner of the university's 1969 outstanding teacher award, and a judge on the state supreme court from 1989 to 1990, Blass, now a partner in the prestigious Gulfport firm of Mize, Blass, Lenoir and Laird, lectured on admiralty law. In the spring of 1993, the chair holder was another alumnus, Charles Clark, class of 1948, who had practiced law in Jackson before being appointed by President Nixon to serve on the U.S. court of appeals for the fifth circuit in 1969. From 1989 until his retirement in 1991, Clark also had served as chair of the federal judicial conference's executive committee. His topic, very appropriately, was appellate law.[81]

An efficient and hardworking staff, meanwhile, remained a core requirement for the efficient management of the law center and for its success in carrying out both its educational and its service functions. The law school student body awarded its outstanding staff member award for 1990–91 to Connie Parham. After earning a B.A. degree at (very appropriately) Lamar University, in Beaumont, Texas, and a masters degree (again very appropriately) in public administration at the University of Mississippi, Parham had joined the law center staff in 1977. After working first with the law student intern program and then with the court education program, in 1984 she was appointed to serve as the registrar for the law school, a position she now, twenty years later, continues to fill very efficiently.[82]

Law Librarian J. Wesley Cochran, after six years of service that had included providing the Eastland law library with its first electronic catalog, and also installing in it the very important and helpful LEXIS and SOLINET electronic legal research aids, left, in 1991, to become the law librarian at Texas Tech University in Lubbock, Texas. He was succeeded as law librarian by Herbert Cihak, who had been serving as the reference librarian since 1988. Cihak, who had earned the B.A., M.A., and M.L.S. degrees at Brigham Young University in Utah and a J.D. degree at the University of Nebraska, had previously served on the staffs of law libraries in San Bernardino, California, and Dallas, Texas. So he was very well qualified to assume the top position, and the library continued to be in very good hands.[83]

One project that Librarian Cihak became very closely identified with was the new legal writing program that was instituted in the fall 1991 semester. The program's director, Greenville native Sylvia Robertshaw, after graduating from the University of the South with top honors had earned a J.D. at Tulane. After practicing law briefly in her family's Greenville law firm and then serving for a while as a staff attorney for the federal Fifth Circuit Court of Appeals in new Orleans, she had been asked to conduct a judicial writing workshop for Mississippi judges and then started to teach legal writing to members of the Mississippi bar in the CLE program. Her assistant, Lois Le Seur, after graduating with top honors from Florida State had gone on to earn both an M.A. in philosophy and a J.D. from Duke. Then she had clerked for a Florida judge and worked as a staff attorney for the Federal Eleventh Circuit in Atlanta before coming to Oxford to practice with Holcomb, Dunbar, Connell, Chaffin and Willard. Now the writing program, under the direction of these two young women, was being separated out from the center's legal research program and made, instead, an integral, and very important, part of the regular law school curriculum. Its launching was much assisted by a visiting session, held in mid-November, to the law center's moot court room by another panel of three judges from the federal fifth circuit court. Judges Edith Jones, of Houston, Texas; Judge Emilio Garza, of San Antonio, Texas; and law school alumnus Judge E. Grady Jolly, of Jackson on this occasion, not only gave the students an opportunity to attend and hear an oral argument but also later met with them informally to discuss and evaluate the arguments that had been made in the court session.[84]

In January 1992, Professor Debbie Bell initiated a new Housing Law Clinic. The fifteen students enrolled in it earned three hours of graded credit by attending one hour of classroom instruction and doing ten hours of clinical work each week, including supervised representation of indigent clients in Justice Court and developing drafting, interviewing, and negotiation skills. By the fall of 1992, Professor Bell was being assisted by "Staff Attorney for the Legal Housing Clinic" Acting Assistant Professor Judith E. Koons, a University of Florida College of Law graduate, who had, in recent years, acted as a trainer for Florida Legal Services, running workshops on federal litigation, trial advocacy, substandard housing, and general legal research and writing.[85]

By the early 1990s, however, a lean state budget was translating into very hard times for the law center. Faculty salaries were lagging more than 20 percent below the average for law schools in the south. Maintaining an adequate collection size and a sufficient equipment budget for the library was very difficult.[86] In spite of all that, however, the law center was managing to do what it had to with what it had. An ABA and AALS team that conducted the required sabbatical inspection of the law school in April 1991 gave it a favorable report; some of the team members were "very complimentary" with regard to its level of teaching and scholarship. An impressive total of 92.7 percent of the Class of 1991 passed the July 1991 state bar exam, compared to an overall passage rate of 88.1 percent. In the spring of 1992, *U.S. News & World Report* published a ranking of the 175 ABA-accredited law schools in which the University of Mississippi's made it into the second quartile together with many much wealthier institutions.[87]

The reason the law school was doing as well as it was, Dean Shipley noted in his "Message" to the 1992 spring/summer issue of the *Law Center News*, was "because of the private support it receive[d] from friends and alumni." Besides the Whitten endowment, the endowments from the McClures and the Dunbars were bringing distinguished lecturers to the campus. Four outstanding members of the law faculty were now earning better than average salaries because their positions benefited from outside endowment funds. Guthrie T. Abbott, J.D. (Mississippi), was now the Butler, Snow, O'Mara, Stevens and Cannada Lecturer and Professor of Law. Richard L. Barnes, J.D. (Arizona) and LL.M. (Northwestern), was the Leonard B. Melvin Lecturer and Professor of Law. And Michael H. Hoffheimer, J.D. (Michigan) and Ph.D. (Chicago) and Ronald J. Rychlak, J.D. (Vanderbilt), were both Mitchell, McNutt, Threadgill, Smith and Sams Lecturers and associate professors of law.[88]

By the summer of 1992, the Lamar Order had a membership of 446, including eighteen affiliate members and seven sustaining members. Its assets totaled around $866,000 and, it was hoped, would reach the one million dollar fig-ure in less than another five years. Also helping in a big way were the 240 or so members of the "Centurial Club," a group of the law school alumni and friends, each of whom had pledged to donate at least one hundred dollars annu-ally to help meet its needs and the Law Alumni Chapter generally. Two phon-a-thons targeting alumni—one, in the fall of 1991, conducted by student mem-bers of the *Law Journal* staff and the moot court board, and one in the spring of 1992, conducted by members of various student groups such as the Black Law Students Association, the Lamar Society, and Phi Delta Phi fraternity brought in a total of just under $54,000. In addition to upgrading faculty salaries, sub-sidizing faculty research and publication projects, funding student scholarships, strengthening the law library's collection holdings and subscription list, and meeting the maintenance costs of the law center building, some of the money raised was also used to underwrite both the *Law Journal*'s and the moot court program's running expenses.[89]

So, by the fall 1992 semester, things in the law center were looking pretty good. The 1992 graduates had achieved the best passage rate in the February and July state bar examinations. With Robert Khayat back after three years working with the NCAA Foundation in Kansas City and again teaching torts, local government law, and general practice and with class of 1986 alumnus Larry Pittman, after practicing for several years in Detroit and then earning an LL.M. from Harvard now on the faculty teaching pretrial practice, law and medicine, and torts and civil procedure, the faculty was just about at full strength and flourishing. All of that being the case, Dean Shipley noted in his message "From the Dean's Office" in the fall 1992 issue of the *Law Center News,* having a staff that was "dedicated and hardworking," and alumni and friends that were both "loyal and generous," it seemed everyone should soon expect to see "an even stronger law school."[90]

When the time for his spring 1993 "Message" came, however, Dean Shipley, although continuing to be "confident" that the University of Mississippi's law school could meet all of the challenges still facing it "and still become an even stronger institution," announced that he was now preparing to leave it to face fresh challenges elsewhere. As of July 1, 1993, he was to begin serving as dean of the law school at the University of Kentucky.[91]

The acting dean of the law school of the University of Mississippi for the 1993–94 academic year was Professor Carolyn Ellis Staton. To her goes the credit for finally having the two circular "conversation pits" that, when the law center building was first built, had been sunk several feet down below floor level in the big open central area of the first floor filled in. Intended to be a trendy example of the fashionably informal modern life style, they, in fact, were recognized almost immediately as having a dangerously high accident potential. The fall of 1993 also was the one that saw the beginning of "institutionalized law school tailgate parties" in the Grove on football game Saturdays. Law school alumni soon learned to look for the big blue tent where they would find a lot of old friends and hospitality.[92]

The year 1993 was the one-hundredth anniversary of the death of the eponymous and undoubtedly single greatest figure in the history of the law center, L. Q. C. Lamar. Early that fall, Lamar biographer Daniel John Meador of the University of Virginia Law School came to the campus to deliver a lecture on the great man's life and career to a large audience of students, faculty, and visitors. Among the visitors were a great, great, great granddaughter; a great, great granddaughter; and a grandson of the law center's great lawyer, scholar, and statesman. Both the historian and the descendants marked the occasion by presenting some Lamar materials to the law library. Acting Dean Staton expressed the hope that other descendants of famous alumni would consider doing the same.[93]

Very appropriately, in the same year that the law center was being administered by its first woman dean, the Whitten chair was filled by its most distinguished female alumnus. In the spring 1994 semester, former Lieutenant Governor Evelyn Gandy (1976–80) taught a course on legislation. That fall, on September 24, the McClure lecture was given by the highly controversial United States Supreme Court Justice, Antonin Scalia, who told his audience: "It is wrong to approach the Constitution as a cure for everything." In the spring semester, the Dunbar lecture in philosophy and law was given by Joel Feinberg, the Regents Professor of Philosophy and Law at the University of Arizona, who, as part of the "Law Weekend" schedule (March 25–26) spoke on "Instigating the Unpredisposed: Bad Luck in Law and Life."[94]

Another major event of that 1994 Law Weekend was a panel discussion held in the Farley Hall auditorium (the old moot court room) by five law school alumni who had gone on to fill at least one of the two highest offices in Mississippi's state government. The participants were Governors William L. Waller (J.D. 1950, 1972–76), William F. Winter (J.D. 1949, 1980–84), and William A. Allain (J.D. 1950, 1984–88), and Lieutenant Governors Evelyn E. Gandy (J.D. 1943,

1976–80) and Brad Dye (J.D. 1954, 1980–92). Their discussion topic was "Can Government Work in the '90's?" and their general conclusion was that it could, though there was plenty of room for improvement in nearly every aspect of it.[95]

Meanwhile, since back in the fall semester, a fourteen-member search committee chaired by Professor "Guff" Abbott had been busy finding a new dean for the law school. The choice they finally made was a somewhat controversial one. By early in the spring 1994 semester, the two finalists for the position were one in-house candidate, Professor Robert Khayat, and one outside candidate, Louis Westerfield, the African American dean of the Loyola University law school in New Orleans. By a very narrow margin, Westerfield was the one finally selected to fill it. Although Khayat had much support among the alumni nationwide and was generally favored by the older members of the law school faculty, he did not get the favorable vote from a majority of the law faculty that ABA accreditation standards required. Probably for a combination of reasons, more than half of the faculty found it hard to think of him as a real colleague and an academic leader for the times ahead. He had been out of the law school for most of the previous decade, serving as a vice chancellor in the Lyceum, from 1984 to 1989, and then in Kansas City for three years heading up the NCAA Foundation. And certainly Dean Westerfield was well qualified for the position. As the holder of not only a J.D. degree from Loyola but also an LL.M. from the Columbia University Law School, he was qualified academically. Also, he had experience as an academic administrator, having served as dean of two accredited law schools: Loyola and North Carolina Central University. He was well known to many of the law center faculty and staff, having been a visiting distinguished professor in the law school for the summer of 1980, a full-time and tenured member of the faculty from 1983 to 1986, and then back as a visiting professor in the summer of 1990.[96]

Doubtless, another important factor leading to Westerfield's appointment was that, as the first African American in the university's long history to become dean of any one of its now seven schools, his appointment gave a strong signal to the outside world that, some thirty years after the Meredith riot and the subsequent expulsion of Cleve McDowell, the University of Mississippi was now a very different place. Westerfield accepted the position, and took up office on July 1, 1994.[97]

CHAPTER 7

THE SESQUICENTENNIAL DECADE
(1994–2004)

Although Robert Khayat did not become the dean of the school of law in 1994, one of the highlights of the Law Weekend on campus March 25–26 that year was the presentation to him, by the law alumni and the student body, of the "Outstanding Professor" award. He was already, by then, the university's vice chancellor for university affairs and that same year was appointed executive director of its upcoming sesquicentennial commemoration. A little over a year later, in June 1995, Khayat would take office as the university's new chancellor and inaugurate his campaign to secure its recognition as one of the nation's "great public universities."[1]

Acting Dean Carolyn Ellis Staton, in the spring of 1994, had been appointed by the government in Washington, D.C., headed up by her Yale law school classmate and good friend Bill Clinton, to serve for three years as a member of "DOCWITS" (the Defense Advisory Commission on Women in the Services), the Defense Department's civilian advisory group charged with enhancing the status of women in the armed services. In the autumn of 1994, she moved into another administrative position on campus, that of associate vice chancellor for academic affairs. In 1997 she was appointed associate provost, and in 1999 she was promoted to provost, thus becoming second only to Chancellor Khayat in the administrative hierarchy of the university.[2]

In the law school, meanwhile, the appointment of the university's first African American dean, Louis Westerfield, was seen by many as ushering in "A New Day At Ole Miss." As an article with that title in the August 1995 issue of *Ebony* magazine told its readers, Dean Westerfield, the grandson of Mississippi sharecroppers, had grown up in a New Orleans slum and might well have embarked on a career as a law breaker rather than becoming the law teacher that he did, and, ultimately, dean, first of the Loyola University law school and then of the law school at the University of Mississippi.[3]

In addition to Dean Westerfield, the twenty-three member, full-time law faculty for 1995–95 included two other African Americans, Associate Professor Robert N. Davis and Assistant Professor Larry J. Pittman, as well as A. C. Wharton, was by then an adjunct professor. The faculty also included four women: Assistant Professor Donna D. Adler, Professor Deborah H. Bell, Professor Karen O. Green, and Associate Professor Barbara Y. Phillips.[4]

The student enrollment in the law school had stabilized at approximately five hundred. The 1994–95 entering class numbered 177, of whom twenty-eight were nonresidents, fifty-eight were females, and seventeen were African Americans. It also included one Asian, four Native Americans, and one Hispanic. Over the course of the year, the J.D. degree was awarded to 181 graduating seniors. Enrollment in the court reporting program continued at approximately thirty, and eleven of its seniors earned the Bachelor of Court Reporting degree.[5]

In 1995, one edition of the *Visions* magazine, published as part of the build-up to the university's sesquicentennial celebration in 1998, was devoted to coverage of "The University of Mississippi School of Law." Co-edited by Elaine Pugh and Barbara Lago of the university's public relations department and funded by both the law alumni chapter and the Lamar Order, in addition to generally describing and discussing the J.D. degree program, it included articles on the *Law Journal,* the moot court program, the new housing law clinic organized and directed by Professor Deborah Bell, the undergraduate court reporting program, the relationship of the law school to the state bar, and on the Mississippi Law Research Institute.

A final article, written by Nancy Crutcher, briefly described the history of the law school from the time of Professor Stearns down to the time of Dean Westerfield. The article ended by noting proudly that, 190 years after its founding, the law school could boast "an enrollment of 504, a distinguished faculty of 28 legal scholars, and a law library comprised of more than 260,000 volumes or volume equivalents. There are 11 endowed lectures or chairs that bring outstanding legal scholars to campus to share their views of the law. More than 65 scholarships help deserving students complete their legal education. Continuing legal education offered by the Center keeps lawyers up-to-date on rapidly changing aspects of the law. Provocative legal lectures open the arena for discussion among legal students as well as legal observers." Not that there was not more to be done, Dean Westerfield was quoted, finally, as remarking. Areas for further enhancement that he had particularly in mind included "developing alumni involvement, increasing diversity, improving the library, and obtaining a chapter of the Order of the Coif, the most prestigious national honor society in legal education."[6]

The publication of *Visions* magazine apparently caused the members of the law center faculty, student body, and staff to want a magazine of their own on a permanent basis. In the spring 1996 semester, volume 1, number 1 of the *Law Center Magazine* was published. Edited again by Elaine Pugh and funded by both the law alumni chapter and the Lamar Order, its focus was on the topic of "Women in Law." A second edition, focusing on the "Pursuit of the Order of the Coif," was published, without a volume number or date, in the spring of 1998. Meanwhile, although the final edition of the law student newspaper, the *Solicitor,* had been, apparently, the one published in the spring of 1992, the *Law Center News* continued to be published, in a glossy newspaper format, once each semester, through the fall 1998 semester. Beginning in the spring 1999 semester, however, the *News* began to be published, once each semester, in a magazine format, until 2002, when it was replaced by the *UM Lawyer,* which is now published twice a year.

News items reported in the 1995–96 academic year included the delivery of the McLure Memorial Lecture by United States Supreme Court Justice Clarence Thomas, the fact that the seventh holder of the Whitten Chair of Law and Government was alumnus Reuben Anderson, and that alumnus Myres S. McDougal, the longtime Sterling Professor of Law at Yale University, had accepted a lifetime achievement award from the law school.[7]

In the law library that year, the new director, Mary Brandt Jensen, oversaw the accessing of several new online services, including RLN, First Search, and CARL/Uncover, which greatly expanded the range of information available to its users. Also, by loading three years of opinions from the northern district of Mississippi federal district court up onto its Web site, the library became the first in the nation to display federal district court opinions. Another very important development was the linking of the law library's Web site to that of the university's main library, which made it accessible not only all over campus but also, worldwide, on the Internet.[8]

The law school's Bachelor of Court Reporting degree was still, in 1995–96, the only one of its kind in the nation. In September 1995, it received a certificate of approval from the Board of Approved Student Education. Its department chair, Janice Bounds, was then a member of the teacher certification committee of the National Court Reporters Association, which that year announced that sometime within the next ten years a university degree would be required of all candidates for the Registered Professional Reporter (R.P.R.) examination.[9]

Meanwhile, the law center's Mississippi Law Research Institute, which had now been part of its program for nearly a quarter of a century, was continuing the vital task of serving as the state's official law revision, research, and reform agency. Its staff of six lawyers, three secretaries, and several law student research associates was working very hard at its task of providing the legislature, state agencies, and local government units with valuable information regarding numerous complex matters of law, such as juvenile justice reform, election laws, lobbying laws, ocean and coastal law matters, and law enforcement. And the center's seven-member Judicial College during 1995–96, in addition to conducting forty training programs for Mississippi court personnel had hosted a conference of judges from both Louisiana and Mississippi, at Vicksburg on August 17–19, 1995, on the topic of "Challenges for the Courts," as well as continuing to publish its quarterly newsletter and a "much needed and requested" updated version of their *Guide to Mississippi Limitations of Actions*.[10]

On Saturday, August 23, 1996, however, tragic news came from Louisiana. Dean Westerfield, while visiting his sister at her home in New Orleans, had suffered a sudden, fatal attack of cardiac arrhythmia. At 5:00 A.M. the next morning, a bus left the law center carrying members of both the faculty and staff to attend his funeral.[11] A few days later, Professor William M. Champion, who had been named the law school's "teacher of the year" for 1995–96, was appointed its acting dean. And, soon a search committee was formed and was looking for a new dean.[12]

By the spring of 1997, that committee had discovered and recruited one who would serve as the law school's chief administrator through its sesquicentennial year. After undergoing a twelve-year period during which it had been administered successively by four different acting deans and three different deans, at last the school and the law center associated with it were going to enjoy a long-time period of administrative continuity under the same dean, Samuel Marion Davis.

A native of Pascagoula, Sam Davis had first come to the law school as a new student in 1966, after earning a bachelor of arts degree in political science and history from the University of Southern Mississippi. During his senior year he served as editor-in-chief of the *Law Journal* and then graduated with honors in May 1969. After spending the 1969–70 academic year at the University of Virginia School of Law as a Dupont Fellow and earning an LL.M. degree there, he had joined the law faculty at the University of Georgia and by 1994 was both their Allen Post professor and a vice-president for academic affairs. A longtime member of the Lamar Order, in the summer of 1979 he had returned to the Lamar Center as a visiting summer school professor. Now, Dean Davis announced that he was "very excited" about what he saw as "a marvelous opportunity to come home to Mississippi and make a difference—to take a good law school and help make it an excellent law school."[13]

By the time the new dean was getting settled in on campus in that summer of 1997, the university was already busily gearing up a major campus-wide public relations campaign in preparation for the celebration of its upcoming sesquicentennial year of 1998–99. The law center already had much that it could boast about. In the spring of 1997, its twenty-seven-year-old Mississippi Judicial College had become the new home location of the American Academy of Judicial Education. Its arrival on campus, Chancellor Khayat commented, was "indeed a momentous occasion. . . . The Academy has for 25 years been in the forefront of providing education for judges throughout this nation as well as those from other countries. We welcome its associates to our campus and look forward to a long and mutually beneficial relationship."[14]

Also that year the law center's Butler, Snow, O'Mara, Stevens and Cannada lecturer in law, Professor Guthrie T. Abbott, succeeded 1967 alumnus Reuben Anderson as president-elect of the Mississippi State Bar. And its 1977 alumnus, University Attorney Mary Ann Connell, became vice-president of the National Association of College and University Attorneys, the non-profit educational organization of some three thousand college and university attorneys in the United States and Canada, and would become its president for 1998–99.[15]

On the down side that year though, although U.S. News & World Report, in its annual assessment of law schools in the United States published in its February 20, 1998, issue, thanks to the great work being done by Director of Career Services Joyce Whittington, out of 174 law schools had ranked the University of Mississippi's thirty-three in placement success; overall, it was ranked in the third tier. The main cause of that low ranking was "inadequate faculty resources," including "expenditures per student," which covered faculty salaries, library, and student support services. And, although the evaluation report issued by the ABA inspection team that came to the campus the first week in March 1998, "overall was very positive," it too made some reference to low faculty salaries and inadequate funding of the library and other support services.[16]

Another unfortunate occurrence around this same time was the tragically rapid demise of the law school's new *Journal of National Security Law.* The brainchild of Professor Robert N. Davis, volume I, number 1, of the *Journal* had been published by the law school in December 1997 in collaboration with both the Center for National Security Law at the University of Virginia School of Law and the Center on Law, Ethics and National Security at the Duke University School of Law. Edited by Sarah M. Falkinham, John W. Eads, and Thomas R. Davis, with the assistance of an editorial and managerial staff made up of seventy-eight other law students, the 118-page volume contained nine articles written by nationally prominent jurists and a book review section. But no other numbers of that volume were later published. And the single number of volume II, published in December 1998, was made up almost entirely of a collection of essays written by students at George Washington University Law School for a course on "The War Powers Resolution: Origins, History, Criticism and Reform." Perhaps the fact that it was dedicated to Professor Davis, who in January 1999 was "sent to Europe to serve in his capacity as a commissioned officer in the U.S. Navy," explains sufficiently why no further issues of the *Journal* were, in fact, ever published.[17]

By the spring of 1999, however, things were beginning to improve. The legislature had just approved a 7.5 percent increase in faculty and staff salaries. Benefits from the first year of a three-year phased tuition increase were already helping meet pressing needs in the areas of instruction, library, and student services. Also private giving was increasing remarkably: a one million dollar pledge from the Jackson law firm of Pittman, Germany, Roberts and Welsh represented the largest single gift ever made to the law school, and membership in the Lamar Order had reached 674, with many of its paid-in-full members continuing to give on a sustaining basis. Back in 1996–97, former Dean Parham Williams had served as the last one-year holder of the Jamie Whitten professorship. Now, Dean Davis held it on a continuing basis, and seven other members of the law faculty occupied endowed positions. Not surprising, therefore, *U.S. News & World Report*, in 1999, for the first time ranked the University of Mississippi's law school in its second tier.[18]

The students were doing their share too. A team made up of Meredith Messer, Alan Burns, Alan Alexander, and Rebecca Jordan, after first winning the southern regional competition and the Best Brief Award in Atlanta, went on to Washington and won the national moot court championship in the "final four" competition against representatives from the three other national regions.[19]

For the last academic year of the twentieth century (1999–2000) the law school received 1,122 applications for admission, of which 469 were accepted and 194 enrolled. The entering class of 138 residents and fifty-six nonresidents was made up of 116 males and seventy-eight females and included thirty-nine minority students (thirty-one African Americans, four Asians, two Native Americans, and two Hispanics). The school's total enrollment for the year was 479. Enrollment for the summer session was 140, and 158 graduates were awarded the Juris Doctor degree.[20]

The joint Juris Doctor/Master of Business Administration degree continued to be an option for law school students. The semester fee was now $2,040.50 for resident law students and $4,001.50 for nonresidents. On-campus residence hall rents ranged from $980 to $1,040 (double occupancy) per semester, and a parking decal cost $25. Capable students who were short of money, however, now had a total of ninety endowed scholarship funds that they could apply to for financial assistance. A student's out-of-the-classroom social, professional, or political life could be enhanced by membership in a variety of student organizations including the Black Law students Association, the Christian Legal Fellowship, the Criminal Law Society, the Federalist Society, the Native Americans Law Students Association, the Lamar Society of International Law, the Public Interest Law Clinic, the Law Association of Women, and the fraternities Phi Delta Phi, Phi Alpha Delta, and Delta Theta Phi, as well as in student divisions of the Mississippi Trial Lawyers Association and the American Bar Association, and in the Law School Student Body Association and the Speakers Bureau.[21]

The very successful summer program, conducted each year by Professor Larry Bush in England at Downing College, Cambridge, was continuing to attract not only University of Mississippi law students but also students from other law schools in both the United States and Canada. In 2000, an agreement was made with both the University of Arkansas-Fayetteville School of Law and the University of Tennessee College of Law whereby they both also became participants in organizing, offering, and administering the program. Beginning in 1997, a second summer program had begun being offered on the other side of the world, in Hawaii. Operated in cooperation with the University of Hawaii on its Manoa campus near Honolulu under the directorship of Professor Richard McLaughlin, it too now was a great success and was attracting law students from all over North America.[22]

By 2000, the law school's Court Reporting Department had turned out a total of 180 graduates. And in July of that year, its chair, Janice K. Bounds, was presented the Outstanding Educator Award at the National Court Reporting Association's annual meeting in San Diego.[23]

In the law library, important improvements were made in the printing and photocopying services, including the purchase of two new photocopiers and the implementation of new printing account management software that enabled students to establish accounts for their printing and use of library computers. Implementation of "Millennium," the new generation of recently purchased software for the library's automation system, was begun, including the fine-tuning of the Web-based catalog and the circulation module. And, in July 2000, Kristy Gilliland, who had been holding the position of associate law librarian for public services at the Georgetown University Law Center, became the library's new director.[24]

The law center's thirty year old Mississippi Judicial College during 1999–2000 conducted more than fifty training programs for court personnel around the state, including certification programs for justice court judges and justice and municipal court clerks. It had also, by then, completed the first edition of its Circuit Clerk's *Deskbook* and published updated versions of its Justice Court and Municipal Court deskbooks. And its quarterly newsletter, *Mississippi Judicial College News*, was now being published online on the World Wide Web.[25]

The twenty-eight-year-old Mississippi Law Research Institute, which, back in the mid-1970s had been staffed by one lawyer, one secretary, and a couple of law student research associates, now employed six lawyers, three secretaries, and as many student research associates as it needed. And, during the year, under its director William Hooper Jr. it completed more than a hundred major and more than 140 minor research projects. The state legislature had been advised with regard to such matters as elder law, teacher standards, the regulation of both swine and poultry processing and the unprecedented election of the governor by the house of representatives. A new pocket book of criminal law and procedures entitled *The Mississippi Law Enforcement Officer's Handbook* had been published and was being distributed to law enforcement departments around the state. And the Mississippi-Alabama Sea Grant Program had published four issues of *Waterlog,* its quarterly legal reporter on ocean and coastal law matters affecting the Gulf Coast and had distributed them to more than one hundred subscribers nationwide.[26]

It is not at all surprising, therefore, that in the spring of 1999 the law school had been moved up into *U.S. News & World Report*'s second tier. In the spring of 2000, it was announced that the Lamar Law Center was soon going to have added to it two very important new divisions. A five hundred thousand dollar grant had been received from the National Aeronautics and Space Agency to establish a National Remote Sensing and Space Law Center that was going to "serve as the recognized research, advisory and training resource for the emerging, commercial geospatial industry, the international legal community, and related user groups." Another pending grant of three million dollars from the Department of Justice in Washington was going to be used to establish the National Center for Justice and the Rule of Law.[27]

The establishment of the Space Law Center at the University of Mississippi was a tribute both to its law class of 1935 alumnus Myres S. McDougal, whose book *Law and Public Order in Space,* published by the Yale University Press in 1963, was still the standard text on the subject, and to its professor emeritus Stephen Gorove, who had organized the first international space law conference on the campus in the summer of 1969 and since 1973 had been overseeing the publication of the *Space Law Journal.*[28]

The National Center for Justice and the Rule of Law in its first year was going to "focus on the criminal justice area, sponsoring research, hosting national and international conferences, and producing educational seminars and training programs for judges and other court personnel on such timely subjects as domestic and international terrorism and drug trafficking." In subsequent years, the center would "expand its focus to include research and educational programs in domestic and international complex litigation; a program of international exchange to promote democratic values, economic development, human rights, and the rule of law in developing nations; and a research, educational, and training program emphasizing the substantive provisions and dispute resolution aspects of international investment agreements."[29]

There can be no doubt that much of the credit for the growth and development of the Law Center as it approached its sesquicentennial anniversary was thanks to the leadership talent demonstrated by so many of its law school alumni at both the state and national levels. The existence of the Stennis Space Center in Hancock County, Mississippi, undoubtedly had helped to strengthen Senator Trent Lott's successful campaign to obtain federal funding for the Space Law Center. And Senator Lott himself had also been largely responsible for getting the National Center for Justice and the Rule of Law funded.[30] By the year 2000, the law school could claim ten governors, six lieutenant governors, twenty-nine state supreme court justices, eleven U.S. representatives, and four U.S. senators among its alumni.[31]

Delivering the law school's fall 1999 Matthews lecture, alumnus and best-selling author John Grisham (1982) had told a packed audience in the school of education auditorium: "We were taught in law school here that the law was and still is an honorable calling. We were taught that lawyers were supposed to use their sense of justice and fair play to protect people, to protect the rights of individuals, and I think that is still true."[32]

And certainly, many of his fellow alumni had been busily proving him right. Among others of whom, by then, the law school was very proud was Assistant District Attorney Bobby DeLaughter (1977) of Greenville, who in 1994 had finally succeeded in convicting Byron De La Beckwith for the murder, twenty-five years earlier, of civil rights activist (and unsuccessful law school applicant) Medgar Evers. In the fall of 1999, DeLaughter, who a short while before had been sworn in as a county court judge in Hinds county, after telling an audience in the law center's moot court room the story of his investigation and ultimately successful prosecution of the case, became the first recipient of the center's newly instituted Alumni Public Service Award.[33]

On July 3, 1997, three more alumni, Attorney General Mike Moore (1976), Richard Scruggs (1976), and Don Barrett (1969), in the rotunda of the state capital in Jackson, had announced the winning of a settlement in their case on behalf of the state against the big tobacco companies whereby the defendant firms had agreed to pay, in installments over the next four years, a total of one billion dollars to cover the state's expenses in caring for its poorer citizens suffering from tobacco-induced illnesses.[34]

Dean Sam Davis, meanwhile, was serving as the 1999–2000 president of the Southeastern Conference of the American Association of Law Schools. In April 2000, a supplement to his book *Rights of Juveniles: The Juvenile Justice System* was published by the West Group. And he was now also one of the three commissioners from Mississippi serving on the National Conference of Commissioners on Uniform State Laws as well as serving as a member of the Professionalism Committee of the Mississippi Bar.[35]

In 2000–2001, another generous gift from alumnus John Grisham made it possible to add a clinical component to Professor Debbie Bell's Legal Problems of Indigence class in the fall semester and also enabled Professor Bell to offer in the spring semester a two-day Poverty Law Symposium that brought to the campus "some of the best poverty lawyers in the South and some of the most interesting thinkers in the country." In addition to giving many members of the law school student body a graphic awareness of the kinds of legal problems faced by their indigent fellow citizens, it also provided many lawyers from the law center's CLE program and on the staff of the North Mississippi Rural Legal Services with a wonderful opportunity to gain some very useful continuing legal education credit combined with some very thought-provoking social data.[36]

In 2001, Professor Thomas Kevin Clancy was appointed director of the law center's newly established National Center for Justice and the Rule of Law (NCJRL). Holder of a B.A. from Notre Dame and a J.D. from the University of Vermont (where he had served as notes editor for the *Vermont Law Review*), Professor Clancy had been employed by the District of Columbia's Legal Services Corporation from 1981 to 1983 and had worked in private practice in D.C. from 1983 to 1989 before serving as an assistant state attorney in Maryland from 1989 to 2000 and then as chairman of the state attorney's post-conviction unit in Prince George's City, Maryland, 2000–2001.[37]

In its first year of operation, NCJRL not only funded but also oversaw the design, development, and implementation of one and a half million dollars in technology upgrades throughout the law center, including the classrooms, the moot court rooms, and portions of the library. And, over the next couple of years, it put into place five programs on issues relating to the criminal justice system. One was the National Programs initiative, in which in association with the National Association of Attorneys General (NAAG) it offers training programs and model projects to facilitate the successful prosecution of persons engaged in computer-related crime. Another, the Fourth Amendment Initiative, develops periodicals and sponsors conferences and lectures with regard to search and seizure principles as well as offering training to staff members of state attorney generals offices regarding the search and seizure of computers. The Prosecution Externship Program provides course work and real-world training to prepare law students for careers as prosecutors. The Criminal Appeals program both trains law students and provides continuing legal education courses with regard to the representation on appeal of persons already convicted of crimes. And, finally, the Special Projects Program supports selected projects that promote the various concepts of justice and the rule of law.[38]

On September 9–11, 2003, the NCJRL co-hosted an advanced cybercrime conference with NAAG that was attended by forty-nine prosecutors and investigators from forty-two states. And on March 2–4, 2004 it hosted a conference on "Computer Hacking, Intrusions and Viruses" that attracted fifty prosecutors from a total of thirty-six states.[39]

On May 15, 2001, Professor Joanne Irene Gabrynowicz became director of the law center's newly established National Remote Sensing and Space Law Center (NRSSLC). An honors graduate of Hunter College at CUNY and a graduate of the Cardozo School of Law of Yeshiva University in New York City, Professor Gabrynowicz had practiced law in New York for six years before joining the faculty of the University of North Dakota's School of Aerospace Sciences. Serving there for thirteen years, she had earned an international reputation in the remote sensing and space law field. Just a few weeks after joining the law center faculty, she was in Europe attending a conference at the University of Cologne at which she lectured on the issues involved in developing remote sensing legislation, and on September 25, 2001, in Washington, D.C., at the annual meeting of Women in Aerospace, she was presented their Outstanding International Award.[40]

In the fall of 2001, the NRSSLC sponsored a forum on the commercial remote sensing industry that brought to the law center during the semester the chief executive officers of five of the corporations in the United States most active in that industry. In the spring of 2002, the center hosted the first International Conference on the State of Remote Sensing Law, April 18–19. Attended by leaders and scholars in the field from the United States, Japan, France, India, and Canada, it was the first time that these key people had come together in one place to exchange valuable information and to try to agree on standards and principles.[41]

In the fall of 2003, the center hired as its associate director Jaqueline Etil Serrao, holder of a J.D. degree (1995) from the Golden Gate University School of Law in California and an LL.M. degree (1999) in International Air and Space Law from McGill University in Montreal, Canada. Also in 2003, the Space Center resumed publication of the *Journal of Space Law*, which had lapsed in 2001 following the sad death of its founder, Professor Stephen Gorove.[42]

On October 1, 2003, Professor Sarrao taught her Aviation Law Class at the law school live from Ulaanbataar, Mongolia, via the Internet. And, a month later, Professor Gabronywicz taught her Remote Sensing law class live from Daejon, Korea, by using the university's grid node video conference facility. In 2004, the center was busy researching the legal rights of passengers on commercial space flights; very obviously it is on the cutting edge of space law research.[43]

Meanwhile, one of the law center's older established programs, the Department of Court Reporting, in July 2001, had been moved over into the university's newly established School of Applied Sciences. In April 2003, because court reporting degrees never had become a nationally recognized professional requirement, the decision was made to begin phasing it out of existence.[44]

Two others programs, however, were continuing to flourish. The Mississippi Judicial College, by 2001–2002, had a full-time staff of thirteen, headed by Leslie Johnson, and was receiving more than a million dollars annually through the state court education fund. Having the American Academy of Judicial Education allied with it was very helpful because it offered the ability to attend national training seminars at a greatly reduced rate, saving in both cost and time for the required national training of new judges, and it offered a greater ability to provide national programs and speakers in Mississippi. During that year, the judicial college conducted more than fifty training programs for in-state court personnel, including justice court judges and local court clerks. Also, in conjunction with Louisiana, the MJC had sponsored a joint meeting of both Mississippi and Louisiana's trial and appellate court judges with regard to psychological issues in fact finding and decision making, and these joint meetings became a regular annual event. The MJC's quarterly newsletter, *Mississippi Judicial College News*, was continuing to expand its circulation annually and also to be published on the World Wide Web. The *Youth Court Manual* and the justice court and municipal court deskbooks continued to be updated. Although in 2003 the relationship with the American Academy of Judicial Education was terminated, a similar relationship was begun with the National Judicial College, which opened an office on campus and provided similar benefits.[45]

The thirty-year-old Mississippi Law Research Institute, by 2001–2002, had a staff of seven lawyers, three secretaries, and as many law student research associates as were needed at any time to do its work. Under the leadership of its director, William Hooper Jr. it was continuing to provide law research and counsel to the state house and senate committees with regard to such topics as redistricting, tort reform, catfish labeling, punitive damages, cellular transmission tower location, compulsory school attendance laws, and environmental protection. Senior Research Counsel Richard L. Carlisle was continuing to update annually the institute's publications *Model Forms for Criminal Affidavits* and *The Mississippi Law Enforcement Officer's Handbook* and was beginning work on a trial and training manual for the state's prosecutors. Senior Research Counsel Jerry L. Patton was continuing the development and maintenance of an online model code of municipal ordinances for use by the state's municipalities[46].

In January 2002, Kristen M. Fletcher, director of the Institute's Mississippi-Alabama Sea Grant Legal Program received exciting news from the National Atmospheric and Oceanic Administration in Washington, D.C. Her program was, for the next four years at least, going to be the home of the National Sea Grant Office, the annual budget of which was $250,000. Two years later, Fletcher resigned to take up a similar position at the Roger Williams University School of Law in Rhode Island, and Stephanie Showalter was directing both the National Sea Grant Law Center and the Mississippi-Alabama Sea Grant Consortium, assisted by Professor Richard McLaughlin, who was providing counsel and research assistance on both programs. In addition to conducting numerous research programs for various state and federal agencies on such topics as aquaculture, fisheries, conservation, and environmental law, each of the two centers was producing and publishing a quarterly legal report, *Waterlog* by the SGLC and *Sandbar* by the NSGLC, containing articles prepared by their research counsel, law students, and guest experts[47].

In the fall of 2003, as the law school began the 150th year of its history, the entering class of 224 was made up of 172 residents and fifty-two nonresidents; 127 males and ninety-seven females; and twenty-seven were minority students (twenty-five African Americans, one Asian, and one Native American). The total enrollment that fall was 576, and 132 students were enrolled for the 2004 summer session. Over the course of the year, the Juris Doctor degree was conferred on a total of 145 students.[48]

The twenty-one full-time faculty and their several part-time or acting colleagues were all very busy doing the teaching research and service work expected of them. Between them, they had written four books and thirteen journal articles that were either published or accepted for publication during the year, and five of them had been invited to lecture off-campus.[49]

For the first time that year, *U.S. News & World Report* ranked the law school in the top one hundred law schools in the country and forty-seventh among public law schools. Getting a chapter of the national law school honor society, the Order of the Coif, seemed to be coming a very real possibility. Dean Sam Davis, as he completed his seventh year in office, was happy and proud to report in the summer 2004 issue of *UM Lawyer*, that the school's team had won the regional championship at the ABA mediation competition. Two students in its criminal appeals clinic had successfully argued a case before the Mississippi Court of Appeals that spring. The average LSAT score for the 2004 entering class was an unprecedented 155.88.[50] As it prepared to embark on the fourth half-century of its history, the future prospects for the University of Mississippi's law school looked very bright indeed.[51]

NOTES

Chapter 1. The Early Days (1854–1874)

1. University of Mississippi, *Catalogue (*1855), 5. "Introductory Lecture delivered to the Senior Class of the University of Mississippi, Oct. 2nd, 1854" (Stearns Papers [hereafter cited as Stearns Papers], U.M. Law Library, Special Collections).
2. David G. Sansing, *The University of Mississippi: A Sesquicentennial History* (Jackson, MS: University Press of Mississippi, 1999), chaps. 1 and 2, passim; University of Mississippi, *Historical Catalogue of the University of Mississippi, 1849–1909* (Nashville: Marshall, Bruce, 1910 [hereafter cited as *HC*]), 81.
3. Faculty Minutes, 1848–74 (U.M. Library, Special Collections [hereafter cited as UMLSC]), 6; *Catalogue* (1852–53), 6.
4. Grover C. Hooker, "The Origin and Development of the University of Mississippi with Special Reference to Its Legislative Control" (Ph.D. diss., Stanford University, 1932), 62 (n.); *Biographical and Historical Memoirs of Mississippi* (2 vols., Chicago: Godspeed Publishing, 1891), I:1144; Steve Sheppard (ed.), *The History of Legal Education in the United States* (2 vols., Pasadena, CA: Salem Press, 1999), 200.
5. Sansing, *University of Mississippi*, 48–49; John N. Waddel, *Memorials of Academic Life. . . .* (Richmond, VA: Presbyterian Committee of Publication, 1891), 279–80; *HC*, 96.
6. *Catalogue* (1852–61), 4, 6.
7. Florence E. Campbell, "Journal of the Minutes of the Board of Trustees of the University of Mississippi, 1845–1860" (M.A. thesis, Univ. of MS, 1939), 409. Rebecca Ann Evans Pegues, Diaries, 1816–89 (8 vols., UMLSC) 7:18. Lamar went back to Georgia in 1852 but returned to Oxford in 1855.
8. *HC*, 81.
9. Ibid.; Campbell, "Journal," 453.
10. *HC*, 81; Campbell, "Journal," 455–56.
11. *Who Was Who* 1897–1942, s.v. Howry, Charles Bowen.
12. *The Rise and Progress of the University of Mississippi School of Government Science and Law* (U.M. Law Library, Rare Book #693), 5–6, 24.
13. Ibid., 14–21.
14. Howry, *Rise and Progress*, 11; Sheppard, *Legal Education* I:15, 19, 317.
15. Campbell, "Journal," 203–4, 204–5.
16. Ibid., 205.
17. *Laws of Mississippi* 1854, chap. 56.
18. *Catalogue* (1853–54), 8.
19. Campbell, "Minutes", 219, 226, 252; *HC*, 81; Dunbar Rowland, *Courts, Judges and Lawyers of Mississippi* (2 vols., Jackson, MS: State Department of Archives and History, 1935) I:257; *Mississippi—Comprising Sketches of Counties, Towns, Events, Institutions and*

Persons (2 vols., Atlanta: Southern Historical Publishing Association, 1907) II:967. Clifton succeeded Wilkinson as a Second Circuit judge.

20. Campbell, "Journal," 229.

21. Frank Moak, "History of the University of Mississippi" (unpublished, UMLSC), chap. 3, 6; Howry, *Rise and Progress*, 11–12; Parham Williams, "The University of Mississippi Law School," *Jurist* 4 (1986), 5.

22. Moak, "History", 6; Sansing, *University of Mississippi*, 42, 338; *Holly Springs Guard*, Aug. 14, 1846.

23. Howry, *Rise and Progress*, 12; "Introductory Lecture," (Stearns Papers). 10.

24. Edward Mayes, *History of Education in Mississippi* (Washington, D.C.: GPO, 1899), 146; "Restoration Converts Depot into Meeting Space," *Oxford Eagle*, Oct. 21, 2002, 1.

25. Mayes, *History*, 146. Also one of the graduating seniors in the undergraduate class of 1854 was Robert Joseph Farley of Panola County (*HC*, 119).

26. *Dictionary of American Biography* (hereafter cited as *DAB*), s.v. Barnard, Frederick Augustus Porter; John Fulton, *Memoirs of Frederick A. P. Barnard* (New York: Macmillan, 1896), 43.

27. *DAB*; Sansing, *University of Mississippi*, 85, 87.

28. *Catalogue* (1854–55), 5; Sansing, *University of Mississippi; Catalogue* (1855–56), 5; *HC*, 82, 102. Townes-Moseley ended up living somewhere in Mississippi called "Wahalak." Thomas ended his days as a clergyman in Oxford.

29. *HC*, 102–5; Mayes, *History*, 146.

30. *HC*, 102–5; Alumni Association Minutes (UMLSC 00-282, K6).

31. *Catalogue* (1860–61), 16–17.

32. A copy of the letter is in the William Nelson Collection (UMLSC).

33. Ibid.

34. *Mississippi Revised Code* 1857, chap. IX, art. 1.

35. *Catalogue* (1857–58), 26.

36. Ibid. 1854–55, 6.

37. Ibid.; ibid. 1856–57, 17; ibid. 1857–58, 28. A copy of the circular is in the Stearns Papers.

38. David J. Langum and Howard P. Walthall, *From Maverick to Mainstream: Cumberland School of Law, 1847–1997* (Athens: University of Georgia Press, 1997), 26–27.

39. *Catalogue* (1854–55), 6.

40. Ibid.; Campbell, "Journal," 290, 299.

41. Campbell, "Journal," 313–15. The other committee members were Isaac N. Davis and Charles Clark.

42. Ibid., 341, 418–19.

43. *Catalogue* (1856–57), 16; *Catalogue* (1857–58), 27.

44. John Wesley Johnson, Notebook, 21–23, UMLSC.

45. Faculty Minutes, 118–20.

46. A copy of the speech is in the Stearns Papers.

47. Campbell, "Journal," 369.

48. Sansing, *University of Mississippi*, 96–97.

49. Undated class lecture text on "Slavery," 20, Stearns Papers.

50. Sansing, *University of Mississippi*, 97.

51. Johnson, Notebook, n.p.

52. Sansing, *University of Mississippi*, 96–98; Campbell, "Journal," 404–7, 412–13; E. V. Capati,"Oxford Intelligencer, 1860–1861" (M.A. thesis, Univ. of MS, 1961), 7–8.

53. Sansing, *University of Mississippi*, 25.

54. Emelda Capati, *A Country Editor Faces Secession: The Story of the Oxford Intelligencer, 1860–1861* (University, MS: Academy Press, ca. 1961), 7, 8, 24, 66; Sansing, *University of Mississippi*, 98.; Howry, *Rise and Progress*, 25.

55. Howry, *Rise and Progress*, 25–27.

56. H. M. Sullivan, *All the Laws and Public Resolutions in Relation to the University of Mississippi* (U.M. Board of Trustees Publication, 1879), 16; *Catalogue* (1860–61), 4; Campbell, "Journal," 234, 355, 367, 425, 428. 472; *Catalogue* (1859–60), 39; *HC*, 87.

57. Campbell, "Journal," 428.

58. Ibid., 419, 447; Lewis Will, "The Story of Banks and Banking Activity in Oxford through the Years" (June 1986, A Contribution to the Celebration of Oxford's Sesquicentennial, 1987, History Research Room, Oxford-Lafayette County Library), 9. A historical map of the Oxford downtown area in the History Research Room shows that the Avent & Lyles Bank occupied the site on the northwest corner of the Square now occupied by the Merchants and Farmers Bank building.

59. Campbell, "Journal," 447.

60. Lecture on "Slavery," Stearns Papers.

61. Sansing, *University of Mississippi*, 103, 106–7; Faculty Minutes, 223–24; Campbell, "Journal," 431; Frances R. Huff, "The Relationship of Oxford and the University of Mississippi, 1848–1947" (M.A. thesis, Univ. of MS, 1947), 95; Allen Cabaniss, *A History of the University of Mississippi* (Oxford, MS: University of Mississippi, 1949), 69.

62. Percy, "Biographical Summary"; Howry, *Rise and Progress*, 28; Campbell, "Journal," 442–48, 472; Mayes, *History*, 152. I am very grateful to Anne D. Percy of Oxford, MS, for the information, based on her own research, regarding Stearns's last few years of life.

63. Percy, notes. Howry, *Rise and Progress*, 28; Lafayette County Chancery Court Records, Deedbook J, 380–81, 445; Deedbook Q, 378–79.

64. Campbell, "Journal," 472; Daniel J. Meador, "Lamar and the Law at the University of Mississippi," *Mississippi Law Journal* XXIV, no. 3 (May 1963), 227–28.

65. Meador, "Lamar," 229–32; Faculty Minutes, 253, 275; Sansing, *University of Mississippi*, 39, 50; *HC*, 106.

66. Howry, *Rise* and *Progress*, 30; Meador, "Lamar," 237, 242.

67. Meador, "Lamar," 235–36, 239–40.

68. Ibid., 234–35.

69. Ibid., 237; *HC*, 107–8.

70. Wiley P. Harris, *Address to the Graduating Class in the Department of Law, University of Mississippi, June 23d, 1869. Published by Order of the Trustees* (Jackson, MS: Clarion Book and Job Publishing, 1869), 3–4, 16. For an autobiography of Harris, see Rowland, *Courts, Judges and Lawyers* I:270–329.

71. Faculty Minutes, 253; Meador, "Lamar," 247–49.

72. Faculty Minutes, 340; Mayes, *History*, 163–64; Meador, "Lamar," 227, 255; Campbell, *Minutes*, 469. Lamar served on the Supreme Court until his death in 1893, in Macon, Georgia.

73. Sansing, *University of Mississippi*, 133–34; *HC*, 108–9; Mayes, *History*, 146.

74. *HC*, 17, 102, 119, 185–86; Rowland, *Courts, Judges and Lawyers* I:103–11, 249.

CHAPTER 2. UP AGAIN AND GOING STRONG (1877–1911)

1. Sansing, *University of Mississippi*, 131–34; Hooker, *Origin and Development*, 134–35.
2. *HC* lists " J.J. Hamm," as the Law Professor, 1877 (p. 87), but there is no record of any lawyer of that name in the state at that time. For James S. Hamm, see Rowland, *Courts, Judges and Lawyers* I:258–60; *Biographical and Historical Memoirs* I:853–54; "Edward Mayes," typescript biography (Verner Holmes Collection, Box 7, Folder 4, UMLSC), 1–2; Mayes, *History*, 212; *HC*, 93.
3. Sansing, *University of Mississippi*, 134; Howry, *Rise and Progress*, 32b; *University Magazine*, Mar. 1880; Hooker, "Origin and Development," 135; Mayes, *History*, 146.
4. *University Magazine*, Mar. 1880, 179; Mayes, *History*, 145.
5. *University Magazine*, Mar. 1880, 179–80. "Judge Hill," presumably, was Federal District Judge Robert A. Hill, who was a member of the board of trustees, 1876–96, and each year delivered a lecture to the law students on federal procedure (*HC*, 62, 82). All of the counsel listed for the cases were graduating members of the 1880 law class, 1888–89 (*Catalogue*, 25).
6. Mayes, *History*, 145.
7. Sheppard, *History of Legal Education* I:552–59. Of the fifty-four institutions covered by the report, forty had two-year courses, seven had one-year courses, and seven had three-year courses.
8. Mayes, *History*, 146; Geo. F. Maynard (class of 1878), "Unwritten Poetry of Law," *University Magazine*, June 1878, 230–35.
9. Sansing, *University of Mississippi*, 150–52; Hooker, "Origin and Development," 128.
10. "Edward Mayes" (UMLSC), n.p.; Mayes, *History*, 178–81; Sansing, *University of Mississippi*, 150–51.
11. Sansing, *University of Mississippi*, 136, 152–54.
12. Michael Landon, "Another False Start: Mississippi's Second State Bar Association, 1886–92," in *The New High Priests: Lawyers in Post–Civil War America, Contributions in Legal Studies, Number* 29 (Westport, CT: Greenwood Press, 1984), 187–93; *American National Biography*, s.v. Mayes, Edward.
13. *American National Biography*, s.v. Mayes, Edward, 6–7. His later publications included *Lucius Q. C. Lamar: His Life, Times and Speeches* (1896) and *Ribs of the Law* (1909), a study guide for law students.
14. Sansing, *University of Mississippi*, 155; Hooker, "Origin and Development," 137.
15. *American National Biography*, s.v. Mayes, Edward, 7–8; Michael de L. Landon, *The Honor and Dignity of the Profession* (Jackson: University of Mississippi Press, 1979), 105.
16. Sansing, *University of Mississippi*, 155–56; Rowland, *Courts, Judges and Lawyers* I:122–26, 164; *HC*, 91, 239; Howry, *Rise and Progress*, 32b.
17. Rowland, *Courts, Judges and Lawyers*, 123, 366; Huff, "Relationship," 78; *Catalogue* (1895–96), 148–49, 152–53, 155–56; *HC*, 82.
18. *Biographical and Historical Memoirs* II:749; Howry, *Rise and Progress*, 32b; Sansing, *University of Mississippi*, 156.
19. *University Magazine*, Oct. 1894, 17, 37, 42; Sansing, *University of Mississippi*, has two pictures of the building.
20. *University Magazine*, Oct. 1894, 44, back cover; *University Magazine*, Apr. 1902, 41; Howry, *Rise and Progress*, 33; *Catalogue* (1895–96), 158–59; *HC*, 62.

21. Sansing, *University of Mississippi*, 63; *University Magazine*, Oct. 1894, 44.
22. *University Magazine*, Oct. 1894, 44–45; *Catalogue* (1895–96), 79; *Catalogue* (1897–98), 110.
23. *Catalogue* (1895–96), 74–75.
24. Ibid., 76–77, 78
25. Ibid., 75–76.
26. Ibid., 72–73.
27. *HC,* 107; *Catalogue* (1998–99), 10. Although the *HC* has only one reference to Edmonds (as a "New Student" in 1897), the James E Edmonds Collection (UMLSC) contains a number of letters written by Edmonds in Oxford to his parents back home in Bolivar, Mississippi, from 1896 to 1900. In a letter dated Feb. 16, 1897, he wrote: "I can finish in third year, take both courses of Law in one year, and in the time it usually takes one to commence one [*sic*] education I can commence mine and get a profession into the bargain" (p. 2). Although there is no record of his receiving any degree, his brilliant academic career, which climaxed with his representing the university in the 1900 Mississippi Inter-Collegiate Oratorical Competition (and coming in second in it) makes it seem likely that he did (*Ole Miss* [1900], 158). He was also the "Historian" of the class of 1900 (*Catalogue* [1898–99], 92).
28. James Blotner, *Faulkner*, 2 vols. (New York, Random House, 1974), 51, 55, 82; *Biographical and Historical Memoirs* II:714; *Catalogue* (1898–99), 10.
29. Rowland, *Courts, Judges and Lawyers*, 107; *Biographical and Historical Memoirs* I:298; *HC,* 100; C. H. Alexander, "Address to the Graduating Law Class, 1900" (John Wesley Johnson Collection, UMLSC), 13–15, 21–22. Alexander had received his B.A. at the university 1877, his A.M. in 1878, and his LL.B. in 1879.
30. "Practical Advice to Young Lawyers" (undated MS, Beckwith/Yerger Collection, Box 7, Folder 7–4, UMLSC). Yerger had graduated with second highest honors in the 1882 law class (*HC,* 112).
31. James Edmonds Collection, UMLSC.
32. Ibid., letters of Feb. 26, 1900, and Mar. 25, 1900.
33. *Ole Miss* (1897), passim; 1898, 7–9.
34. Ibid., 1898, 103, 141–50.
35. *Mississippi Law Journal* II, no. 4 (May 1930), 454; *Bulletin* (1929–30), 24.
36. *Catalogues* (1897–1903), *passim; Catalogue* (1906–1907), 233; *Alumni Minutes Collection, 1853–1976,* June 3, 1902, UMLSC; Faculty Minutes, 1.
37. *Catalogue* (1895–96), 17, 21; *Catalogue* (1905–1906), 11, 171; Sansing, *University of Mississippi,* 161–62.
38. Landon, *Honor and Dignity,* 3, 5–12.
39. Sansing, *University of Mississippi,* 178–80.
40. *HC,* 151, 288, 301; Sansing, *University of Mississippi,* 179–80; Landon, *Honor and Dignity,* 19. Shands apparently had a family connection at Tulane—the U.M. alumni, at their 1902 annual meeting, were lectured by a "Dr. Harley Shands" about the Tulane Alumni's support of their alma mater (*Alumni Minutes Collection,* June 3, 1902, 2).
41. *HC,* 87, 236; *Biographical and Historical Memoirs* II:784; Landon, *Honor and Dignity,* 11, 12, 13, 19.
42. *HC,* 264; *Ole Miss* (1898), 150; Robert J. Farley, "The School of Law—Since 1854," *Mississippi Law Journal* XX, no.3, (1948–49), 250.

43. *HC,* 203; *Ole Miss* (1911), 29; Sansing, *University of Mississippi,* 186.
44. *Catalogue* (1910–11), 87; Landon, *Honor and Dignity,* 179; *Ole Miss* (1898), 150; *HC,* 96, 248, 264.
45. *HC,* 102–13, 215–320.
46. *Catalogue* (1910–11), 87–92.
47. Alumni Minutes; Hooker, "Origin and Development," appendix H, 3–4.
48. Sansing, *University of Mississippi,* 186; *Catalogue* (1910–11), 88.

CHAPTER 3. THE VENTRESS HALL YEARS (1911–1930)

1. *Catalogue* (1911–12), passim. *Ole Miss* (1913), 137–38 and passim.
2. Charles Ferriday Byrnes Correspondence, 1907–17 (UMLSC), letters of Oct. 1, 1911, Oct. 15, 1911, Oct. 30, 1911, Dec. 14, 1911, Dec. 18, 1911, Dec. 20, 1911, Jan. 4, 1912.
3. Ibid., letters of Jan. 4, 1912, Mar. 27, 1912, Apr. 23, 1912, Apr. 26, 1912, Apr. 28, 1912, May 12, 1912.
4. *Ole Miss* (1913), 64, 137; *Catalogue* (1913–14), 150. Two popular recreation facilities in north Mississippi are the Wall Doxey State Park and the John W. Kyle State Park.
5. *Ole Miss* (1911), 70; book of *Daniel,* chap. 5. Byrnes did not smoke his cigar that evening: "I pocketed mine for 'chic,'" he told Roane (Byrnes Correspondence, letter of Feb. 1, 1913).
6. Byrnes Correspondence, letters of fall term (n.d.) 1912, Jan. 7, Feb. 1, Feb. 23, Mar. 20, May 29, May 30, 1913; *Catalogue* (1913–14), 150. Wall Doxey received his LL.B. degree one year later (*Catalogue* [1914–15], 161); *Ole Miss* (1913), 62–66; Rowland, *Courts, Judges and Lawyers,* 252.
7. Byrnes Correspondence, letter of Feb. 23, 1913; *Catalogue* (1913–14), 15, 88. Dean Somerville's law office on the Square was located immediately next door to the Federal Building (now City Hall) in the building that today belongs to his great-grandsons, the Howorth brothers. His home, 304 South Fifth Street, is today owned and occupied by his granddaughter, Vasser Bishop.
8. Landon, *Honor and Dignity,* 43; *Catalogue* (1914–15), 154, 155; *Catalogue* (1915–16), 169; *Ole Miss* (1915), 66, 69, 70, 71, 183—Linda Brown and Ruth Watkins can be seen in the junior law class photograph on p.70.
9. *Catalogue* (1916–17), 173; *Ole Miss* (1915), 69; Jay Watson, *Forensic Fictions: The Lawyer Figure in Faulkner* (Athens, GA: University of Georgia Press, 1993), 7, 9, 10–11, 233–34.
10. *HC,* 230, 243; *Catalogue* (1915–16), 163; *Catalogue* (1916–17), 13, 152, 165, 171; *Ole Miss* (1915), 22.
11. *Catalogue* (1917–18), 173–74; *Catalogue* (1918–19), 10, 15, 171–72; *Ole Miss* (1919), 26.
12. *Catalogue* (1919–20), 11, 190; *Catalogue* (1920–21), 188–89; *Ole Miss* (1919), 26, 47.
13. *Catalogue* (1920–21), 10, 17, 187; *Catalogue* (1921–22), 167; *Ole Miss* (1928), 24; "Historical Sketch of the Law Department of the University of Mississippi," *Mississippi Law Journal* I, no.2 (Oct. 1928), 175.
14. *Ole Miss* (1924), 208; *Ole Miss* (1928), 24; "The Spoils System Enters College: Governor Bilbo and Higher Education in Mississippi," *New Republic* (Sept. 17, 1930), 123–25; *Mississippi Law Journal* I, no 2 (Oct. 1928), 175–76; *Catalogue* (1921–22), 8, 9, 164; *Catalogue* (1922–23), 9, 12; Landon, *Honor and Dignity,* 39–40. Dean Kimbrough's

having played on the University's first football team (organized and coached by Professor Alexander Bondurant) in 1893 was noted, with great approval, by the University's alumni at their meeting on Oct. 16, 1926 (Alumni Association Minutes).

15. *Catalogue* (1921–22), 38, 91–93, 164; *Mississippi Law Review* I, no. 4 (Mar. 1923), 75.

16. Ibid., 91–93.

17. Michael de L. Landon, "The Origins of the Mississippi Law Journal," *Mississippi Law Journal* 50 (1979), 3.

18. Ibid., 3–4; *Mississippi Law Review* I, no. 3 (Feb. 1923), 41–63.

19. *Mississippi Law Review* I, no. 4 (Mar. 1923), 74. 76; *Catalogue* (1924–25), 95.

20. *Catalogue* (1922–23), 186–88; *Who's Who in the South and Southwest* (1950), s.v. Howorth, Lucy (Somerville); Landon, *Honor and Dignity*, 53–54. Susie Blue Buchanan of Brandon had been admitted to the state Bar Association in 1918 and Sarah L. Buchanan of Booneville in 1921.

21. *Catalogue* (1923–24), 184; *Mississippi Law Review* I, no. 5, passim; *Who's Who in the South and Southwest* (1950), loc. cit.

22. Landon, "Origins of the Mississippi Law Journal," 4; *Mississippi Law Review* I, passim. The OCLC (#1758366) lists no copies of any volume II numbers anywhere in the country. As of 1978, the University of Mississippi Law library did not have a copy of volume I; it now has three copies, however.

23. *Catalogue* (1924–25), 188–89; *Ole Miss* (1924), 46; Landon, *Honor and Dignity*, 50, 61–62, 69, 80, 93–94, 96, 99–100, 107, 117. Jiggitts died, at a tragically early age, of a heart attack during World War II.

24. *Ole Miss* (1924), 45; *Who's Who in America* (1972–75), s.v. Farley, Robert Joseph.

25. Landon, *Honor and Dignity*, 61.

26. *HC*, 100, 108, 83, 85, 149. He had served on the board of trustees, 1890–1906, and on its executive committee, 1891–94 (Alumni Association Minutes).

27. "A Lecture," by Judge R.H. Thompson (UMLSC), 6–7. On June 2, 1930, the Alumni Association, meeting on campus, voted to send Judge Thompson a telegram congratulating him on being the last surviving member of the 1869 class (Alumni Association Minutes).

28. *Bulletin* 1925–26, 42; *Bulletin* 1927–28, 53; *Bulletin* 1928–29, 31.

29. *Bulletins*, passim.

30. *Bulletin* 1924–25, 25; *Bulletin* 1925–26, 13, 39; *Bulletin* 1928–29, 56; *Bulletin* 1929–30, 27.

31. Landon, *Honor and Dignity*, 63–64.

32. Ibid., 64; Hardy P. Graham, "Bilbo and the University of Mississippi" (M.A. thesis, University of Mississippi, 1965), 2–4.

33. Alumni Association Minutes, 11/5/27; Landon, *Honor and Dignity*, 65–66; $200,000 of the $1.6 million was used to build the new graduate building, today known as Bondurant Hall.

34. Landon, "Origins of the Mississippi Law Journal," 4–5, and *Honor and Dignity*, 69

35. Landon, "Origins of the Mississippi Law Journal," 5.

36. Ibid., 6.

37. *Mississippi Law Journal* II, no. 1 (July 1929), 115–17; author's interview with Dean Emeritus Robert J Farley, Aug. 25, 1977.

38. *Mississippian* (Apr. 20, 1935), 1, 8; *Ole Miss* (1948), 307, 314. The campaign to get a Phi

Delta Phi chapter was led by Conwell Sykes, a transfer from the University of Alabama Law School, who had been initiated into the chapter there. New chapters were also established in 1929 at LSU and the University of South Carolina.

39. *Mississippian* II, no. 4 (May 1930), 454; *Bulletin* 1929–30, 24, 116; *Bulletin* 1930–31, 226; Frances R. Huff, "The Relationship of Oxford and the University of Mississippi" (M.A. thesis, University of Mississippi, 1947), 72–73.

40. Volume II, no. 3 (Feb. 1930), 286–92.

41. *Mississippi Law Journal* II, no.4 (May 1930), 363–64.

42. Sansing, *University of Mississippi*, 216–27; Graham, "Bilbo and the University of Mississippi," 14.

43. Board Minutes, June 27, 1930; Sansing, *University of Mississippi*, 211–12, 234–35; John B. Hudson, "The Spoils System Enters College," *New Republic* 64 (Sept. 17, 1930), 123–34.

44. *Bulletin* 1930–31, 23, 113; Hudson, "Spoils System," 124; Sansing, *University of Mississippi*, 237.

45. Hooker, "Origin and Development," 279–80.

46. Ibid., 280–81.

CHAPTER 4. THE EARLY DECADES IN FARLEY HALL (1930–1962)

1. Board Minutes; Sansing, *University of Mississippi*, 243–44; *Making Haste Slowly*, 109, 262.

2. *Bulletin* 1932–33, 9–12; *Bulletin* 1933–34, 14; *Who's Who in America* (1950), s.v. Farley, Robert Joseph; Sansing, interview with Dean Robert J. Farley, Oxford, MS, May 15, 1979, 53; *Mississippian* (Apr. 20, 1935), 7. Dean Stone Deavours had returned home to Laurel, where he died a year later, on Sept. 20, 1933 (*Who Was Who in America 1897–1942*), s.v. Deavours, Stone; *HC*, 294.

3. *Bulletin* 1932–33, 204; *Bulletin* 1933–34, 218; *Higher Education in Mississippi* (Nashville, TN: George Peabody College, 1933), 10.

4. *Bulletin* 1931–32, 123.

5. Author interview with Hugh N. Clayton, New Albany, MS, Aug. 17, 1977.

6. *Bulletin* 1932–33, 123.

7. *Bulletin* 1930–31, 117; *Bulletin* 1935, 5; *Bulletin* 1936, 5; *Bulletin* 1937, 5, 12; *Bulletin* 1938, 5, 13, 14. Rhoda C. Bass, in 1937, had been the first winner of the Phi Delta Phi award. The Registrar and Secretary in 1937–38, Miss Lulie Reynolds Eddins, did not have a degree.

8. Sansing, *University of Mississippi*, 245–47; *Bulletin* 1939, 18.

9. *Who's Who in America* (1972–73), s.v. McDougal, Myres Smith; Law faculty minutes, May 8, 1935; *Bulletin* 1935–36, 231.

10. *Bulletin* 1936, 13–15.

11. Faculty Minutes, May 21, 1935; *Who's Who in the South and Southwest* (1950), s.v. Lenoir, James Jefferson, and Wade, John Webster; *Bulletin* 1936, 5; *Bulletin* 1937, 5; *Bulletin* 1939, 5.

12. Sansing, interview with Farley, May 15, 1979, 1–2.

13. Ibid., 2; *Bulletins* 1935–43, passim; Sansing, *University of Mississippi*, 254; Robert J. Farley, "The School of Law—Since 1854," *Mississippi Law Journal* XX (no. 3), 250.

14. *Bulletins* 1934–41, passim; *Higher Education in Mississippi* (1933), 64.

15. *Bulletin*s 1934–43, passim.

16. Ibid. 1935–36, 28, 30.

17. Ibid. 1935, 7.

18. Ibid., 11.

19. Ibid. 1935, 12.

20. Law Faculty Minutes, May 8, 1935.

21. *Bulletin* 1936, 13–14.

22. Ibid. 1937, 11.

23. Faculty Minutes, May 16, Sept. 11, Nov. 13, and Nov. 19, 1935.

24. Landon, *Honor and Dignity*, 88–92; Michael de L. Landon, *The Challenge of Service: A History of the Mississippi Bar's Young Lawyers, 1936–1986* (Jackson, MS: Fellows of the Young Lawyers of the Mississippi Bar, 1995), 4–6.

25. Landon, *Honor and Dignity*, 92, and *Challenge of Service*, 6–9; Landon, interview with Clayton, Aug. 17, 1977, 2.

26. Faculty Minutes, Feb. 11, Dec. 15, 1936 and passim, Jan. 29, Sept. 10, 1937 and passim.

27. *Bulletin* 1938, 10.

28. Ibid. 1935, 9.

29. Ibid. 1937, 11.

30. Ibid., 12; Faculty Minutes, Oct. 29, 1938. The plaque now hangs on the right wall just inside the main front entrance of the Lamar Law Center. The first winner recorded was a woman, Rhoda C. Bass, in 1937.

31. *Bulletin* 1941, 7, 10, 22–24; Faculty Minutes, Feb. 3, 1941; Farley, "School of Law," 252.

32. Faculty Minutes, Feb. 3, May 5, Sept. 13, Oct. 22, 1941.

33. Faculty Minutes, 1939, 3; Faculty Minutes, Oct. 22, 1941.

34. Ibid., Dec. 12, 1941; *Bulletin* 1943, 21. Two of the out-of-state students were from Memphis, and one was from Washington, D.C., and another from Bangor, PA.

35. *Bulletin* 1943, 7; *Who's Who in the South and Southwest* (1950), s.v. Ethridge, William Nathaniel, Jr.; Farley, "School of Law," 251.

36. *Bulletin* 1943, 11–12.

37. Ibid. 1946, 21–23.

38. Ibid. 1939, 5; *Bulletin* 1944, 7; *Bulletin* 1946, 7; *Who's Who in the South and Southwest* (1950), s.v. O'Neal, F(orest) Hodge; Farley, "School of Law," 252. A student named "Corinne Bass" (a niece?) was enrolled in the law school, 1947–49 (*Bulletin* 1949, 22).

39. Landon, *Honor and Dignity*, 162; Sansing, interview with Farley, May 15, 1979), 2.

40. Sansing, *University of Mississippi*, 260–61.

41. Faculty Minutes, Jan. 19, Jan. 31, and May 27, 1946.

42. *Bulletin* 1947, 7, 21–24; *Who's Who in the South and Southwest* (1950), s.v. Wade, John W(ebster); Faculty Minutes, May 19, 1947.

43. *Bulletin* 1947, 17; Faculty Minutes, Feb. 4, 1946), 2.

44. *Mississippian* (Feb. 12, 1954), 2; Sansing, *University of Mississippi*, 254; *Bulletin* 1947, 17.

45. *Bulletin* 1949, 8, 20–26; *Who's Who in the South and Southwest*, s.v. Cross, Roscoe; Ethridge, William Nathaniel, Jr.; O'Neal, F(orest) Hodge; Farley, "School of Law," 252.

46. Faculty Minutes, Nov. 7, 1949 and passim.

47. Ibid., Feb. 11 and Nov. 7, 1949.

48. Ibid., Mar. 7 and Nov. 7, 1949, Mar. 2 and Apr. 6, 1950.

49. Ibid., Jan. 11, Mar. 8, May 25, 1951.

50. Ibid., Jan. 11 and Apr. 6, 1951.

51. Ibid., spring 1952, passim.

52. Ibid., spring 1953, passim, Aug. 26, 1952.

53. *Bulletin* 1954; "The Centennial of the School of Law," 18–20.

54. "Centennial of the School of Law," 7; *Bulletin* 1949, 8; Farley, "School of Law," 90; *Who's Who in the South and Southwest* (1956), s.v. Ethridge, William Nathaniel, Jr.

55. *Mississippi Lawyer* (Aug. 1955), 1, 4; *Bulletin* 1956, 7; *Bulletin* 1958, 7.

56. *Bulletin* 1954, 8–11, 15.

57. Ibid., 13–14.

58. *Mississippi Lawyer* (Apr. 1954), 4, 7.

59. Ibid. (July 1954), 1, 7; ibid. (Aug. 1954), 7.

60. Ibid. (Nov. 1954), 1, 8; ibid. (Dec. 1954), 1.

61. Ibid. (Jan. 1955), 1; ibid. (Mar. 1955), 7.

62. Ibid. (Feb. 1955), 1; *Who's Who in America* (1972), s.v. Taft, Charles Phelps; *Who's Who in the South and Southwest* (1950), s.v. Davis, Clifford, and Arnold, Thurman Wesley.

63. *Mississippi Lawyer* (Apr. 1955), 1; *HC,* index, passim. The story says thirteen nineteenth-century graduates were honored, but only twelve names are listed.

64. Ibid., 3, 6.

65. *Bulletin* 1955, 18; *Mississippi Lawyer* (Aug. 1955), 2; *Mississippi Lawyer* (Oct. 1955), 2.

66. "The School of Law—Since 1854," *Mississippi Law Journal* XX, no. 3 (May 1949), 251. "The School of Law—The First Hundred years," *Mississippi Law Journal* XXV, no. 2 (Mar. 1954), 91; *Bulletin* 1949, 15; *Bulletin* 1955, 13.

67. "Dead House" historical marker. *Bulletin* 1959, 15.

68. Sansing, *University of Mississippi,* 272.

69. Ibid.; Sansing, interview with Farley, 7–8.

70. Sansing, *University of Mississippi,* 142–43; Board Minutes, Aug. 16, 1954, Dec. 16, 1954.

71. *Bulletin* 1954, 7; Sansing, interview with Farley, 6; Devereux, interview with Murphy, Jan. 17, 1978 (Murphy Papers, UMLSC).

72. Stennis letters, June 29 and July 9, 1954 (Murphy Papers, UMLSC).

73. *Summit Sun,* July 12, 1954), 2, 7.

74. Sansing, interview with Farley, 3; Board Minutes, July 19, 1956; *Time Magazine,* July 29, 1957, 38.

75. Murphy File, passim; Sansing, interview with Farley, 10; *Mississippi Law Journal* XXIX, no. 1 (Dec. 1957), 110.

76. Murphy file, passim; Sansing, *Making Haste Slowly,* 146–48; Sansing, *University of Mississippi,* 278–79; Board Minutes, Aug. 27, 1959.

77. Senate Concurrent Resolution No. 155. A copy is in the Murphy file.

78. A copy of the petition, with the signatures attached, is in the Murphy file.

79. Murphy file, passim; *Bulletin* 1961, 5; *Bulletin* 1962, 7.

80. Sansing, interview with Farley, 11; Board Minutes, Mar. 17, 1960), June 29, 1961, May 29, 1962.

81. Devereaux, interview with Murphy, Jan. 17, 1978 (Southern Oral History Program Collection, UNC, Chapel Hill), 24.

CHAPTER 5. FROM LAW SCHOOL TO LAW CENTER (1963–1975)

1. Sansing, interview with Farley, May 15, 1979, 2

2. *Who's Who in America* (1982–83), s.v. Morse, Joshua Marion; *Bulletin* 1963, 6; *Bulletin* 1964, 6; "A New Dean at Ole Miss," *Time Magazine,* July 18, 1969, 53–54; Sansing, *Making Haste Slowly,* 212–13; Ken Vinson, "Mississippi: Signs of Life. 1. The Lawyers of Ole Miss," *Nation,* June 13, 1969, 791.

3. *Bulletin* 1964, 6. A printed program of the proceedings is in the Farley papers in the U.M. Library.

4. *Bulletin*s 1964–1973, passim.

5. Sansing, *University of Mississippi,* 308–9; Board Minutes, May 24, 1963.

6. Sansing, *University of Mississippi,* 309; Sansing, interview with Farley, 15.

7. Sansing, *University of Mississippi,* 309–10; Board Minutes, Nov. 16, 1964; Faculty Minutes, Dec. 7, 1964; Sansing, interview with Farley, 15.

8. Nadine Cahodas, *The Band Played Dixie* (New York: The Free Press, 1997), 109; *Martindale-Hubbell Law Directory* 2003, MS11P; Sansing, *University of Mississippi,* 310.

9. Faculty Minutes, Oct. 22, 1962, Mar. 18, 1965; *Bulletin* 1963, 8.

10. *Bulletin* 1964, 6, 22–28.

11. Landon, *Honor and Dignity,* 139. *Law Center Magazine* I:1 (spring 1996), 25.

12. *Law Center Magazine* I:1 (spring 1996), 25; Board Minutes, Oct. 22, 1964; School of Law Annual Report (1965–66), 7; *Bulletin* 1965, 6; *AALS Directory of Law Teachers* (1970), s.v. Brown, James Milton; *AALS Directory* (1979–80), s.v. Katz, Michael P.; *AALS Directory* (2004), s.v. Vinson, Kenneth. Landon, interview with J. R. Bradley, Jan. 2, 2004.

13. *Bulletin* 1965, 8 and passim; Board Minutes, Aug. 16, 1965.

14. Faculty Minutes, May 1, 1965 and passim; Alumni Association Minutes, Oct. 8, 1965.

15. Alumni Association Minutes, letter of Dec. 8, 1965, signed by Robert Khayat, acting law alumni secretary.

16. Faculty Minutes, Jan. 28, 1966, Nov. 21, 1967, Jan. 10, 1968; Board Minutes, Jan. 18, 1968. Reportedly, the motive for upgrading law school graduates' degrees to doctoral status was the fact that federal government departments paid holders of any doctoral degree at a higher rate than holders of bachelors or masters degrees.

17. *AALS Directory* (1970), s.v. Gorove, Stephen; *Bulletin* 1966, 6, 14–15. Professor Arthur B. Custy is listed as the 1965–66 graduate program chair but also as being on leave of absence that year.

18. *Bulletin* 1966, 14–15; School of Law Annual Report (1965–66), 4.

19. Board Minutes, Dec. 5, 1960, Apr. 20, 1961, July 27, 1968.

20. Ibid., Oct. 8, 1965, Oct. 15, 1966, Oct. 19, 1968, Oct. 18, 1969 (Chancellor's Papers, box 12, folder 4 (UMLSC); Board Minutes, Dec. 14, 1967.

21. Wynne Trust Fund papers (UMLSC); *Who's Who in the South and Southwest* (1950), s.v. Wynn, William Thomas; Alumni Association Minutes, Nov. 7, 1958.

22. Chancellor's Papers, box 12, folder 4 (UMLSC).

23. *Bulletin* 1966, 8–9; School of Law Annual Report (1965–66*),* 4.

24. *Bulletin* 1966, 18; School of Law Annual Report (1965–66), 8–9.

25. Cahodas, *Dixie,* 120, 122–23; Sansing, *University of Mississippi,* 311; author's recollections.

26. Author's recollections.

27. Board Minutes, Apr. 21, 1966, Nov. 17, 1966; Cahodas, *Dixie*, 121; Sansing, *Making Haste Slowly*, 213–14.

28. *Bulletin* 1966, 16.

29. Ibid., 6–7; ibid. 1967, 6–7; School of Law Annual Report (1965–66), 2.

30. Ibid., 7–8; ibid. 1967, 7–8; School of Law Annual Report (1965–66), 6; *AALS Directory* (1970), s.v. Bradley, John R., Jr.; Condon, Aaron S.; Edmonds, Thomas A.; Khayat, Robert.

31. Bulletin 1967, 6–7; School of Law Annual Report (1965–66), 2–3; *AALS Directory* (1970), s.v Dellinger, Walter E., III; *AALS Directory* (1979–80), s.v. Strickler, George Marion, Jr.; Landon, interview with Bradley.

32. *Time Magazine,* Sept. 23, 1966, 76.

33. Board Minutes, Oct. 22, 1964; School of Law Annual Report (1965–66), 7.

34. *Bulletin* 1966, 6–7; *Bulletin* 1967, 6; *AALS Directory* (1970), s.v. Champion, William M.

35. School of Law Annual Report (1965–66), 3; School of Law Annual Report (1969–70), 2–3; Board Minutes, July 20, 1967. Professor Chryst, who was informed by the board in late July 1969 that, because most of the responsibility for the program was going to be transferred over to a member of the Mississippi State University faculty, his appointment would terminate as of July 1, 1970, died from a heart attack while watching a football game on Sept. 11, 1969 (Board Minutes, July 25, 1969; *Bulletin* 1970, 6).

36. Faculty Minutes, Mar. 28, 1966, Mar. 29, 1967, Aug. 9, 1967; *Bulletin* 1968, 18.

37. "Strengthening Mississippi's Higher Education through Diversification, Cooperation, and Coordination" (A Report of a Study of the Role and Scope of Higher Educational Institutions in Mississippi, November, 1966), 25–26.

38. Faculty Minutes.

39. Faculty Minutes, July 26 and Aug. 2, 1967, Apr. 17 and Apr. 12, 1968, Mar. 19, 1969; *Bulletin* 1968, 15; *Bulletin* 1969, 15.

40. Faculty Minutes, Apr. 3, 1968. Author's recollections—on a research trip to England a couple of months later, the author met several people who had seen extracts from the speech on television news broadcasts.

41. Annual Report (1967–68), 1–3; Vinson, "Mississippi," 791.

42. Annual Report (1967–68), 4–5; Annual Report (1966–67), 9, 11–12.

43. Annual Report (1966–67), 9.

44. Michael B. Trister, draft curriculum, July 18, 1967.

45. Annual Report (1966–67), 9; Annual Report (1967–68), 12.

46. *Clarion Ledger,* Dec. 5, 1966; Board Minutes, spring 1968, passim; Cahodas, *Dixie*, 125.

47. Cahodas, *Dixie*, 125–26; Sansing, *University of Mississippi*, 311–12; Vinson, "Mississippi," 791–92; *Bulletin* 1968, 7; *Bulletin* 1969, 6; *Time Magazine,* Aug. 30, 1968, 37.

48. Board Minutes, Aug. 15 and Sept. 19, 1968. Semmes Luckett of Clarksdale was hired to defend Chancellor Fortune and Lowell Grisham of Oxford to defend Dean Morse.

49. Vinson, "Mississippi," 791–92; *Time Magazine,* July 18, 1969, 53–54.

50. His annual salary was to be $23,500 (Board Minutes).

51. "Report on Law School Accreditation Problems," *Mississippi Lawyer* XVII, no. 3, 3.

52. Chancellors Papers, box 39, Jan.–June 1970 folder (UMLSC); Faculty Minutes, Jan. 19 and Jan. 21, 1970; *AALS Directory* (1979–80), s.v. Strickler, George Marion, Jr.; Vinson, Kenneth; McDougal, Luther L., III.

53. "Accreditation problems," *Mississippi Lawyer* XVII, no. 3, 3; Faculty Minutes, Apr. 9 and Apr. 16, 1969; John R. Bradley, letter to Chancellor Porter L. Fortune, May 22, 1969 (Chancellor's Papers, UMLSC).

54. *Mississippi Lawyer* XVII, no. 3, 3.

55. Ibid., 3, 6.

56. Ibid., 6, 8.

57. The motion supporting Dean Bunkley was Professor Luther McDougal's idea (Faculty Minutes, Jan. 19, 1970).

58. A. B. Carthy, letter, Mar. 30, 1970 (Chancellors Papers, box 39 [UMLSC]); Faculty Minutes, Oct. 12, 1970.

59. *Who's Who in the South and Southwest* (2003), s.v. Anderson, Reuben V.; Law School and State Bar Records.

60. BALSA–Law School Records.

61. Cahodas, *Dixie*, 133–34, 150–51.

62. Ibid., 146–49, 152–54. Author's personal recollections—the author recalls with some pride that he was the mover of the "legitimate grievances" resolution that passed on the first night and also the author and mover of the five committees resolution that was adopted the second night as well as a member of the academic grievances committee. Donald left campus at the end of the year and finished up his law school work at Howard University in Washington, D.C. Eugene McLemore transferred to Jackson State University and became both a minister of religion and a Hinds County administrator.

63. Annual Report (1971–72), 1.

64. Annual Report (1969–70), 3–4; Annual Report (1970–71), 2; *Bulletin* 1971, 6; *AALS Directory*, s.v. Condon, Aaron; Shaw, William Burns.

65. Annual Report (1970–71), 4–5. *AALS Directory*, s.v. Fruge, Don L; Ethridge, Thomas R.; Sweat, Noah Spurgeon, Jr.; *Bulletin* 1971, 6.

66. Annual Report (1971–72), 2–3.

67. Faculty Minutes, Oct. 3, 1971.

68. Board Minutes, Oct. 22, 1971); *Who's Who in America* (1982–83), s.v. Williams, Parham Henry, Jr.; *AALS Directory* (1979–80), s.v. Williams, Parham H., Jr.; *Oxford Eagle*, Oct. 25, 1971, 1A, 8A.

69. Faculty Minutes, Nov. 15, 1971. A copy of Sander's letters can be seen in Chancellor's papers, box 41 (UMLSC).

70. Chancellor's Papers, box 40 (UMLSC).

71. Ibid.

72. Law School Registration Files (1971–76).

73. Chancellors Papers, box 40 (UMLSC).

74. Ibid.; *Bulletin* 1971, 8.

75. Chancellors Papers, Box 40 (UMLSC); Law School Registration Files (1971–76); Faculty Minutes, Mar. 20, Apr. 17, Apr. 20, and May 3, 1972.

76. "Chancellor Stands in Path of Effort to Move Mississippi Law School," *Commercial Appeal*, Nov. 24, 1971, 1; "Junior Bar Studies Law School Sites," *Clarion Ledger*, 11 Dec. 1971; "Move Law School Or Build New One?" *Jackson Daily News*, Mar. 3, 1972.

77. Chancellor's Papers, box 38, letters, newspaper clippings, 1971–72 (UMLSC); *Clarion Ledger*, June 23, 1972, 4.

78. Ibid.; H.E. Taylor, letter to Chancellor Fortune, Jan. 25, 1972); Dean Williams, letter

to state bar membership, Oct. 9, 1972; Faculty Minutes, Feb. 8, 1973; "UM Opens Law School in Jackson," *Clarion Ledger,* Mar. 9, 1973), 1A, 16A.

79. Board of Trustees Exec. Secretary, letter to House and Senate appropriations committees' chairs, Mar. 5, 1973.

80. Annual Report (1972–73), 3–4; *AALS Directory* (1979–80), s.v. Cochran, George C.; Featherstone, D. Michael; Mason, Tom R.; Chancellor's Papers, box 40 (UMLSC).

81. Faculty Minutes.

82. Ibid., Mar. 24, Apr. 27, May 25, 1971. Students now can check out monographs.

83. Annual Report (1972–73), 28–29; Faculty Minutes, Apr. 8, 1970; PLF, letter to Dr. E. E. Thrash, Dec. 13, 1971 (Chancellor's Papers, box 40 [UMLSC]).

84. Annual Report (1972–73), 24–29.

85. *Bulletin* 1973, 19. Professor J. R. Bradley informed the author that the "Employer-Employee Relations" course never was, in fact, actually required.

86. Ibid., 17, 19–29.

87. Faculty Minutes, Apr. 17, 1972.

88. Poster in *Journal of Space Law* files.

89. Chancellor's Papers, box 40 (UMLSC).

90. *The Journal of Space Law* I (1973), title page, v.

91. Parham Williams, *The University of Mississippi Law School* (1979), 8; Annual Report (1972–73), 36–38.

92. Annual Report (1972–73), 39–40; *Oxford Eagle,* July 25, 1973, 12A.

93. Chancellor's Papers, box 38 (UMLSC); Annual Report (1972–73), 38, 47.

94. Faculty Minutes, Aug. 4, 1973; Williams, *Law School,* 8, 9. Brass plaque inside law center main entrance (3rd floor).

95. "America's Lawyers: A Sick Profession?" *U.S. News & World Report,* Mar. 25, 1974, 23–28; Annual Report (1974–75), 2.

96. Williams, *Law School,* 9; Annual Report (1973–74), 3–4; *AALS Directory* (1979–80), s.v. Sullivan, Catherine A.

97. Annual Report (1973–74), 10–11; Annual Report (1974–75), 7, 11.

98. Chancellor's Papers, box 41 (UMLSC).

CHAPTER 6. THE RECENT PAST (1975–1994)

1. *Newsletter* I (1), 1 (no later editions of the newsletter seem to have survived); *Meridian Star,* Jan. 12, 1976, 1.

2. *Women in Law* (a law center recruiting brochure, 1974 [UMLSC]); Annual Report (1976–77), 2–3; Faculty Minutes, July 31 and Sept. 15, 1975; AALS *Directory* (1979–80), s.v. Ellis, Mary Carolyn; Green, Karen Oakes; Sullivan, Catherine A.

3. *Women in Law,* passim; Dean P. Williams, memo to Vice Chancellor A. De Rosier), Oct. 24, 1975.

4. Annual Report (1974–74), 3–4; Annual Report (1976–77), 5–6; Annual Report (1977–78), 3; *Bulletin* 1979, 40; *AALS Directory* (1979–80), s.v. Minor, James D.

5. Faculty Minutes, Sept. 15, 1975, Apr. 22 and June 25, 1976; Annual Report (1976–77), 11.

6. Faculty Minutes, Nov. 5 and Oct. 22, 1975; *Newsletter* I (1), 3. The Lamar portrait is now to be seen in Senator Trent Lott's office in Washington, D.C. A copy of it can be seen in the main entrance hallway on the third floor of the law center.

7. Williams, *Law School*, 8–9. Faculty Minutes, Feb. 15, 1977.

8. *Newsletter* 1, 2; Annual Report (1976–77), 10; *Who's Who in the South and Southwest* (1950), s.v. Matthews, Burnita Shelton.

9. Williams, *Law School*, 9; *Biloxi Daily Herald*, Feb. 23, 1976, 1; Faculty Minutes, July 12, 1977.

10. Chancellor's Papers, box 41, July 1974–June 1975 folder (UMLSC); Board Minutes, Mar. 24, 1977; Williams, *Law School*, 9.

11. Chancellors Papers, box 41, July 1975–June 1976 folder (UMLSC).

12. Faculty Minutes, Sept. 14, 1976.

13. *Catalogue* (1978), passim; *Catalogue* (1980), 4; Faculty Minutes, May 6, 1977.

14. Board Minutes.

15. Ibid., Apr. 28, Sept. 15, Dec. 15, 1977; Jan. 19, Mar. 16, Aug. 17, Oct. 19, Dec. 21, 1978; Jan. 18, Apr. 19, 1979.

16. Ibid., Aug. 17, 1978; Feb. 15, Sept. 15, Sept. 20, 1979. Williams, *Law School*, 9, and Annual Report (1978–79), 2, both say that building was so named "to honor three generations of Farleys," including the Robert Joseph Farley "who was a member of the first law class enrolled at the University and who later gave his life for the Confederacy at Gettysburg." In fact, no Farley was enrolled in the first law class of the fall 1854 semester. A Robert Joseph Farley from Panola County, however, did graduate from the university with a B.A. in the spring of 1854 and was still alive in 1910 (*HC*, 119).

17. Annual Report (1978–79), 1.

18. Annual Report (1979–80), 2; *Oxford Eagle*, Mar. 24, 1980, 5. Plaque on *Law Review* office door.

19. Michael de L. Landon, *The Challenge of Service: A History of the Mississippi Bar's Young Lawyers* (Jackson, MS, 1995), 114.

20. Ibid., 115.

21. Ibid., 116.

22. Ibid., 116–17; *General Laws of the State of Mississippi* (1979), chap. 486.

23. Landon, *Challenge of Service*, 117.

24. Lamar Order Records.

25. Annual Report (1979–80), 15

26. Williams, *History*, 9

27. Ibid., 1995 McClure Memorial Lecture Program.

28. Ibid.

29. *LS Catalog* (1979), 39–40; Annual Report (1979–80), 8; *AALS Directory*, s.v. Davis, Samuel Marion.

30. Annual Report (1979–80), 3, 9, 12–14.

31. Memo distributed to new students, 1972.

32. Ibid.

33. *Bulletin* 1973, 14; *LS Catalog* (1979), 25–26.

34. Annual Report (1978–79), 11–12.

35. Ibid., 14–15.

36. Ibid., 17–18.

37. Ibid., 18.

38. Ibid., 18–19.

39. Ibid., 19–20.

40. Ibid., 21.
41. Annual Report of the Chancellor (1984–85), 240; *LS Catalog* (1985), 52–54.
42. Law School files.
43. *LS Catalog* (1983), 40, and *LS Catalog* (1984–89), passim.
44. Faculty Minutes, Sept. 10, 1980; *LS Catalog* (1982), 21.
45. *AALS Directory* (2004), s.v. Bush, Larry Steven; Landon, interview with Bush, Nov. 15, 2001, 10–12.
46. Faculty Minutes, Sept. 6, 1984, Sept. 7, 2004, passim.
47. Ibid., Sept. 6, 2004, 2.
48. *Solicitor* (Mar. 1984), 2–3; *Solicitor* (Nov. 1984), 2, 4.
49. Chancellor's Annual Review (1984–85), 252–55; *LS Catalog* (1985), 5.
50. Chancellor's Annual Review, 246.
51. Author's recollection.
52. Langum and Walthall, *From Maverick to Mainstream*, 144, 244–45.
53. Ibid., 246–47.
54. Faculty Minutes, 1984–85, *passim*. Williams served as dean at the Cumberland School, 1985–96, and, since 1997, has been serving as dean of the Chapman University Law School in Orange, California (*AALS Directory* [2004]).
55. Chancellor's Annual Report (1985–86), 236; *Law Center News* (fall 1985, winter 1985–86).
56. *Who's Who in America* (2001), s.v. Edmonds, Thomas
57. Ibid.; Landon, interview with Bush.
58. *Law Center News* (winter 1985–86); *LS Catalog* (1985), 56; *LS Catalog* (1986), 56; *LS Catalog* (1989), 59; Chancellor's Annual Report (1986–87), 289.
59. *LCN* (spring 1986, winter 1986–87).
60. Ibid.(winter 1985–86); Chancellor's Annual Report (1884–85), 241; Chancellor's Annual Report (1985–86), 236.
61. Landon, interview with Bush; Chancellor's Annual Report (1985–86), 239.
62. *LCN* (spring 1988); *AALS Directory* (1979–80), s.v. Cox, Archibald.
63. Annual Report (1988–88), 6; Landon, interview with Bradley; *LCN* (fall 1988), 1.
64. *LCN* (fall 1988).
65. Chancellor's Annual Report (1988–89), 259.
66. Landon, interview with Bush; Chancellor's Annual Report (1988–89), 255–56.
67. *LCN* (summer 1989), 3.
68. Ibid., 2; Annual Report (1989–90), 2; *LS Catalog* (1990), 58–59.
69. Annual Report (1989–90), 1, 5.
70. *LS Catalog* (1990), 8, 20, 24–29; *LCN* (spring/summer 1992), 2.
71. Chancellor's Annual Report (1989–90), 304–6.
72. Ibid., 300–10; *LCN* (fall 1989), 3.
73. Ibid., 301–4; *LS Catalog* (1990), 60.
74. Chancellor's Annual Report (1989–90), 307–10; *LS Catalog* (1990), 60.
75. *LCN* (fall 1989), 1, 5.
76. Ibid.; Chancellor's Annual Report (1989–90), 298.
77. *Who's Who in America* (1996); *AALS Directory* (2004), s.v. Shipley, David E.; *LCN* (spring 1990), 1.
78. *LCN* (fall 1990), 5; *AALS Directory*, s.v. Harges, Bobby Marzine; Adler, Donna D.

79. Faculty Minutes, Dec. 13, 1990.
80. *LCN* (spring 1991), 1, 5.
81. *LCN* (fall 1990), 1,7; *LCN* (fall 1991), 1,4; *LCN* (fall 1992), 1, 5.
82. Ibid. (spring 1991), 9.
83. Ibid., 6.
84. Ibid. (fall 1991), 1, 3.
85. Ibid. (spring/summer 1992), 3; ibid. (fall 1992), 2, 8.
86. Ibid. (fall 1990), 2; ibid. (spring 1991), 2.
87. Ibid. (spring 1991), 2; ibid. (fall 1991), 2; ibid. (spring/summer 1992), 2, 8.
88. *LCN* (spring/summer 1992), 2; *LS Catalog* (1993), 63–64).
89. *LCN* (spring/summer 1992), 2, 6, 9, 13, 16.
90. Ibid. (fall 1992), 2.
91. Ibid. (spring 1993), 2.
92. Ibid. (fall 1993), 2.
93. Ibid. (fall 1993), 1, 2, 5, 15.
94. Ibid. (spring 1994), 8–9.
95. *LCN* (spring 1994), 1.
96. Ibid. The author was one of the two non-law school faculty on the search committee.
97. Ibid. (fall 1994), 1.

Chapter 7. The Sesquicentennial Decade (1994–2004)

1. *LCN* (spring 1994), 4; Sansing, *University of Mississippi*, 344–45.
2. Bill Clinton, *My Life* (New York: Knopf, 2004),183; LCN (spring 1994), 22; *AALS Directory* (2004), s.v. Staton, Mary Carolyn E.
3. "Black Law Dean Ushers in A NEW DAY AT OLE MISS," *Ebony* (Aug. 1995), 128–32.
4. *Ebony*, "A NEW DAY," 130; *LS Catalog* (1995), 63–65.
5. Annual Report (1994–95), 1.
6. *Visions*, 27.
7. Annual Report (1995–96), 6.
8. Ibid., 8–9.
9. Ibid., 12–13.
10. Ibid., 11–12, 14–15.
11. The author is grateful to John Sobotka for this information.
12. *LCN* (fall 1996), 1, 2.
13. Ibid. (spring 1997),1, 9; *AALS Directory* (2004), s.v. Davis, Samuel Marion.
14. *LCN* (spring 1997), 1.
15. Ibid., 2.
16. Ibid. (spring 1998), 2, 3, 6; ibid. (fall 1998), 2.
17. U.M. Law School library records.
18. *LCN* (spring 1999); "From the Dean's Office," Annual Report (1996–97), 7; *LS Catalog* (1999), 68–70.
19. *LCN* (spring 1999), 10–11.
20. Annual Report (1999–2000), 2.
21. *LS Catalog* (2000), 6, 9, 24–25, 28–35; Annual Report (1999–2000), 6.

22. *Ibid.*, 4; *LCN* (spring 2000), 18–19.
23. Annual Report (1999–2000), 12–13.
24. Ibid., 8–9.
25. Ibid., 10–11.
26. Ibid., 14–16.
27. *LCN* (spring 2000), "From the Dean"; *LCN* (spring 2001), "From the Dean."
28. *LCN* (spring 2001), "From the Dean," 17.
29. Ibid.
30. Ibid.
31. *LCN* (fall 1999), 14; "The Sesquicentennial Celebration" (U.M. Development Office, Nov. 21, 1996).
32. *LCN* (fall 1999), 10–11.
33. Ibid., 16.
34. Ibid., 8–9.
35. Ibid (spring 2000), 23.
36. Ibid (spring 2001), 22–23.
37. AALS *Directory* (2004), s.v. Clancy, Thomas K.
38. Annual Report (2001–02), 18–22; "Focusing on the Criminal Justice System" (NCJRL brochure).
39. Annual Report (2003–04), 19.
40. *LCN* (spring 2001), "From the Dean," 5; AALS *Directory* (2004), s.v. Gabrynowicz, Joanne I. Women in Aerospace award wall plaque.
41. *LCN* (fall 2001), 10; NRSSLC Annual Report (2001–02), 10.
42. NRSSLC Annual Report (2003–04), 3, Appendix 2.
43. Ibid., 4–5; *Space News,* Apr. 5, 2004, 22.
44. SAPS records.
45. Annual Report (2001–02), 11–12; Annual Report (2002–2003), 14.
46. Ibid. (2001–02), 14–16.
47. Ibid. (2003–04), 16; *Inside Ole Miss* I:61 (July 15, 2002), 1.
48. Annual Report (2003–04), 2.
49. Ibid., 2–5.
50. Ibid., 7.
51. *UM Lawyer* (summer 2004), "From the Dean."

INDEX